EVERYTHING IN ITS PLACE

Social Order and Land Use
in America

CONSTANCE PERIN

Everything in Its Place

SOCIAL ORDER AND LAND USE

IN AMERICA

Princeton University Press

PRINCETON, N.J.

To the memory of my parents
Lee *and* Simon Perin

Contents

Contents

As issues of housing and educational discrimination keep coming up in city councils, legislatures, and the courts, they themselves raise another important social question: whether we have the ability to discuss and debate important social questions. This book is devoted to widening our vocabulary for doing so.

Land-use regulations and development practices in metropolitan areas, where about 73 percent of Americans live, work, and go to school, are major social mechanisms with which we determine "a place for everything" and put "everything in its place." The criteria used in making those judgments reveal much about American culture, for they condense the particular ways that we as Americans agree that "God's in his heaven—All's right with the world." This book treats those technical conventions, economic practices, and social customs as "elemental facts" in their own right: the "most elemental and important facts about a society—those that are seldom debated and generally regarded as settled," Louis Wirth once put it.

The technicalities of defining zoning districts in terms of their permitted and forbidden buildings and activities, classifying parts of cities and suburbs by housing types and levels of population density, arranging the layouts of subdivisions: these also express our taken-for-granted understandings of what social order is and how it is best obtained. Whatever governs relationships among land uses I take to be as well organizing principles for relationships among land users. What those principles are and what they mean are my conclusions. They are not solutions to vexing questions but a vocabulary of social meanings underlying them that might carry us further in debating and finding judicious remedies.

I analyze directly the social meanings of homeownership, sprawl, newcomers, mortgages, housing styles, forms of tenure, the life cycle, status, and local control over zoning. These meanings arise from American conceptions of transition, citizenship, honor, marginality, success, and self-esteem, cultural conceptions customarily addressed indirectly in deciding about "a place for everything" in terms of density levels, housing types, price levels, subdivision layouts, and neighborhood and community character.

Shelter, the single most significant mediator between each household and the larger society, putting each into touch with the other, is never a simple matter in complex society, determining as it does access to many other necessities: education, work, social life, and political participation.

Comprehending the many meanings in American society of the single-family-detached house seems to me prerequisite to remedies for reducing discrimination and making new departures for improving both the availability and quality of living environments. But a developer who uses market research told me: "It's very difficult in talking about something as personal as housing to get people to talk about their real reasons. What you're really feeling about your neighbors and how you live and why you like privacy and this sort of thing. People always seem to couch reasons in socially acceptable norm-giving ways, which I think are frequently misleading" (Pope: 21). What some of these "real reasons" of both housing producers and consumers might be is the question I am looking into from the perspective of cultural anthropology.

This search for meanings reconstructs the whole cloth from which most current research in land use is necessarily cut. As a cultural anthropologist, I put much stock in the configurative tradition. The subjects I cover only appear to range widely, for this tradition arrives at the interpretation of social facts not by decontaminating and reducing them but by considering them in the very media where they thrive. John Dewey said "there is no immaculate conception to meanings and purposes." Once having these meanings—and their sources—to debate, we can better decide whether to change them and their consequences, social, economic, and symbolic.

In working out the problem of studying my own culture, it was necessary to become something of an outsider to it in order to get more deeply into it. I decided that by concentrating on how people now actively and responsibly involved in metropolitan development describe what they are doing and why they are doing it—listening to them as though for the first time—I might arrive at some new understandings of matters that have been of professional concern to me over the past twenty years or so. Mortgage bankers and lenders, appraisers and developers, planners and architects, politicians and civic leaders told me what they believe about consumers' needs and preferences and the kinds of neighborhoods and communities they think will result from the types of housing and community plans they have so much say in. Their ideas about

x

how society is and ought to be organized also came through and my interpretations of these conceptions of social order provide a different perspective on many long-standing issues in metropolitan development and American society.

A word is perhaps in order to account for my coming to take a systematic interest in the assumptions underlying the American system of land use, and, like much else in social research, it is partly autobiographical. After writing *With Man in Mind*, a book proposing new grounds for collaboration between human scientists and environmental designers, I carried out a study that asked: left to their own ideas and definitions, how do people evaluate their physical environment at home, at work, in the neighborhood? Do they share the same concerns about it as those producing it? I began by studying the physical environment of the house in a middle-to-low-income population (Perin 1972). Instantly finding that the small size of their housing was a constant preoccupation, I went on to interview housing producers, talking to developers, architects, and financiers then putting together subsidized housing "packages" for non-profit groups. I asked them for particulars about the marginal costs of providing room sizes that were, say, 20 percent larger than customary. First I concluded that I was getting the run-around from this group of experts and professionals. They hemmed and hawed. They ultimately avoided an answer by claiming that the zoning would never allow the taller buildings necessitated (larger units would mean additional units in order to pay the mortgage). Solid information was not forthcoming and the best they could offer was a "rule of thumb" of "something like" $4 per square foot marginal cost added onto the $14 per square foot that was the cost of new construction at the time in the Chicago metropolitan area. Nevertheless they had made no definitive analyses because the possibility of going beyond the minimum legal requirements had not occurred to them.

Thinking over the resistance in these conversations, I concluded that consumers were getting what producers believe they ought to have. Previously my research had found that there is a dearth of studies into the human necessities for light and space, for example. Not only that, but often enough producers are the authors of those "standards" promulgated in various model codes for building, housing, and health (Perin 1970: 142). The cost of producing larger-size housing units was perhaps not the issue needing attention, but rather that in our culture a high price axiomatically attaches to greater amounts of living space. Producers may ration space as a reasonable consequence of various constraints they face, but the outstanding fact is that new larger housing is always—should be, it is believed—higher-priced housing even though the going price may be out of proportion to the marginal costs of production.

Even in public housing, where price makes little difference, the functional needs of large families for greater floor area had long been overlooked, and only in recent years have some public housing authorities begun to convert into a single apartment for larger families what had formerly been two or three apartments. Visiting single-family house models in the suburbs selling then to moderate-income households for $35–$40,000, I found them so tight on floor area that to give an illusion of spaciousness, furnishings were wherever possible attached to walls, so that only two legs of chairs or tables used up floor space. I was led to look into the question of standards for housing size and the size of housing being built and in the course of that study, came upon this exchange between a congressman and a representative of the building industry during a 1969 congressional hearing on industrialized housing:

> Mr. Biderman. These townhouses ($15,000 to $19,500) go from a two-bedroom, one-story unit of 985 square feet to a two-story, three-bedroom unit of 1,450 square feet.
> Representative Widnall. Would they be too small for public housing?
> Mr. Biderman. Oh, no. They would be too large. (Perin 1974: 34)

The reasons for small housing are complex and may have to do more with city and suburban land pricing than with building costs. What I *had* found was that the practices of housing producers had little if anything to do either with hard-headed cost analyses or with the functional needs of families in carrying out their ordinary living activities. Where my concerns had previously been with research bringing about environments more realistically reflecting an understanding of their users, I moved on to study the beliefs and ideas of producers who also, as I have said, often control the rules by which they come into being. What shared assumptions about social rewards—about society's structure—underlie these ostensibly technical activities?

Echoes of a chord lost to economic analysis! Thorstein Veblen at the turn of the century:

> . . . he insisted on bringing into technical academic discussion the usages of the common man. Thus . . . he argued that "capital" can only be defined by empirical observation of how businessmen use the term—there is no point in a more refined definition. Indeed, the study of economics becomes the study of businessmen's habits of thought; changes in businessmen's linguistic usage, therefore, reflect changes in what they do. . . . he stresses that price, interest, value, and other categories are conventions, not given in the nature of things or in human nature but through the institutional processes and social learnings we would today summarize as culture. (Riesman 1954: 278)

These "habits of thought" do not, of course, explain social or economic systems, but they do provide the raw data for cultural analysis. Here I have sought out the common usages of entrepreneurs and public leaders in metropolitan development not, I want to emphasize, to criticize or to disprove, but to *understand*. These are often enough, it will become clear, assumptions we all share as social scientists, consumers, policymakers—as Americans.

This is, then, a study largely about ourselves, as people who have some say in which "habits of thought" are those commonly used. I have not looked into the cultural conceptions of an alien group elsewhere on the globe, or of a deprived and isolated group of Americans, or of a group deviant in any way. These are terms we all use in constructing the social order we have, and if there is an enemy to our quest for a better society, he is, as Pogo put it, us.

I begin by discusssing the relationship I see between land use and social order in the context of the culminations visible in growing shortages of land, energy, and capital along with the new-found impetus from the judiciary for enforcement of civil rights legislation in both housing and education. I explain the scope and design of the study and certain particulars of my approach to cultural analysis. Chapter Two examines the differences believed to exist between owners and renters—single-family houses, row houses, and apartments—that figure importantly in land-use and investment decisions. I analyze the American Dream of homeownership sociologically, as differences in relationships with bankers and landlords, and culturally, in terms of the significance of the stages of the life cycle. Chapter Three discusses suburban social conflict and avoidance and social homogeneity and compatibility by uncovering American conceptions of marginality and transition underlying ideas about social categories and their possible mixture.

Chapters Four and Five outline certain elements I see belonging in a social theory of metropolitan development. I distinguish among three kinds of property markets in terms of the different risks investors face in each and I propose that, because of the social and economic significance of homeownership for the majority of Americans, they, more than they might like, share with producers many of the same conceptions of American social order. Persistently localized control over land use, in city neighborhoods as well as in suburbs, is explained as a social response both to change and to the basic problem of social order faced by every society, that of incorporating newcomers. Defining resources locally is seen as part of a process of renegotiating social place in the face of newcomers who change its meaning. In Chapter Six, I suggest that having now this vocabulary of meanings with which to examine some of the organizing principles of the American system of land use may make it possible to reunify moral and technical questions and so serve the cause of equal justice under law.

Throughout, I have taken as data what others take for problems. I intentionally speak less about what ought to be—prescriptions and specific solutions—and more about what is actually happening, trying to understand why. Disagreeing with my interpretations is equally important in changing the way we think about these long-standing issues. For as a study in the humanistic tradition, it will succeed in that spirit if, in providing new knowledge, it raises scientific questions not raised by scientists.

C. P.

Washington, D.C.
January 1977

xiv

Acknowledgments

Edwin T. Haefele originally provided both the intellectual and institutional support for embarking on this work, and his sustained encouragement has been, with no exaggeration, indispensable.

I do, of course, take full responsibility for the entire work, and especially its errors, and I am grateful to many friends and colleagues who have responded to versions along the way. Allen W. Batteau has been a faithfully querying reader of several drafts, and he taught me much. The interest and informed criticism of William Doebele, Robert Gutman, Daniel Mandelker, Ralph Nicholas, Marshall Sahlins, and Roy Wagner have been invaluable. I am much in debt to those who took the time to read and think with me: Geoffrey Burkhart, Ernest Callenbach, Phyllis Pease Chock, Jarl E. Dyrud, Tom Dinnell, Gary A. Fuller, Katharine S. Halpern, George L. Harris, Everett C. Hughes, John Mixon, and Melvin M. Tumin.

To those who shared their time and thoughts with me, and to those who helped arrange these interviews, I am grateful indeed.

I carried out this study at Resources For The Future in Washington, D.C., April 1973 through September 1976, and I appreciate the interest and support shown by staff members there. Joseph L. Fisher, then President, made that appointment possible.

Laura Walker of the Brookings Institution library staff eased my searches greatly. Sylvia Steadham contributed both her typing and editorial skills. My editor Edward Tenner and my copy editor Pamela Long have, in fine style, brought me through.

EVERYTHING IN ITS PLACE

*Social Order and Land Use
in America*

Chapter One

—*All's Right with the World?*
Land Use in American
Society

LAND USE AND SOCIAL ORDER

What have been thought of as singularly technical concerns in land-use matters I take to be value-laden, that is, moral. American land-use classifications, definitions, and standards—alongside all their concrete tasks—name cultural and social categories and define what are believed to be the correct relationships among them. Why are some kinds of land-use relationships regularly prohibited? Why do zoning districts contain the specifics they do? Why do changes in land-use categories meet with widespread resistance, and on whose part? What implications are there for the way society is and should be organized in the definitions used to estimate how one land use will affect the value of another? Once made explicit, these beliefs and categories reveal much about our social structure and our moral world.

Land-use planning, zoning, and development practices are a shorthand of the unstated rules governing what are widely regarded as correct social categories and relationships—that is, not only how land uses should be arranged, but how land users, as social categories, are to be related to one another. In undertaking to decipher the glyphs of this shorthand, I have discovered several conceptions being used to define these social relations and assign them their different values. These have to do with the life cycle, transition, renting and homeownership, citizenship, social homogeneity, social conflict, newcomers—and ideas about the consequences each entails. Not idle thoughts, these conceptions are used as principles of social organization in metropolitan areas. They are different in kind from those factors more familiarly used to explain metropolitan growth and change, such as income, race, occupation, nationality, and prestige.

I have found those conceptions by examining the maps of society, as it were, guiding those who today largely control the form

3

of metropolitan development. Their ideas about how society is and ought to be organized—not as the ideas of a single "interest group," but as *American* ideas—influence profoundly the entries in our catalog of land use. From my understandings of these assumptions, beliefs, and definitions I draw most of my interpretations of still other sorts of social and cultural data.

In current analyses of land-use matters, most often the grounds on which—the principles by which—social relationships exist are discussed as: economic, through exchange in markets; political, through mechanisms allocating power; legal, through the distribution and enforcement of rights, obligations, and sanctions; ideological, through the conflict and consensus of diverse interests; governmental, in the distribution of authority and taxing powers. Less familiarly, the grounds I examine are cultural in the sense of the criteria used to define categories, social in the sense of people who occupy the categories, and sociological in the sense of kinds of relationships among the categories.

For the very reason that we understand them less well than we can see the political and economic patterns they result in, if left unexamined, these criteria and categories can continue to produce the less-than-ideal conditions so clearly manifested in the built landscape of metropolitan areas, still best described in older metropolitan areas (where the majority of the population lives) as a white noose around the blacks and poor of central cities. Citizens everywhere have been asking whether our system of land use helps in creating a social order—social categories and the relationships among them—consonant with the ideals of a great industrial democracy, and have been finding that system wanting, importantly.

These findings provide a perspective on the land-use system as a moral system that both reflects and assures social order.

The social order of a society is its amicable coherence apparent to its members. American social order includes its Constitutional ideals for non-discrimination in the opportunities to share in its material and social goods of wealth, esteem, and power. The actual distribution of those resources and opportunities, without asking how it relates to the ideals—that is the status quo. The continuous evaluation of the disparity between actuality and ideals, together with shared strivings to lessen it is implicit in this definition of American social order.

Cultural and social categories and our ideas about their rela-

4

tionships both shape and result from the distribution of those goods. Why these categories are as they are is, then, the basic question. At the end of the French monarchy in the nineteenth century Lamartine declared: "It is a problem of this time to classify things and men. . . . The world has jumbled its catalog." With all we know about the consequences of our land-use catalog, we know too little about the sources of its entries.

In anthropology and in general, conventional assumptions and beliefs are often termed "world views," "values," or "ethos." I find those inadequate tags for the problems of explanation we face in industrial societies. In working the way I do, I am trying at the same time to breathe into the construct "culture" the vitality it actually has in social and economic systems. Those systems, too, are constructs; their subjects are only believed to be more specific, phenomenal, and measurable. Culture, as values, beliefs, assumptions, rules, and definitions, should not be regarded "on the one hand," as inexorably given, static, and abstract while, "on the other," social events are dynamically generated, variable, and concrete. By identifying those definitions and rules as the principles underlying events, I hope instead to convey how actively, variably, and concretely "values" and "world views" are at work. If the organizing principles were different, the events would be different: only by artifice do we separate thoughts from actions and their observable, sometimes measurable, consequences.

Those items covered by the construct culture—beliefs, premises, rules, assumptions, definitions: Social scientists have been reluctant not to name them but to study them, largely because they have not resolved the issue of how to "concretize" them. What I now understand about the American cultural system from studying the system of land use is put into a context of current action and historical events. As I will show, there are many kinds of evidence with which we can assure ourselves that this complex of items we call culture has real effects and is justifiably analyzed in its own right.

Measuring the incidence of those elements is, however, the least and last of our worries: whether cultural analysis brings to the fore worthwhile variables is the more important, and difficult, challenge. Later in this chapter I explain more about the analytic approach I take.

I claim not much more than a partial glimmering of the cultural

5

elements with which Americans construct social order. The whole collection is a great circulating library of public assumptions, premises, beliefs, and lore from which we all borrow. We would need parallel investigations of major institutional systems such as education, health, religion, and politics to discover still other elements of it: the shared understandings from which the social categories important in those systems are shaped, together with the sociological principles by which they are evaluated. Then we would begin to have the data from which an integrated theory of American culture might be formed. If and how these might be transformed or combined into a single, consistent "pattern" must remain an empirical question. This book is an annotated bibliography, as it were, of the collection of cultural conceptions as used in this one American system, land use. It demonstrates how far still there is to go.

CULMINATIONS: SCARCITY, JUSTICE, AND CHANGE

An unusual coalition of interests among the producers of new housing, consumers, and groups pursuing some public interest has recently arisen, unusual because historically these interests have been antagonists. One consists of the environmentalists and conservationists, who favor land-use practices that reduce air pollution resulting from the levels of automobile use that suburban sprawl imposes and that leave undeveloped areas of natural beauty, wildlife preserves, streambeds, and land for recreation to serve regional needs. Supporters of the enforcement of open housing and civil rights laws are another significant group finding the inhibition on suburban sprawl rewarding, in that high prices for single-family housing by definition exclude those with lower incomes, and blacks are a population group whose incomes are, occupation by occupation, generally lower than whites'. Producers wanting to sell to a lower-income market tend to favor both environmentalists' and civil libertarians' goals: higher density, more compact development—now that well-located land is scarcer and prices higher—and an end to the exclusionary zoning in city neighborhoods as well as in suburbs which amounts to de facto discrimination in housing.

De facto housing discrimination arises from housing prices

6

only whites can afford; racially discriminatory practices via restrictive covenants were declared unconstitutional in 1948 and
1953, and in 1962 the first federal action to prohibit discrimination in housing took the form of an Executive Order on Equal
Opportunity in Housing, applying only to housing receiving federal financial assistance (National Committee Against Discrimination In Housing and The Urban Land Institute 1974: 7-9).
Under Title VI of the Civil Rights Act of 1964, no government
benefit may be provided on a discriminatory basis, including any
of those provided through the programs of the U.S. Department
of Housing and Urban Development, as in federal mortgage insurance, housing subsidies, urban renewal and community development funds, sewer and water grants, and so on. Under Title
VIII of the Fair Housing Act of 1968 all housing, except that sold
by an individual without the assistance of a broker or advertising
or that rented by an individual in a house in which he/she lives
(and which does not contain more than four units), must be made
available without discrimination on account of race, color, religion,
or national origin.

An interest group so far not heard from: fuel conservationists,
who, it might be thought, would be in favor of development patterns that create a pool of people among whom public transportation becomes a feasible and attractive alternative in their job
commuting. With about 73 percent of Americans now living in
metropolitan areas, whether energy conservation at an effective
scale can actually ever occur depends on changing the structure
of their consumption of energy. That has to mean changes in the
framework of consumers' living patterns—not changing their habits through exhortation or incentives alone but also through the
concrete reorganization of home, work, school, transportation, and
recreation. In one form or another, future land-use patterns attentive to conserving gas will tend more to concentrate than scatter
population. Transit depends on large numbers of people to make
it a good public investment. Shorter driving distances will also
mean that work and shopping are not so far from home. Green
breathing spaces, as recreation or beauty spots, take on ever
greater importance, and they should be accessible quickly for frequent refreshment. But ecological preserves also decrease the supply of land for development. So, circularly, higher prices for land

7

more often than not necessitate higher densities—and development more compact than suburbanites, whether in rolling acres or the sprawl of tract subdivisions, have been accustomed to.

With ever higher prices of land in metropolitan areas, and with population growth, together with greatly increased building costs, in labor and in materials, compact development has also become the only certain route to housing most consumers can afford. It most often implies higher density housing, in the form of row houses or townhouses having two or three levels, shared walls, no front yard to speak of, and a private, walled patio or backyard. The Federal Housing Administration has been making available a special form of mortgage insurance covering developments of this kind: called a Planned Unit Development, or PUD, the row houses are clustered together under overall density regulations in order to lower the costs of spread-out sewer, water, and road systems. The land area thus saved becomes common open space, shared by all those living there, and the residents must also work out ways of taking it over from the developer and subsequently maintaining and operating it. The establishment and operation of community homeowner associations are an intrinsic aspect of PUD developments, and the FHA provides developers with written guidelines for forming them.

Historically, wherever higher density development is to be found, it is in response to land prices high enough to make it impossible to sell or rent housing at an affordable price, so it is clear that one feature of our economic system for so long making possible the single-family-detached house has been pervasively low land prices. In contrast, city land prices, set as they are by the values attaching to quick and inexpensive communication—whether in the form of comparison shopping or the efficiencies of manufacturing with ready access to railroads and labor supply—are, almost by definition, always higher, hence the customary urban high density apartment buildings or town and row house developments.

Although the increasingly expensive single-family-detached housing with its four private yards continues to be built and sold, it is within reach of an increasingly smaller group. The Secretary of the Department of Housing and Urban Development reported in 1975 that in three years the prices of new houses had risen 33 percent:

8

From the first quarter of 1971 to the fourth quarter of 1974 land costs went up 62 percent; construction financing 148 percent; labor costs 39 percent; materials 36 percent; overhead 54 percent; and marketing costs 73 percent. Put all of these figures in the hopper, sift in the leveler of competition, and prices of new homes have risen 33 percent in these three years . . . the median family income today is $13,000 which by rule of thumb tells you that the median affordable house should cost no more than $32,500. In truth the median new home today actually costs $39,000, and the median existing home is priced at over $35,000.

Looking back a decade, in 1965, prior to the current inflationary spiral, 44 percent of American families had sufficient income to purchase a new home as compared with 31 percent today, and 46 percent could buy an existing home as compared with 32 percent today. (Hills 1975: 2, 3)

The costs of maintenance, not to mention heating and cooling, have increased drastically too: maintenance and repair are estimated to have jumped 105 percent in ten years, mortgage interest up 56 percent, fuel and utilities 70 percent, and property taxes 70 percent (Hills 1975: 3).

The lower prices of more compacted housing may attract the middle-to-low-income consumer, but suburbs have been repelling its construction, especially suburbs having mostly single-family-detached housing. These suburbs have zoning laws that permit only more of the same, in regulations setting forth minimum house-size requirements, minimum lot size and minimum frontage requirements, the outright prohibition of multi-family housing or more subtle restrictions on the number of bedrooms, prohibition of mobile homes, and zoning land for nonresidential use to prevent its residential development. Singly or in combination, these may be present in local zoning ordinances.

Housing producers aiming at the market represented by the broadest group of consumers have come to support the efforts of open housing groups trying, mainly through the courts, to prevent municipalities from using or abusing these devices, all of which tend to limit an increase in density or population, or both. The United States Supreme Court on June 25, 1975, issued an opinion on the pivotal subject of standing to sue, finding against the proposition that persons not now residents of a municipality using exclusionary devices have standing on that issue; if they wanted to litigate the denial of a specific building permit, however, federal standing would be conferred. This opinion (*Warth* v.

9

Seldin) in effect asks a plaintiff on any general issue of permit denial to prove his case in court in order to be in the position of getting it to court. The U.S. Court of Appeals for the Ninth Circuit in California in August 1975, following this new dictum, found in favor of a growth-limiting zoning ordinance both on the procedural grounds that the housing producers seeking to overturn it did not have standing to sue and on grounds that a substantive federal question was lacking (*Construction Industry Association of Sonoma County* v. *City of Petaluma*).

In a decision that also broadened the basis for standing, the Supreme Court of New Jersey has, oppositely, raised hopes that municipal parochialism might be seeing the beginning of its end. In March 1975, it decided unanimously against any municipal regulations that foreclose housing opportunities for low- and moderate-income people; more importantly, the decision specifies that the locality's regulations should reflect the municipality's fair share of the present and prospective regional need (*Southern Burlington County NAACP* v. *Township of Mount Laurel*). On April 20, 1976, the United States Supreme Court unanimously held that it is within the purview of federal courts to order the U.S. Department of Housing and Urban Development to fund low-cost housing within a metropolitan area, not just its central city, in order to comply with the Constitution (Fifth Amendment) and federal statutes (Civil Rights Act of 1964) (*Hills* v. *Gautreaux et al.*). The regionalization of the housing market in which lower-income people can participate is now well underway, constitutionally at any rate.

These are historic moments only because, during these past forty years or so of great population growth and industrial expansion, the American Dream of owning the single-family-detached house on its own lot has been so ubiquituously realized. Rising incomes, especially after World War II, permitted people to leave concrete and brick downtowns, make use of commuter railroads, and provide their families with the benefits of greenery, good air, and better schools. With the federal highway and mortgage insurance programs, growing metropolitan populations were more free than ever before to settle in the older suburbs and create new ones (Muth 1969). These incentives brought into development rural land, a land-use conversion still going on. The British New Towns, built out in the countryside in the immediate post-war years, were widely publicized, and these "garden cities," combining residence and nearby employment, provided the models for the good planning so often overlooked in the speculative rush. "New communities," a nearly defunct program now, was a federal attempt to control and rationalize the processes of growth from the beginning of subdividing, including as well the constitutional objectives of open housing for all. The "urban renewal" of central cities and their older residential neighborhoods was less an expression of any widespread interest in city living and more a governmental response to nervous merchants feeling the pinch of population shifts to suburban shopping centers. In forty years the suburbs have come to accommodate only a distorted profile of the American population.

We sit now on the brink of another historic period being outlined by the energy shortage, the rise in land prices all over metropolitan areas, and the competition for capital with which to build and buy housing of any kind. This period will introduce, I believe, a pronounced change in the glorification of the single-family-detached house as the ideal. Families may still dream of it, but producers will sell something else.

The trend is already visible even in land-rich Houston where, as recently as 1973, developers, bankers, and builders finally came to acknowledge that the flood plain of Harris County would have to be mapped and buyers made aware of the hazards, if federal insurance were to be accepted. Before the severe floods during the spring of 1973, building occurred anywhere at all without the safety of stilts and without any legal requirement that the floodplain contours be disclosed to buyers. During my fieldwork I found that two civic leaders had had the personal experience of flooding in their houses. Even in Houston, then, there has been an unheard-of talking-up of higher density development, most often taking the form of townhouses and apartments.

THE DESIGN OF THE STUDY

During 1973, I interviewed people active in responsible positions influencing aspects of development in metropolitan Houston and Philadelphia. These are people somehow figuring out the market for housing, neighborhoods, and shopping centers. My questions in our discussions were meant to elicit their views on the pressures of growth and its implications for the quality of life. Each person was chosen on the basis of a reputation for concern with development as a public responsibility. Each had a record of successful development activities guided not only by the ledger but by an awareness of larger obligations to the general welfare.

In wanting to take a fresh look at the familiar, I chose to interview in Houston, as it represented, I thought, a major source of ideas about land use possibly contrasting with what I already know: Houston is the one city of its size in the United States still to have no zoning ordinance after defeating the adoption of municipal land-use regulations in public referenda held over the past ten years. Though city-wide ordinances regulate the provision of off-street parking, and building codes limit structural features, both of which may have some of the effects of zoning regulations, there are no zoning districts nor municipally codified classifications of land-use relationships. As land is developed, subdivisions are protected in their original use through private deed restriction, a form of private contract among all the property owners. Since 1965, the State Legislature enabled the city attorney's office to enforce these upon complaints from citizens, a situation never tested for its constitutionality but one so satisfying to Houston's civic associations that no challenge has been brought. There are about 200 of these, each one organized around its particular set of deed restrictions, some more active than others in preventing violations. In the Appendix a typical deed restriction and examples of zoning ordinances are reprinted.

One person put my reasons for choosing Houston perfectly: in Houston you "have to use your head" about land-use matters.

In other words, land, as we in the appraisal business say, land can then rise to its highest and best use. The appraisers consider Houston the hardest town in the United States to appraise in, and it is because you have to make a statement as to what is the highest and best use of the land. And you don't have zoning that does it for you. You have to use you head to figure out what the highest and best use of land is. (Wing: 3)

I thought I would find more familiar ideas in Philadelphia. It represents the older East Coast metropolitan areas with a long history of zoning. Although development continues, open land is

scarcer and past development is in need of renewal or replacement. Houston, in contrast, is a classic boom town, where land is
still plentiful and accelerated development is recent. These two situations of land availability and regulation would, I thought, provide me with a wide range of American land-use beliefs and practices. I was not concerned with comparing their histories, their
current problems, or their particular governmental arrangements,
but only with generating a wide array of the assumptions used in
land-use matters.

Indeed, my first finding is that by and large there is one dom-
inant set of ideas and assumptions operating: one person finds it
is "all mental," the difference between Houston and everywhere
else:

> One of the things that is strange to me, I have been aware ever
> since we moved to Houston that we didn't have zoning—that it
> was good and it was bad, depending on who you were talking
> with. And yet I don't get the feeling when I go to other cities,
> I don't see any difference in the communities. You see strip
> shopping centers here. You go to other cities that have zoning,
> you have strip shopping centers. I don't see having or not hav-
> ing zoning—in the overall picture of the community has had any
> real significant difference. You talk to the developers or you
> talk to some of the politicians, the real estate people here, they
> say, the reason we're so great is because we don't have zoning,
> other people in other cities say the reason we're doing great is
> we have zoning, and I don't see any difference. It may all be
> mental, I don't know. (Peat: 28-29)

Others also disclaimed that Houston's lack of zoning made any
difference to the way land uses were arranged and they thought
Houston was physically similar to other American cities. One
source of this similarity is clearly the federal system of mortgage
insurance and availability:

> *What I was wondering is when you are processing your mort-
> gage business to what extent do you find it easier, harder, or
> whatever for local ideas about development to take precedence
> over FHA or national standards, and how does that get dealt
> with?* First of all we have never found anything that we do in
> conflict with the requirements of FHA or VA. (Wing: 1-2)

13

Originally, I had thought to divide evenly the number of interviews, expecting regional differences in ideas to be significant. In Houston, where I began interviewing, I found that several people I talked with had come from elsewhere within the past ten years or so and others had work experience or education elsewhere, mainly on the East Coast. They were using these experiences and their training in their current work.

More significantly, I found that the rules governing capital investment are not regional but national (and perhaps even international): "New York money" was in Houston and it was in Philadelphia. The Shah of Iran was said to have invested in Houston developments. The land-use conditions to be met for "guaranteeing" that these investments will be "good" compete with conditions everywhere else. For example, one Houston developer with a novel idea, to be carried out on a very large scale, could not get financing within the Houston metropolitan area; he had to interest New York money in his project. In Philadelphia a mortgage banker and one-time member of its redevelopment authority told me that local bankers and others would not invest in projects because they knew too much about local politics—not a sure enough deal! Outside money came in.

I asked whether the Federal Housing Administration in Houston ever did battle with the national regulations of the FHA in order to preserve some regional distinctions, whatever they might be in the way of neighborhood layout or housing style: ". . . I think FHA's been instrumental, having been here for so long, and Houston developed along the FHA line for so many years that our [federal] patterns and our [federal] forms [for subdivisions] and all were followed by the local attorneys." Though Houston's subdivisions are controlled by private deed restrictions and though many developers do not seek FHA insurance, they often request from the FHA detailed site analyses, an FHA function its personnel regard as "missionary" work. The national standards of the FHA are thereby influential even beyond the development it insures. In Houston one appraiser of property referred to the volumes on his shelves as "bibles": these are national publications setting out criteria for judging the worth of building materials, of construction types, and so on. For these reasons, in Philadelphia I sought out people in comparable positions simply in order to generate more

14

data on the subject as a whole, not to contrast the assumptions used in each city, nor to evenly match the numbers of interviews.

The system of land use, its beliefs and practices, is, then, in important aspects a national one, due to federal government standards and regulations, to the freedom of capital to invest anywhere with the same expectations of return, and to the employment mobility of a group having a high-level of skill in finance, development, architecture, planning, and management.

In my interviewing, I wanted people's beliefs and judgments to emerge at their own pace and judiciousness, as each person discussed any of the topics below. The discussions reflect their own ideas, definitions, and associations: the interview not only was open-ended but it was as much as possible under their control—where his/her ideas went, mine followed. The ideal interview was one in which the person kept up a steady stream of talk on the topics I introduced. The best possible answer was a question, "Do you mean . . . ?" to which I could respond, "However you see it is what I'm interested in." In that way I elicited their own definitions of terms, the import the question had for them, and the relations they saw it having to other subjects. Their spontaneity is attested by the length of time they went on talking without requiring any questioning or prompting. My questions and comments are italicized in the text excerpts. With their permission, all discussions were tape-recorded.

The transcripts have been minimally edited, to retain the natural language and trains of thought. They are sometimes a strain to read, with their repetition, incomplete phrases, and poor syntax. Reading as though listening to them may help. I made this choice in order to guarantee the opportunity for other interpretations of the social thought being articulated.

To insure the anonymity of those I talked with, I do not identify each pseudonym with occupation, race, or locale, although the city identification will come through sometimes in their own remarks; sometimes, in order to clarify the particular context for certain statements, I add information about race or occupation. The page numbers following the text excerpts are those of the interview transcript.

My data are not people's answers to the questions asked; the questions were put not because I was interested in the substance of

15

the answers per se, but because I wanted to generate fresh and spontaneous responses that would as naturally as possible contain their assumptions about many aspects of land use. Neither are their responses to be evaluated for their analytic sophistication or truth-content, nor for the differing points of view such a heterogeneous group could be expected to have. For these people are not, and were not intended to be, statistically representative. Rather, I have generated a body of public, not private, conventions and understandings—a "universe of discourse" as it were—of the American system of land use from those centrally active in it. Not using the canons of survey research, I had no pretested interview schedule designed to generate data of uniform character for quantitative analysis; instead, my fieldwork was intended to produce a "native's account" of the American land-use system from the points of view of those largely in control of it. I interviewed the people I did simply to get a reasonably complete configuration, for I was not concerned that each person should cover the same ground. On the contrary, to delineate this universe each person's discussion is one star in a total constellation. What one might miss others might emphasize, but the configurative outline would be unmistakable (Werner and Fenton 1973).

The responses often include quotations of consumers' opinions and state what the interviewee thinks others think, perhaps disagreeing ironically or skeptically. Or some may mention a prevalent belief that they know has been tested in research and found untrue. These statements too are analyzed without respect to their sources or their truth-content, and are regarded also as part of this body of publicly shared conventions and understandings.

Furthermore, before starting fieldwork I decided that for reasons I discuss shortly, interviewees' education, life history, marital status, sex, age, and race were not variables on which my analysis would depend. I asked no questions about these matters, so that whatever appears on these topics was volunteered. All persons occupied executive positions of one sort or another, closely involved with decisions made in various phases of metropolitan development. I do not distinguish between those persons having private enterprise roles and those in public service. The significant fact is that professional positions are highly interchangeable in the actual workings of the land-use system, attested by their own experiences: An elected public official was also in the real estate business; a

16

private developer now engaged in profit-making residential development had spent two years in government working in a less-developed country on public housing finance and construction; a planning consultant to public agencies as well as to private developers was also teaching graduate courses in a private university; a mortgage banker had served as chairman of his city's publicly constituted urban renewal authority; another mortgage banker was on the city planning commission; a large-scale private developer was a member of his state's housing authority. Not only would it be infeasible to trace out with any certainty the influences on these persons' ideas of such life experiences in light of their present position; it would, moreover, overlook the ethnographic fact that the American system of land use is populated by people in positions interchangeably public and private, pragmatic and scholarly.

This interchangeability of professional role and of organizations in which people work may itself be a clue to understanding why change in the system comes so slowly. Any new constraints or incentives that are proposed in federal or local legislation are viewed in the round, for these are people who can see the consequences from all sides. What constrains someone else today may be one's own harness tomorow. This is the reason, moreover, that I refer to the institution of land use as a system, for it reflects the enduring interdependency of public and private, producers' prices and consumers' taxable income, of property-tax policies and land-use regulations—to name only a few such pragmatic relationships.

In the interviews, I used the various technical terms customary in land development—planning, investing, writing mortgages, appraising. The scope of the questions reflects many of the major problems previous studies in economics, law, and political science have identified (Clawson 1971). I also asked questions specific to their answers, and I would, as well, venture my opinions in order to further elicit theirs, to provide a mutuality of concern with the topics (Dexter 1970). Every interview was unique in the sequence of topics, the probing I did, and emphasis—evidence for my claim that the interviewees generated the data.

The development professionals and public figures I talked to consist of three mortgage bankers, an appraiser in a private firm, a public assessor, one city councilman (also in real estate), two

17

developers, one elected municipal executive officer, two federal government executives, three executives of large oil, insurance, and development firms acting as liaisons between public officials and citizens, and four civic leaders concerned with development issues. I also spoke with one architect and planner, and recorded a group discussion of a large project, just then on the drawing boards, with six development executives in marketing, architecture, planning, and financing, called here the Goss Group.

I introduced subjects intended to bring out ideas about the economic relationship between land-use values, how they arise and are maintained, what values people can and cannot directly control, how effective zoning is and what its objectives are:

What do you think economists mean by their expression "contagion of value"?

Are there any conventions that you question, relating to "what will sell"? Have there been any developments that were surprisingly successful?

Have you been involved in any investment deals that did not go through, and why? Innovative? How?

Do you think that there are local, regional, and national differences in the ways that investment risk, property appreciation and depreciation, and so on, are defined?

What about the present system of development seems to you to be unfair? How should things be, ideally? What role do you see for yourself?

What is your evaluation of zoning as a means of dealing with the separation and mixture of land uses?

What do you think of the proposal that zoning should be administered regionally and not by each municipality?

I was also interested in the interviewees' ideas about the relationships between land uses and property values, their explanations of land-use trends in metropolitan areas, and their ideas about social relationships as a function of land-use relationships:

What do you think the homeowner thinks works for and against his investment?

Is there a difference between the populations who own and those who rent?

What causes neighborhoods to decline?

Do you think that there are many people who own or are buying their houses who are "house-poor" (overcommitted in terms of income)?

Do you think homeowners expect to make a profit on the re-sale of their houses?

How much social life do you think goes on within the residential neighborhood?

Compared to his education level and his occupation, how important to his reputation is a person's residence—house and neighborhood?

Compared to roads and shopping centers, why are low-income housing proposals always disruptive?

What do you think contributes to neighborliness among people living in both the city and the suburbs?

Why do people put boundaries around their neighborhoods?

What disappointments do people seem to have about new suburbs as compared to older ones or to the central city?

Do you think the suburbs are still a symbol of "arrival" socially?

I present the interviewees' responses at length throughout, and although they raise many interesting subjects, it is their assumptions and beliefs that have engaged my interest. From them I generate my initial interpretations with which I also reanalyze data of many other kinds (legal, economic, social). My analysis also draws on my professional career in land-use matters, a stint of participation and observation that began in 1957 with experiences ranging from local government (representative town-meeting form) to federal government (policy planning in the Office of Metropolitan Development at the U.S. Department of Housing and Urban Development); practical (working on the revision of a town's zoning law and evaluating appeals for variances) as well as theoretical (a book proposing new grounds for evaluating environments responsive to human use).

This work owes much to many specialists in land use and housing who also have addressed and are addressing these long-standing issues from their particular perspectives in law, economics, and planning. The major figures of the American housing and planning movement—Charles Abrams, Percival and Paul Goodman, Jane Jacobs, Lewis Mumford, Catherine Bauer Wurster—have laid an enduring and fertile groundwork, and I could not have made my departures without them. Thirty years ago, at the brink of those policies now come to flower, John P. Dean, a sociologist and anthropologist, published *Home Ownership: Is It Sound?* with a foreword by Robert S. Lynd. Dean's work laid out for consumers facts not then generally available, scrutinizing the ideology itself. Friedrich Engels first published "The Housing Question" in 1872: "The worker who owns a little house to the value of a thousand thalers is certainly no longer a proletarian, but one must be Dr. Sax [a commentator of the times] to call him a capitalist" (Burns 1935: 346).

Henry Nash Smith and Carl Sauer have ploughed the meaning in American life of homeowning as homesteading. Architects and critics have always dwelt on the significance of personality and spirit in the design of the house, and anthropologists have long since recorded the integration, symbolic and functional, of setting and society (Warner 1959; Rapoport 1969). The community sociologists—Louis Wirth, Robert Park, Maurice Stein, and the many who have come after—document the uses and significance of hearth and neighborhood in urban society. There is—will be—no end to asking after the implications of the ways we go about sheltering ourselves for the kind of society we are building.

THE ANALYSIS OF AMERICAN CULTURE

First and foremost, this is a study of concepts Americans use in thinking about land use especially, and, inevitably, about other things. Not an inventory of the diverse ways in which the American system of land use actually works, nor a comparison of the ways its many professionals, politicians, and citizens carry out their roles, this study seeks out the social forms, functions, applications, and origins of public thoughts:

> Human thought is consummately social: social in its origins, social in its functions, social in its forms, social in its applications. At base, thinking is a public activity—its natural habitat is the houseyard, the marketplace, and the town square. The implications of this fact for the anthropological analysis of culture . . . are enormous, subtle, and insufficiently appreciated. . . .
>
> [I]deas are more difficult to handle scientifically than the economic, political, and social relations among individuals and groups

20

which those ideas inform. And this is all the more true when the ideas involved are not the explicit doctrines of a Luther or an Erasmus . . . but the half-formed, taken-for-granted, indifferently systematized notions that guide the normal activities of ordinary men in everyday life. (Geertz 1973: 360, 362)

Raising these "taken-for-granted notions" to the status of data, doing epistemologically in my own society what anthropologists customarily do in others, brings up several general issues of interest, I hope, to many besides anthropologists.

Social thought, in being a public activity, is therefore best explained at the same level—that is, by reference to society-wide events. Private thoughts, on the other hand, are best explained by looking into the psychology and structure of the emotions and the intellect. I try to discuss those definitions and premises that I find are guiding public behavior, then, always in the context of social, political, and economic activities. The purpose is to find out what those activities and events—which are so much more often described—mean from a society-wide point of view. Man is an animal, writes Clifford Geertz, "suspended in webs of significance he himself has spun," and taking "culture to be those webs," its analysis is "not an experimental science in search of law but an interpretative one in search of meaning" (1973: 5).

The ideas and methods of this science of social meaning in part derive from the branch of semantics called semiotics, the study of signs.[1] Those conventions we take for granted, students of social meaning take apart. A sign is "*everything* that, on the grounds of a previously established social convention, can be taken as *something standing for something else*" (Eco 1976: 16). Those conventions have to be elucidated, in each case, for in them is the explanation for the inevitability of the connotation.

[1] The early contributors to semiotics were Ferdinand de Saussure (1916) and Charles S. Peirce (1932). Recent interpreters extending the theory of signs to include social and cultural evidence are Barthes 1967 and Eco 1976.

The bibliography lists several classics demonstrating the interdependence of cultural and sociological analysis (Durkheim and Mauss 1963 [1903]; Geertz 1973; Leach 1954, 1976; Schneider 1968, 1972; Tambiah 1969; Turner 1957). A collection of estimable commentaries, articles, and bibliography is in Douglas 1973. Keesing provides a tour through various definitions of culture in addition to his own alternative (1974). Fernea and Malarky discuss ways in which the social anthropology of the Middle East and North Africa might now benefit from a deeper venturing into the semiotic approach (1976).

Looking upon everything—events, rules, and actions—as signs standing for still others is the province of cultural anthropology. Semiotics only extends its traditional interest in symbols, ever a preoccupation once the ethnographer in an alien society is faced with learning how to hear, speak, and interpret another language, itself one kind of system of signs. Always, objects, rules, and practices stand for others and finding out by what system rituals, songs, myths, and customs differ from and relate to one another is perhaps what social and cultural anthropology is best known for. Specifying the organization and structure of the system of differences in order to interpret it in the same way its members do is the ultimate goal.

As I use the term, therefore, the "system" of culture consists of relationships among those constituents such as rules, definitions, categories, conventions, and premises, and the actions and artifacts in which they are embedded. These relationships occur for some good reason or other that it is the task of cultural analysis to propose. Each comes to our attention because of its difference from every other, defined and actual. These *differences* carry meaning, for it is by not being that we distinguish one thing from another. To know culture is to know how and why the differences are as they are, and to get that information it is necessary to study people's behavior and the signs and symbols with which they communicate these differences.

This search for social meanings embedded in the American system of land use ranges over many subjects because its signs point to them. Our everyday vocabulary for discussing zoning, renting, homeownership, and neighborhoods compresses relationships that a semiotic analysis has to take apart in order to connect afresh. The referents I identify are found in social practice, in the written law, in the structure of economic incentives, in historical events, in the tools of industrialization, and in American ideology.

As I have said, I have not sought out referents in the structure of individual cognition, attitudes, or affect less because I know they are not relevant, for I do not, but more because ethnographically there is so much concrete sociological and cultural evidence needing first to be put on the record.

With one exception, these perspectives are no longer unique to anthropology, only especially emphasized by it. Examining beliefs as themselves data does perhaps call for a turn of mind that may be

22

a unique hallmark of anthropology. We are more accustomed to read beliefs or ideologies as positions with which we feel impelled to agree or disagree, amend or extend. Here, beliefs are data, about which no such decisions are to be made: they simply are. The research question is to find what fuels them.[2]

For that reason, whatever the persons interviewed said I have looked upon as objective data, just as neutral and accessible to further analysis as the incidence of bankruptcies or the age profile of a population. I take it that these assumptions, definitions, and beliefs guide the actions of people in the land-use system in the same way that last quarter's earnings statement does. Our own beliefs may be the same or not, but, as partners in a "collective contract," we understand what is being said. That is, within this particular social institution of land use there is a universe of discourse that, like language, "is essentially a collective contract which one must accept in its entirety if one wishes to communicate" (Barthes 1970 [1964]: 14).

The interviews therefore appear to tell us what we already know. I have pored over them, reexamining my own experiences

[2] "Social" and "cultural" anthropology are both engaged in the comparative analysis of social organization and principles of social structure. This construct "cultural system" is meant only to round out the convenient vocabulary in wide use—"social system," "political system," "economic system." Just as political and economic systems are made up of activities said to be related according to particular principles, so are cultural systems made up of elements (units) having relationships with one another (Schneider 1968). Identifying both the elements and the principles by which they are related is the subject of cultural analysis.

This approach sees culture and social action in conjunction and it differs in several respects from that of those anthropologists calling themselves ethnoscientists whose main interests are in the cognitive processes involved in constructing, learning, and internalizing norms and rules. For the latter, see Goodenough 1970 and 1974 and Colby 1975; for the former, see Geertz 1973, Leach 1976, Parsons 1973, and Schneider 1976.

Another clarification: except as already mentioned, the difference between the disciplines of sociology and social anthropology is minimal in terms of theoretical outlook, and anthropologists, too, study the comparative sociology of politics, status, the professions, race relations, migration, and religion. Methodologically, anthropologists are eclectic, even sharing sociology's priority for quantitative representativeness and statistical test when warranted by the problem, but more often they remain "committed to a different kind of thoroughness—one based on the depth and comprehensiveness" of their observations and study of a given topic or group (Wagner 1975: 3).

and understandings, in order to raise questions about the sources of our shared commonplaces, legends, and lore. As such, the interviews are treated as ethnographic texts, in the way that traditionally recorded definitions, rules, and myths of exotic societies are. Only those texts are reproduced that struck me, after reading and pondering, as worth looking into further, in ways and for reasons I explain shortly. I sometimes treat data and findings from other sources (sociological, legal, economic) also as cultural evidence, and equally as manifestations of the social thought that is my subject.

I interpret the texts systematically, by which I mean they are discussed in terms of other features of our social, political, and economic systems, not in terms of the personality, nationality, occupation, or religion of the interviewees. Their role, age, and race are, for my purposes, superfluities, for I do not have the objective of analyzing either "American national character" or the motivations of "interest groups," two familiar tacks taken on the subject of culture and values.[3]

The distinction between psychological and cultural analysis is particularly important. Magnifying states of individual mind and

[3] *The Lonely Crowd: A Study of the Changing American Character*, by David Riesman with Nathan Glazer and Reuel Denney, has had the greatest impact of any in the last twenty-five years. *The American Business Creed* by Francis X. Sutton, Seymour E. Harris, Carl Kaysen, and James Tobin, published nearly twenty years ago, is based on the premise that creed and belief are but tissues of rationalization mending the psychological conflicts businessmen experience in their public and private lives, through their business and institutional interests, and in their ideals and compromises with them. One survey of American-character studies, beginning from Frederick Jackson Turner's 1893 hypothesis that "the traits of the frontier" distinguish Americans, finds that whichever traits were proposed, by journalists, novelists, poets, literary critics, historians, and—only since the 1930s—social scientists, each was "simply a vehicle for the delivery of opinions on the contemporary scene, and the national character itself was relatively unimportant" (Hartshorne 1968: 189). He finds two details of character so employed: the American either as a materialist conformist or as an idealistic individualist. Calling these "national caricatures," Hartshorne proposes that they represent an attempt to retain as long as possible the traditional Jeffersonian theme of agrarianism, which Turner had so appealingly re-stated. Only when industrialism proved to rescue the nation in World War II did commentators begin to identify a positive relationship between industrialization and representative democracy.

24

emotion into states of social systems is one kind of psychological reductionism to which cultural analysis as I practice it is intended as antidote. The problem from my perspective is to explain social matters in terms of collective, not individual, behavior. When American culture is treated as though it is American character or personality, analysis necessarily depends on those metaphors and constructs, such as attitudes, dispositions, and motives, developed to account for the operations of individual mind and emotion. Social psychological analysis can be illuminating in appealing to our own understandings of personal relationships and experiences with fear, envy, love, prejudice, hope, self-interest, insecurity, anxiety, confusion, dissonance, and conflict. Often, though, it does not also examine those situations structured by the impersonal, collective elements of political, legal, economic, and social systems that provoke, precipitate, or reinforce our passions, attitudes, and dispositions. There are meanings to social events and social behaviors that cannot be explained by reference to psychological processes as we know them, and trying to may even obscure their society-wide sources and significance.

Instead, considering culture to be a shared system of signs—and not an American mind regarded as an individual mind writ large—improves the prospect that cultural analysis may help to explain aspects of society previously less accessible to study. By postulating that ideas, beliefs, premises, assumptions, and definitions (and the signs and symbols standing for them) are independent data and that they are evident in the collective consequences of individuals' behaviors, those social practices (not the attitudes and behavior of an imaginary actor) can be the subjects of inquiry.

Earlier I said that I was avoiding the term "values" in the hope of drawing conclusions more useful for the analysis of the structure of social and economic systems. Values in one sense are general norms or agreed ways of going about things, spoken of in terms such as achievement and success, efficiency and practicality, individualism, material comfort, conformity, rationality. In another sense, values are categorized into sets of objectives or "systems," as in the several "isms"—liberalism, conservatism, socialism. In a sense I prefer, values are specific ratings used in the operations of a social system: in the system of land use they are socially shared propositions about the relative merits of various levels of density in settlement patterns, types and styles of housing, subdivision layouts and land-use arrangements, configurations of population composition, and so on.

These shared criteria for defining those relative merits are built up out of a rich stock of axioms: untested, taken-for-granted, tacit, irreducible, and unquestioned—our cultural apparatus. With these axioms we go on to construct the propositions of a social geometry—many social geometries—to guide ourselves in many endeavors. That is, we encircle a subject or triangulate a problem by using these axioms and propositions: We mark off social categories, make moral judgments, and identify public and scientific problems on the basis of conventional understandings. Here I am looking only at those conventions in this artificial slice of life I call the system of land use; the effort to raise up their invisible social geometries should be made for other important institutions—public education, health care, governance, law enforcement, and industrial organizations. Having always imperfect knowledge of how such domains are put together and why they work as they do, we "explain" in the everyday with such propositions and conventions far more than we do by means of proven generalizations. Social geometries are in much wider use than are the social sciences.

I adopt this metaphor of a "geometry" to draw attention to our undefined terms and unproved propositions for two reasons: To shift the vocabulary away from psychological concepts, and to concentrate on a form of cultural analysis aimed at putting cultural evidence on the same footing as those other empirically available social facts such as census data, market operations, and voting patterns. Understanding and evaluating the performance of large-scale industrial societies requires that culture be analyzed as objectively and as rigorously as markets and migration. As will be seen, I try to document the existence of cutural conceptions by tracking down their concrete consequences in order to demonstrate the active role—the public, empirical role—of the elements of culture.

The very act of analyzing what we take for granted addresses our attention to our own subjectivity, as we, as citizens, scholars, researchers, and policymakers, work in our worlds of research questions and public problems. By definition, members of every society share conventions and understandings, which, obviously, in literate, democratic societies, once revealed, are simultaneously open to affirmation, to question, and to change. One contribution

of the anthropologist as professionally concerned with beliefs is to
help maintain an objective social science, watchful that the problems as defined are less tainted with the biases cultural membership necessarily implicates us all in.

But despite the importance of becoming more aware of our own
subjectivity as a screen and despite my concern with the limitations of social psychological analysis, it is equally my position that
subjectivity and imagination are at the same time essential if we
are ever to discover the meanings of the events that we try to explain. Long ago, Democritus posed an argument between intellect
and the senses about what is real. Says intellect: "Ostensibly there
is color, obstensibly sweetness, ostensibly bitterness, actually only
atoms and the void." Responds the senses: "Poor intellect, do you
hope to defeat us while from us you borrow your evidence? Your
victory is your defeat" (Schrödinger 1967: 177). Without our subjectivity tuned as a sounding board, we can be acquainted with
many facts but be defeated in comprehending them (Weber 1947).

Not psychological understanding, but contextual: it is that anthropological and semiotic perspective I emphasize. The quanti-
fied data that are more familiarly the products of social scientific
investigations are, we need to remember, only ciphers standing for
people's activities. Unless replaced in the contexts yielding them,
they are defeats to understanding masquerading as victories. For
meaning is a product of the relationships among elements that, in
belonging together, by definition share a context and that, in so
doing, differ from other relationships and their context.

My working methods are a consequence of the search for context and for those differences. They are also a result of the fact that
I am an American studying my own society, not reporting on people and their actual relationships, but unearthing the conceptual
framework for their activities. The ethnographic unit is not a
village, tribe, or region, but a major institution or what Americans
consider a subsystem of complex society. In first examining my
interview data (and once confronting its familiarity, despairing
even more of discovery than ethnographers usually do), I concentrated on several pairs of consistently salient categories, one half
of the pair defined in part by the other: owner–renter, single-
family-house–apartment, suburb–city, home–work, oldtimer–newcomer, high- and low-density, stability–change, homogeneity–
heterogeneity, among others. Familiar as they are, I decided to

27

regard these as bottled messages that, in arising from this one domain, would help to decode each other. Next, asking what composed the differences within each pair led straight to the contexts from which each half draws its edges, the media in which it thrives: those details of custom, convention, relationship, and event giving rise to the distinguishing features of each.

I did not look to every possible context but at those my perspective classically emphasizes: social relationships and the social practices and mechanisms through which they are realized (Mauss 1967 [1925]; Firth 1967; Sahlins 1972). Those relationships and forms defined the differences within each pair. Then I put them under the light of certain American beacons: those uniquely American ideals embodied both in our basic documents (the Constitution and the Declaration of Independence) and in the American ideologies of opportunity and progress. I of course found contradictions between these ideals and social practices in the system of land use, but rather than stopping at criticism I take these disparities to be themselves cultural products. What are more commonly labelled problems are here taken as data, in order to ask about the origins and uses of these American contradictions. The puzzle being worked consists of those misfitting pieces of ideology and practice, asking the same questions of them as we ask of other products such as norms, rules, rights, and obligations: where do they come from, who uses them, for what purposes, and how do they relate to other cultural products? Contradictions, paradoxes, and inconsistencies are thereby substantive elements and points of departure for analysis.

Regarding contradictions this way provides a key, perhaps, to working in one's own society. Observing at home does not provide that immediacy of contrast available abroad that throws all of one's conceptions into doubt, the doubt that provides the anthropologist of one culture with the certainty of what there is to be said about another. Instead, I had to provide my own contrast and doubt in order to reach beyond what I already knew.

And, indeed, the field research with which every anthropological career begins is the mother and wet-nurse of doubt, the philosophical attitude par excellence. This "anthropological doubt" does not only consist of knowing that one knows nothing, but of resolutely exposing what one thought one knew, and indeed one's very own ignorance, to the buffetings and denials which are directed at one's most cherished ideas and habits by other ideas and habits

28

which must needs contradict them to the highest degree. (Lévi-Strauss 1967: 43-44)

Nor was an exotic society providing me with insights about my own:

> The anthropologist's efforts to understand the subjects of his research, to make them and their ways meaningful, and to communicate this meaningfulness to others, will grow out of his abilities to make meanings within his own culture. Whatever he "learns" from his subjects will therefore take the form of an extension or superstructure, built upon that which he already knows, and built *of* that which he already knows. . . . And this is why it is worthwhile studying other peoples, because every understanding of another culture is an experiment with our own. (Wagner 1975: 8, 12)

Those pairs of opposites: they are not entirely my ideas, but are those I found in use. The texts here, from interviews or other sources, are not used because they fit *my* themes: *they are* my findings, these pronounced, indigeneous definitions and distinctions. Those are the presenting reality I am after. Nor, I add, are these the same as the "binary oppositions" Lévi-Strauss manipulates in order to discover universal properties or structures of the mind. I am not at all interested in their formal or logical properties, but only in their substantive sources and sociological properties.

In that deceptively simple distinction between prefiguring categories and finding them rests what is probably the major theoretical difference between the anthropological perspective and that of other social sciences. Anthropologists are consistently cautious that their own categories may be wide of the mark, narrowing down observation, screening out telling behavior and events. By beginning from the premise that classifications and categories are themselves of social manufacture, anthropology concentrates on the apparatus itself. So ingrained is this traditional open-mindedness—an inductive or naturalistic perspective—that it has been leading anthropology itself to doubt two of its most traditional analytic categories, kinship and belief (Schneider 1972; Needham 1972). For example, their study of Balinese kinship leads Geertz and Geertz to conclude that

> what once seemed so indubitable—that kinship forms a definable object of study to be found in a readily recognizable form everywhere, a contained universe of internally organized relationships awaiting only an anthropologist to explore it—now seems very

much less so. . . . When one sets out to study "kinship" and ends up talking as much as we have found ourselves doing about status rivalry, political combat, and, especially, religious style, the idea begins to dawn that whatever system there is in all this (and we hope we have shown there is a great deal) is not likely to be formulable in terms of the sentiments, the norms, or the categories pertaining to "consanguinity and affinity." (1975: 153, 155)

Another influential broadside has been made on the analytic category of beliefs. Ethnographers have always reported "what people believe," but, Rodney Needham has asked, whose category is that? "Clearly, it was one thing to report the received ideas to which a people subscribed, but it was quite another matter to say what was their inner state (belief, for instance) when they expressed or entertained such ideas. . . . [The purpose of this inquiry is to show that] the first task of social anthropology is . . . the undermining of categories throughout the entire range of cultural varieties in the conception of human experience" (Needham 1972: 2, 203).

C. Reinold Noyes, a legal scholar, cautions in his classic *The Institution of Property* along these very same lines. One must "distinguish between the legal form and the real substance of the . . . institution of property" because that substance "consists of a certain system of relations among men which are devised, developed and practiced in social economic life. These relations exist as independent phenomena. They are social habits, capable of being viewed in many different aspects. . . . But the legal clothes in which this institution is wrapped, and the so-called rights, according to which these relations are analyzed and classified . . . are but conventionalized abstractions from the facts themselves" (1936: 18). Noyes, too, would have us question the conventions in order to look twice at the original forms.

Last, the milieu I live and work in has itself influenced my choice of this approach. Allowing as we do for divisions between scientific and humanistic thought and endeavor, we perpetuate a separation between the technical (as neutral) and the moral (as evaluative). In so pragmatic a realm as provisioning a growing society with housing, jobs, schools, parks, roads, and amenities there has come to be a technical vocabulary for thinking about these functions: neutrally stating costs and benefits, counting demand and estimating preferences, scheduling priorities and expenditures. A powerful terminology, it dominates thought and controls the definition of problems. Hard: concrete, empirical about objective matters, so it is believed. Alongside its charts and trend lines are the social and moral civic objectives enunciated in legislation, in the Constitution, in the common law: soft, qualitative, idealistic, subjective, unreliable. Intellectually I find the technical-moral distinction one born of expediency masquerading as sophistication. But ethnographically, it is the fact that upon this duality turn matters of tremendous importance: decisions about what problems there are, how scarce resources will be expended on them, whose professional advice is esteemed—in all, what Americans decide knowledge is and what it is for.

I, too, am an American pragmatist, hoping to demonstrate that these two believed-in poles are just that. In observing an all-too-ready psychologizing and personalizing by otherwise rigorous analysts when they attempt social and cultural interpretation, I did not want to reinforce that tendency. Circularly, in downgrading the worth of nonquantitative studies there is a dearth of them, and in their absence, personal experiences are substituted for ethnographic and sociological data and analysis. Then, justifiably, those interpretations are set aside, never to enter analysis. Far from solving the problem of blending cultural evidence with other kinds, this study states it as thoroughly as I have been able for one existential domain.

Around each of our existential concerns are formed institutions, each having special assumptions, definitions, and rules. Both public and private, these are a major feature of industrial society. Individual action is constrained in their terms, providing persons with greater or lesser degrees of freedom. We know that individual differences under the same conditions can be great. To specify the structure of these institutions, as the constants from which psychologists and sociologists can measure variation, should be the work of the cultural sciences. Education, health, religion, law, community development, industry, science—each has become a specialized institution manufacturing and using systems of meanings, some unique, some shared. A science of social meanings enables us to find out how those systems affect the structure and the performance of these institutions and, ultimately, the quality of each person's right to life, liberty, and happiness.

31

Chapter Two

The Ladder of Life: From Renter to Owner

In American society the form of tenure—whether a household owns or rents its place of residence—is read as a primary social sign, used in categorizing and evaluating people, in much the same way that race, income, occupation, and education are. There are, of course, people who actually own and people who actually rent, and there are likely to be as many differences as similarities within each group. But besides those social realities, there are also meanings attached to each, axioms circulating in the general currency of social exchange. The categories of owner and renter are, then, real and symbolic. What the symbolic meanings are and why they take the form they do is what needs to be explained.

In this chapter I explore the reasons why the two forms of tenure are so widely viewed as inherently distinctive, setting people in each category apart along so many dimensions: in personal attributes, in social esteem, in the spatial arrangements of new developments, in zoning district classifications, in building codes governing occupancy, and in their differing rights under the law. I will be giving my account of the reasons why renters have lower social status than owners, why the spatial separation between housing for each tenure group and between income levels is a consistent feature of American land-use priorities, especially in the design and marketing of new development, and why people in settled neighborhoods so often object to renters and to multifamily structures.

The people I talked to make the proposition that the life cycle is composed of a sequence of events to be lived out in a correct order, each stage matched by appropriate marital status, amount of income, ages of children, school years completed, leisure tastes, tenure form, and housing type. In distinguishing between the characteristics of renters and of owners, they see the correct sequence of the life cycle as being an intrinsic feature of these differences— first a renter, then an owner. Further, this pervasive belief in a single correct chronology of life events etches the meaning of the transitions from one stage to the next, for what matters is the perfect attainment of each stage, that is, not being in-between. In turn, these stages provide clues to the meanings of the differences in social status the categories signify, but not, I find, differences attributable to income, age, or occupation. With these ideas I take a new look at the social and economic functions of the widespread homeownership that is so central a fact of the American residential domain.

Historically, both Philadelphia and Houston are metropolitan areas having high rates of homeownership. The texts therefore speak to questions similar to those being posed today by the many suburban areas today not accustomed either to renters or to higher population densities. People more familiar with neighborhoods where rental units and multifamily structures are more common, as in Manhattan or in the central parts of Chicago for example, would not, I expect, be joining in this laughter:

I was staggered. I met someone last night who lived in an apartment for eight years, and I couldn't believe that. Eight years in the same damn apartment, you know! [Laughter] (Goss Group: 24)

Nor would they make this analysis, knowing of the generations of apartment dwellers raised and educated in stable city neighborhoods.

Renters, I think, will tolerate—renters I think are more value or more dollar oriented in the sense that they will seek out the best value for their renting dollar and put up with characteristics in a neighborhood which are—unstable characteristics, or that is, unstab*lizing* characteristics. They will live where the school district perhaps is not so good because they're in a different stage of the family cycle. Renters, I think, you'll find have fewer children of school age than owners. They will live perhaps closer—they'll want to be perhaps closer to their job location but in a neighborhood which is not quite so desirable to own. They therefore I guess will have better transportation opportunities but lesser recreational, lesser environmental. I think I could characterize a renter as a person who is willing to sacrifice something, either for cost of living or accessibility to work—so he will tend to live in a less stable—I don't want to mix the words. (Pope: 19)

RENTERS, OWNERS, AND THOSE BETWEEN

Here are some succinct previews of definitions from texts quoted fully later:

RENTER

-just keeping afloat, using up all monthly income
-young
-not saving
-have no choice
-job situation very mobile
-float from job to job
-gray collar, not blue collar, just keeping even with the economy
-empty nester, investing capital elsewhere
-wants a carefree situation
-apartment is an intermediate step
-he's older now, safer in an apartment than in a townhouse
-historically anyone who rented in the South is a temporary sort of person
-in the South particularly you're just not the best type person if you're a renter
-we're in a transition stage in adopting the renter as being the full-fledged citizen
-not just an attitude, but it's really true that these people live differently
-tenants do live differently, they think differently and they're not as conservative as homeowners tend to be
-in the real slum areas, they don't own the property, that's the problem
-not truly indigenous to the neighborhood
-not as likely to maintain property
-always prefer to own
-could be gone tomorrow
-can't afford to own

OWNER

-homeowners' ethic means a very high value on you
-a step up the ladder of social as well as economic standing
-great deal of pride even in the ownership of very modest dwellings
-people display the fact that they own that house even though it may not be much of a house

-display the fact that they are independent

-they have reached a certain stage in their lives where they can tell the world that this is mine

-predominant thing in people's minds as being a mark of quality of the person

-generally speaking the homeowner takes better care of his property

-more safe, nontransient in nature

-neighborhood of homeowners is very residential

-can function better

-have the ability to make decisions about where they will live and what they'll do

These texts provide still a third category, that of the townhouse or condominium owner, that is, the owner of a unit that is not a single-family-detached housing unit, a category that interviewees see as having to be explained, partly because it is a category new to them and partly because it is a category combining, as they see it, features of both owning and renting:

TOWNHOUSE OWNER (*or condominium owner*)

-doesn't compete with single-family house for square footage

-it's the last stop

-people are tired of the yard

-children have left home

-young couples who don't need a larger house

-young couples not ready for the yard tools and the maintenance

-lazy man's style, and everyone wants to be lazy if he can afford it

-poor man's way of living like a rich man because he has the lawn taken care of, swimming pool cleaned by someone else, exterior of house maintained

-the roof leaks, he picks up the phone

-a natural transition from being a tenant to a homeowner

-everyone ought to go through that stage

-some people just aren't ready for homeownership

-the townhouses have caught on because a lot of people . . . want that owner's feeling so they're catching on pretty well

-townhouses [as distinguished from single-family] are somewhat less conducive to children ages 7-16. They're okay for young children, and they're okay for much older children. They're [townhouses] right down the middle of the child-rearing time.

35

One widespread axiom is that renters and any units not single-family-detached within the vicinity of owner-occupied single-family-detached housing will lower the resale value of the latter. One person suggests the strength of that belief in finding that even when renters are persons having very high prestige they do not change that perception, nor the actual market values based on it:

I suppose there is a theory that anytime you rent that you're bringing the quality of the neighborhood down because the theory is that anybody who rents is less desirable than someone who owns. And in the case of Pasadena, probably in the case of some sections in Bel Air where there's a large leasing market, it's probably true. Your house is worth less by virtue of the fact that the house on either side of you is leased to Michael De-Bakey or Denton Cooley [famous surgeons] respectively. *That's an appraiser's rule of thumb?* That goes through people's minds. I don't think there is any real rule of thumb if you're going to be objective about it, it is too easy to categorize things, to put labels on things. (Fare: 16)

Another person speaks of public reactions "to apartments next door" that he has observed:

Well, while there is some overbuilding in apartments, I think that they're acceptable. I think that the question of acceptability is not so much a question of whether there should be apartments or whether there shouldn't be apartments. It is whether it should be apartments *next door to them.* I don't think that the people in the subdivisions are objecting to there being apartments in town—they don't have objections to people *living* in apartments, they just don't want them living next to them. I think from that standpoint they are acceptable, it is a question of where they are. (Peat: 35-36)

A calculated judgment from the appraisal perspective classifies apartments as "reasonably domestic," but barely so:

Generally, unless we get too far out off the scale, apartments can exist practically next to practically anything. As long as it is—what do I want to say—reasonably domestic atmosphere as opposed to a—well apartments would do better next to a bad strip joint than they would next to a light industrial user. (Fare: 27)

In a similar vein, another person reports that homeowners are seen to be "very residential" and "apartment dwellers" less so:

Another one is that when you are getting into a very residential type neighborhood, largely occupied by homeowners, which are found in Philadelphia except in the very central part, they just don't consider the apartment dweller as being truly indigenous to the neighborhood. They just don't. *And the homeowners are there first, is that what you're saying?* They have a very proprietary attitude about the neighborhood. (Gale: 12)

Here, Pope is asserting that even if the housing types they live in are the same, renters and owners cannot be mixed; although each can occupy adjacent blocks, no mixture within blocks has ever been "intentionally" proposed to a developer:

I think—no lender has ever told me this, but I would have to think that lenders would be somewhat reluctant to see a mixture in the same identifiable project. I am not talking about a PUD where you've got a rental project on one block and an ownership project on the next block. This is a different kettle of fish. But if you mix the two in the same—you can take the same *housing* type, the same design almost, and segregate the two groups, and you will be okay. But if you mix them, I don't think it works. *So what you are really saying is that this sort of thing was probably never proposed to a lender.* Not intentionally. *Not intentionally, yes.* I shouldn't say never, it may work elsewhere in the country. But it has not *here* been successful. (Pope: 8)

The Goss Group also finds that a plan mixing renters and owners will not see light of day:

It may be that there is this sort of feeling usually on the part of owners that people who rent are transient and I guess less culturally rooted and able to care for their property or just different, and consequently there is also a real difference in management and handling of the property. There are all kinds of legal and other kinds of things that cause you to end up segregating in your plan, projects and housing, let's say, that's rented from that which is owned. I guess we are all—some of us are pluralistic in our—I can see functional and environmental ways of mixing these things that I think would have some social benefit but I have yet to be able to achieve it in a plan. *So you can achieve it in a plan, but you can't sell it, [to the boss] is that what you are saying?* By achieving it in a plan I mean make the programming of that a believable thing so that it is reasonable to put it on a plan and then assume that the plan will be implemented. (Goss Group: 6)

Pope finds that houses for sale will not find takers if there are people renting them too:

Do you find that there are differences in definitions made about owners and renters? What do you mean "in definition"? *Are they conceived to be separate categories of people?* Yes, very definitely so. *How? How so?* Renters are nonpermanent, renters have different motivations in terms of maintaining their units, in terms of commitment to community, in terms of involvement in community. Owners view renters as having different attitudes. Therefore, it becomes very difficult to mix owners and renters in a single project, i.e., if you took a ten-acre parcel and put 200 units on it or whatever, and you tried to and you willy nilly tried to sell or rent those units, you would be, I think, almost universally unsuccessful at *selling*. You could get renters in. I have seen this happen as a matter of fact in one specific project here. In a rental situation the management of the project reacts in different ways than in an ownership situation. And the owners of this specific project, which are in the minority, are not satisfied. They don't feel as though they are getting the kind of service that they deserve, given the fact that they *own* their units, whereas if they rented them they might be content. The renters appear to be quite content with the kind of service they are getting. (Pope: 8)

One person with long experience in evaluating subdivision plans terms any mixing of renters and owners "planting a booby trap":

What is the appraiser's attitude, in terms of owners and renters living side-by-side or next door? This may not be the answer you are looking for. When you mix them you are just planting a booby trap. For eventual devaluation, renters and homeowners do not mix well regardless of what the hope may be. *What happens?* There is a decline in the area when the renters come in. *How come? What causes it? What goes on?* The old-fashioned pride in homeownership. The difference between a tenant renter and a homeowner is in the majority of cases quite marked. *What are these differences? How do they show themselves?* You can tell when a house is being rented and when it is being owned. From the maintenance of its yard, its appearance and so on, its upkeep. *Are the people themselves different?* No, not the people. But their motivation is different. *Really. That the homeowner is reselling his house every day, is that what you are saying?* He has an economic stake and he is going to protect his investment. The tenant is not under that compulsion.

Well, is it protecting his investment or is it enhancing his investment? Maybe there's not much difference? No. When the average homeowner is going to be there six years and he knows he is going to have to sell his property, is he protecting it or enhancing it? *Yes. Did you say—is that the average length of stay for a homeowner here or is that*—Nationally. The average homeowner on a national basis owns his home six years. *Do we know how much it appreciates in that time, do we have any figures on*—In some cases it appreciates—the value of the land climbs so fast and the replacement cost of materials and labor cost so much that it's actually appreciating. *So he is moving up, upward and onward?* In a twenty-year period I owned three homes and made a profit on all three of them. And as a Civil Service worker that's on a very low economic level. (Dole: 7-9)

A survey reporting currently received conventions provides still another kind of cultural data. The acceptability of various housing types was assessed in eleven New Jersey suburbs, which were studied as a cross-section of growing localities (New Jersey County and Municipal Government Study Commission 1974). Local leaders in and out of government—106 in all—discussed their "perceptions and attitudes" toward multifamily development. The authors of the study regarded them as "community 'gatekeepers,'" officials who decide "whether or not multifamily housing will be constructed, what types of housing are constructed, and where in the community they are to be located" (75). The leaders were asked not only about their own positions on these subjects but also what they thought residents' positions were. This fieldwork was part of a larger effort designed also to find out about the costs of development of various kinds, in a fiscal analysis comparing tax revenues and expenditures in terms of added population and increased requirements for schooling and other public services. Therefore, the study also evaluates these perceived differences among housing types and their occupants for the degree to which they agree with the facts of fiscal impact. I discuss those data in Chapter Five.

These are the main findings about apartments in general, that is, those developments not associated with subsidized housing. The majority of those local leaders say that residents consider apartment dwellers to be different, and they "saw their constitutents as being hostile to apartments and apartment residents, generally on visual or social grounds" (83). Comments leaders heard from other residents reported as "typical" include:

> They're ugly; all packed together; will be future slums.
> Wild things going on there.
> They're flooding our schools.
> Costs us too much money.
> They don't care about the community. (83)

SUBURBAN RESIDENTS' ATTITUDES TOWARD APARTMENTS
AND THEIR OCCUPANTS AS REPORTED BY SUBURBAN LEADERS
(Frequency of Mention)

	Percentage
Apartments are undesirable housing types (look bad; don't fit into community; too urban; too high density)	23.3
Apartments are fiscally damaging to the community (don't pay fair share of taxes; don't pay their way)	20.8
Apartment residents are transient and don't care about community; don't get involved	20.0
Apartment residents have too many schoolchildren; place burdens on local school system	12.5
Apartment residents are socially undesirable (welfare recipients; hold wild parties)	9.2
Apartments place particular burdens on specified municipal services (traffic; fire)	5.0
Other unclassified negative comments	6.7
Positive comments	2.5

(1974: Table 5-9, p. 84)

That is how apartment residents generally are perceived: persons living in subsidized developments (by definition, apartments) "are considered particularly undesirable" (86). Almost three-quarters of the suburban leaders (73.5 percent) felt that "low- and moderate-income housing would be unacceptable in their community" (85).

SUBURBAN LEADERS' ESTIMATES OF LOW-
AND MODERATE INCOME MULTIFAMILY HOUSING

A. *Nature of Impact*		*Percentage*
Social/Racial Conflict		42.6
Social problems	18.8	
Racial problems	12.5	
Ghetto/slum creation	11.3	
Community Hostility		23.8
Fiscal Problems		21.3
School Problems		6.3
Public Safety Problems		2.5
Positive Impact		3.8
B. *Reasons Given for Impact*		
Tenant Social/Racial		
Characteristics		43.7
Community Prejudice		15.5
Physical Deterioration		14.1
Service Demands		5.6
School Demands		5.6
Unclassified		11.3
Positive Reasons		4.2

(1974: Table 5-11, pp. 85 and 86)

On the question of where apartment residents come from, suburban leaders themselves thought that "the majority of apartment residents in their community had migrated from a major core city." In one suburb, 7 out of 10 residents "felt that the greater part of garden apartment residents in that town came from major cities in New Jersey (typically Newark or Jersey City)" (84). In the same suburb, however, only thirty-one of 493 garden apartment residents (6.3 percent) had come from those cities (84). A more general survey of about 4,000 New Jersey households reports these findings:

41

Present Housing Type Occupied	Previous Place of Residence			
	Same Town	New Jersey Major City	New Jersey Elsewhere	Outside New Jersey
		(Percentage)		
Garden Apartment	23.0	6.1	43.6	31.3
Townhouse	7.5	3.1	43.6	45.7
High-Rise Apartment	19.1	5.5	28.5	46.9
Single-family House	17.2	2.4	54.6	25.9

(1974: Table 4-3, p. 55)

THE CORRECT CHRONOLOGY OF LIFE

A correct sequence of life—"the straight line"—is laid out and to be followed:

I think so, I think there is a definite difference between owners and renters. I think even renters and owners recognize those differences. I think there is a negative syndrome against renting by people who own. It's almost no matter, even the price range doesn't seem to make that much difference but the guy who owns feels that he has made a commitment and he has done the right thing. He has done the thing that he was, you know, his parents told him he ought to do and he has followed the straight line and he's, you know, he's doing the right thing. "The renters tend to be more transient. They're a lower class of people. They haven't been able to raise the down payment and decide what they want to do with their lives, they haven't grown up, they're not mature and so forth."

These are all exotic generalizations. But there is a grain of truth in almost every one of them. On the other hand, I think the society is beginning to break up, the patterns are breaking up. Take a look at the divorce rates anywhere in the United States. . . . And so the society is breaking down and renting becomes more and more of, less of a fixed type situation. It offers the flexibility. We've noticed in the rental patterns here in Houston, for example, almost 100 percent turnover in rental projects on an annual basis. . . . And transient type people always create unrest amongst people who tend to be more stable. So I think there's a social thing. You know, that the other guy's got to be somebody to watch a little bit because he is going to pick up in the middle of the night and steal away. (Goss Group: 47-48)

Another text ties the progression of career to neighborhood choice:

Don't you think, really—I don't care what anybody's government tries to do, people prefer to seek their own level. They prefer to live in a neighborhood of the same type of people they're working in. I think if people are successful, that they advance. Let's take somebody that starts out as a teller at a bank and advances to be president. As a teller of the bank he lived in one neighborhood. When he becomes bank president he wants to move to another neighborhood. I mean I don't think you shun your friends, but I think that economically . . . I mean—gee, I've got friends that are still friends of mine that I knew when I worked at Sears Roebuck, but by the same token you do— you are drawn into the neighborhood that you can afford, and I think that the people who didn't have anything—they've given their kids too much—all of us do—but we want to move into a neighborhood where we can give our children more, we can give our children things we didn't have. (Case: 25)

Apartments are equated with an "intermediate step," not a permanent choice:

Do you see a difference in the populations that own and rent? Well, there are two differences, I think. Maybe more than two, but at least two. One is, typically, the renter is the guy that can't afford to own, that is to say, he is using up all of his monthly income just simply to keep afloat, he doesn't acquire any savings to speak of, and so you have that kind of situation, which is a large number of young people, and, again, what I'd call maybe not blue collar but gray collar people who are just kind of keeping even with the economy, and those people simply live there because they don't have a choice, economic choice. And then the second category, I think, is again the person whose employment situation is very mobile. Let's take a case where a construction worker may float around from town to town simply because that is where the work is. . . . I guess the third is, again, the same people who make up this sort of empty-nester category, the person who wants not to have his savings tied up in a resi-

43

dence but would rather invest it in some other thing and wants the carefree sort of a situation. My mother is a good example of that, living in an apartment and not having any responsibility for having to sell it if she gets ill or living there alone. . . . So, you have a variety of reasons for the apartment dweller, but I think those are the most predominant ones. I guess there's some people that just like apartments, and I don't know who they are. . . . The apartment tends to be an intermediate step or a step dictated by sort of convenience rather than, "I've always lived in apartments and I want to live there forever," you know —that's not a large segment of our market. (Hale: 4-5)

SACRED HOUSE, MUNDANE APARTMENTS

What is getting said and why is it being said? The key was provided by one person, who upon being asked whether he thought there were differences between owners and renters, replied immediately:

You mean character differences, moral differences? *However you see it. Whatever there are.* Of course, historically, anyone that rented in the South is a temporary sort of a person. This is the attitude. Homeownership is the predominant thing in people's minds as being a mark of quality of the person, and I think probably this is one reason why minorities will not adopt a townhouse. They will not have it. It doesn't have the significance in their minds, the prestige and all. I've talked about this subject several times to my Equal Opportunities expert here who's a Houstonian, originally from Atlanta, and—but he's an appraiser, been in the mortgage business, the real estate business, and he's black. And he knows these things. We've worked very well together because we think alike. He used to work for me, and he knows my problems and I think I understand his. The real thing has been that in the South particularly you're just not the best type person if you're a renter. Now this is changing. Big influx of people from elsewhere who talk differently, and but basically this is a homeowner town in attitude. So this is the reason minorities haven't taken to the liberal life styles, as I call them, of apartments, townhouses, or highrises, here pretty much a failure, conventional, FHA, and otherwise. We don't really need highrise because our land isn't that expensive. Our freeway system is still adequate and we get out where land is cheaper. So I'd say that we're in a transition stage in adopting the renter as being the full-fledged citizen. You'll find this, that this is reflected also in church locations, and church giving. They watch their pocketbook like everyone else, so in church surveys and all when they find that they're in an area that's changing, and areas here do change from single to multifamily, and if they find that they're becoming surrounded by apartments, they find that their collection plate is not as full as it has been, and the people attending the churches are fewer, and so it's a fact. It's not just an attitude, but it's really true that these people live differently. Tenants do live differently, they think differently, and they're not, as you might say, conservative, I guess, as homeowners tend to be. And I think it's partly dictated by fact or fantasy as far as our part of the country is concerned. (Moon: 12)

I begin by examining the special qualities that culturally define the American family and the single-family house in the American system of land use. Later I ask how these qualities relate to the meaning of renting.

In its legal instruments—zoning ordinances, deed restrictions— the American system of land use is defined into a hierarchy of uses at whose apex is the single-family-detached house. The size of its lot and its four private yards varies from zoning ordinance to zoning ordinance, as well as within them, but the designation of the figure "1" or "A" to mark the category never does. (Examples of zoning regulations appear in Appendices 1 and 3.) Land for commercial and industrial uses may sell for more per acre and the buildings on them may cost more per square foot to occupy, but none is valued socially as highly as the single-family house on its own lot. One legal scholar, commenting on the landmark case in the United States Supreme Court, which in 1926 established the constitutionality of zoning as a valid exercise of the local police power, has said:

> . . . Regulation of land use separations based on taste must necessarily carry with it the implicit acceptance of value judgments about the ordering of land development. Certainly this is true of residential zoning, in which the conventional separation of single family dwellings from apartments can only be defended by judgmental preference. Zoning strategies based on this preference carry

with them an implicit hierarchal model of residential development in which single family development is favored. . . . These assumptions provide the theoretic underpinning for the fountainhead *Euclid* case, and for much of what passes as municipal zoning. . . . Zoning imported from the nuisance cases [of the common law] a simple model of residential development based on a taste hierarchy in which single family residences stand at the peak. Apartments are accorded a secondary buffer role between the preferred single family use and other uses, which are supposedly even more obnoxious to the single family home dweller. (Mandelker 1971: 32,84)

Another lawyer, active in current land-use practice and proposals for reform, has written:

> . . . zoning caught on as an effective technique to further an eminently conservative purpose: the protection of the single-family house neighborhood. In spite of all the subsequent embellishments that objective remains paramount. (Babcock 1966: 115)

In 1935, on their return to Middletown, Robert and Helen Lynd compiled a "rough pattern of things Middletown is *for* and *against* —in short, its values," culled from "local editorials, club programs, civic-club and other addresses and papers, and from conversations" that "represent widely-held Middletown attitudes" (1937: 403-4).

> By and large Middletown believes . . .
> That "progress is the law of life."
> That "the natural and orderly processes of progress"
>   should be followed. . . .
> That a man owes it to himself, to his family, and to society to
>   "succeed." . . .
> That "the strongest and best should survive, for that
>   is the law of nature, after all." . . .
> That competition is what makes progress and has made
>   the United States great. . . .
> That the poor-boy-to-president way is the American
>   way to get ahead. . . .
> That the family is a sacred institution and the funda-
>   mental institution of our society.
> That the monogamous family is the outcome of evolution
>   from lower forms of life and is the final, divinely
>   ordained form. . . .
> That home ownership is a good thing for the family and
>   also makes for good citizenship. (1937: 405, 406, 407,
>   409, 410, 411)

46

The family "is a sacred institution and the fundamental institution of our society." The family and the good citizenship that homeownership is believed to instill are equally idealized and, thereby, equated. A sacred quality endows both the family and its "home," sacred in the sense of being set apart from the mundane and having a distinctive aura. The proposition is, I suggest, that in the hierarchy of land uses all those below the apex partake of less of this sacred quality, but when one follows those "natural and orderly processes of progress," if one engages in "competition" and "gets ahead," then one can achieve the ideal family existence, fulfilling both the American Dream and the American Creed. Any other residential dwelling, the Goss Group puts it, is a "compromise" with those ideals.

The hierarchy of land uses is at the same time the ladder of life: one climbs the ladder as the "natural progression" through the stages of the life cycle—from renting an apartment or townhouse, duplex, or attached row house, to owning, as still another step, any one of those, along the way to the ultimate rung, that of owning a single-family-detached house. In taking the ladder rung by rung, the movement is altogether upward, an evolutionary progress as well, toward salvation from "lower forms" to a "final, divinely ordained form."

In the landmark decision maintaining the constitutionality of zoning, the apartment house, presumably to be occupied by families along with other household types, is there classified *as a business or trade, properly excluded from residential districts.* The Supreme Court held that the "open spaces and attractive surroundings" of detached house developments are destroyed by an apartment house, a "mere parasite" taking advantage of "residential character."

> The serious question in the case arises over the provisions of the [Euclid] ordinance excluding from residential districts, apartment houses, business houses, retail stores and shops. . . . This question involves the validity of what is really the crux of the more recent zoning legislation, namely, the creation and maintenance of residential districts, from which business and trade of every sort, including hotels and apartment houses, are excluded. . . .
>
> With particular reference to apartment houses, it is pointed out that the development of detached house sections is greatly retarded by the coming of apartment houses, which has sometimes resulted in destroying the entire section for private house purposes; that in

47

such sections very often the apartment house is a mere parasite, constructed in order to take advantage of the open spaces and attractive surroundings created by the residential character of the district. . . .
Village of Euclid v. *Ambler Realty Co.* (1926) (quoted in Haar 1959: 163)

"Detached houses" are thus to be set apart from all other places in which people might live. They produce their own aura or "character"—a sacred aura, I suggest.

In 1974, the Supreme Court, through the majority decision in *Village of Belle Terre* v. *Boraas*, defined the characteristics of single-family residential areas, from which more than two unrelated persons living together in a single-family house, are, in its decision, properly excluded.

> A quiet place where yards are wide, people few, and motor vehicles restricted are legitimate guidelines in a land use project addressed to family needs. . . . The police power is not confined to elimination of filth, stench, and unhealthy places. It is ample to lay out zones where family values, youth values, and the blessings of quiet seclusion, and clean air make the area a sanctuary for people. (416 U.S. 9)

Again, connotations of the sacred: residential areas provide "blessings" and are a "sanctuary."

In his dissent Justice Marshall spotlights the privilege afforded the blood relatives of the family, in that "two or twenty" of its members can live in one single house, a privilege not accorded those making a free choice in associations.

> The choice of household companions—of whether a person's "intellectual and emotional needs" are best met by living with family, friends, professional associates or others—involves deeply personal considerations as to the kind and quality of intimate relationships within the home. . . . The instant ordinance discriminates on the basis of just such a personal lifestyle choice as to household companions. It permits any number of persons related by blood or marriage, be it two or twenty, to live in a single household, but it limits to two the number of unrelated persons bound by professional, love, friendship, religious or political affiliation or mere economics who can occupy a single home. Belle Terre imposes on those who deviate from the community norm in their choice of living companions significantly greater restrictions than are applied to residential groups who are related by blood or marriage, and compose the established order within the community. The village has, in effect, acted to fence out those individuals

48

The Ladder of Life

whose choice of lifestyle differs from that of its current residents.
. . . There is not a shred of evidence in the record indicating
that if Belle Terre permitted a limited number of unrelated persons to live together, the residential, familial character of the community would be fundamentally affected. (416 U.S. 16, 17, 20)

Not defined to be a family, a *group* living together is mundane:
all of the effects it has by virtue of its size, in terms of the traffic
and noise its numbers may generate, are, unlike those equally to
be produced by a *family* of "twenty," regarded as earthly nuisances. Indeed, in the words of its attorney during the oral argument, that is the "crux" of the Village's case:

> At this point I think we come to the crux issues [*sic*] in the
> case. Are there any circumstances in which the village can treat
> the family, because of what it is, because of the value it has for our
> society, can it treat the family different [*sic*] from the unrelated
> group? (U.S. Supreme Court: 7)

He is asking the court to set the "single-family" apart constitutionally—and it has done so—as a legitimate classification under the
First Amendment, the grounds of Marshall's dissent. Violation
of Belle Terre's zoning ordinance results in the charge of "dis-
orderly conduct."[1]

MOVING UP THE LADDER: THE DANGERS OF TRANSITION

There is an "order of things" that people "strive for" and their
"arrival" is mediated directly by the "house with lawn and trees
and flowers."

> I think that insofar as the land use problem is concerned,
> that when people buy a house, they buy a neighborhood. They
> buy a chunk of a piece of neighborhood. They really want that
> to make them middle class even if they don't have the educa-
> tion and the job that are commensurate with middle class, you
> see. In my view, they are willing to buy—I don't care—a guy

---

[1] One analysis hostile to this decision finds a contradiction in it. Earlier,
in a decision concerning food stamps, Justice Brennan, writing for the majority (which decided against the United States government), deemed the
government's assumption of differences between households of related and
unrelated persons to be "wholly unsubstantiated." The author goes on to
ask whether, in the case of Belle Terre, "the Court holds the word 'zoning'
in special reverence." (Marquis 1975: 430)

may work as a construction worker, construction workers make a lot of money. So if he makes enough money to buy a house with a lawn and trees and flowers, and all his other neighbors are doctors, and lawyers and Indian chiefs, as far as he is concerned he has arrived at the middle class status, the education and the job thing—he *bought* his stake in it. I think that is what people are more concerned with.

Now, as to whether they really feel middle class or not because of job, I think that's an individual thing. I think that's part of this insecurity about status which makes them oppose low income housing. See, I think that they believe that, well, if there is any public housing in their neighborhood it is going to affect their status. They want their neighborhood to be recognized by its *name* as a middle class neighborhood. I live in a section called Windfield. People who live there primarily want you to understand when they say Windfield, that you're talking about an upper middle class neighborhood. *Who do they say this to, who are they trying to impress in this way? Friends, relatives, people on the job?* I don't even think that the individuals identify that themselves. They don't recognize it, that they're trying to impress anyone. It's just that they feel threatened. I don't think they sit down and analyze why they feel threatened because they may change their minds, they just feel threatened, the order of things is being changed, and the things which they strove for are being changed. (Dock: 4-5)

Residential land use patterns are, then, embodiments of the stages of life that are tied to natural, evolutionary processes over time. *What is out of place spatially is thereby out of place chronologically.*

What unifies people socially and spatially is that they are moving up the rungs of the ladder at the same time, according to Gale:

Do you think people do spend much social life in their neighborhood these days? I think they do. This might sound heretical but I'm not opposed to the neighborhood concept of living, I'm not. I think it's very fundamental to our way of life. If I looked for the smallest unit of our democracy, it would be the family, and I'd say the next unit going up in our democracy is the neighborhood. O.K.? When you take that and use it in a way, in an attempt to justify unwholesome things, then it kind of turns me off, because I don't like people to use that concept to buttress then something that I would not agree with. Now, what is a neighborhood? I don't agree that it ought to be a melting pot of Americana. I don't think it *can* be, but the people there should have some common interests which says that they don't all have to be black, or all have to be white, but there is a certain economic-socio status which is somewhat of a spectrum, but not the total thing, which tends to pull them together because that's the determinant of mutual interests—where you came from, what you're doing, and where you're going. This is what tends to bring people together in a group. (Gale: 9-10)

". . . where you came from, what you're doing, and where you're going"—but is there not a contradiction? Renters are described as transient, unstable, not thrifty, without pride, immature, lower class, not full-fledged citizens, indifferent to property maintenance —all opprobrious characterizations. Renters have to be doubly thrifty, in fact: saving up their downpayment at the same time as they are paying rent. But the emphasis is distinctly on "moral" or "character" inferiorities of various kinds. These axioms do not frame "transiency" as an expression of improving one's job ("where you're going"), a deepening of skills ("what you're doing"), or any other positive features of progressing. Indeed, renters are also thought *not* to be progressing—but as permanently renters.

Why the opprobrium? According to the correct chronology of life, living in a rental unit is the natural and normal thing for single people and for young couples without children; a young couple with enough money for a downpayment upsets expectations. And, even after renters are finished with that stage, they display the same attitudes:

Our experience on the thing is that it's, generally speaking, the planners and developers try to keep it from getting all mixed up, because their feeling is that the market—people who are buying—don't want the houses mixed up with the apartments. . . . There was a large open tract of land just west of our subdivision and it was sold and they're building apartments all over the place and all the residents got all upset. They extended the street on through to the thing, and they got indignant and went down to City Council and raised hell because all the traffic was going to come through and all those bad apartments people would be using *our* very own streets. And this is the kind of a attitude on things—so I think there is a feeling there, and of course, I think when people are living in apartments and then turn around and buy a house they have the same kind of feeling. And so it seems to be perpetuated. As a result I think this attitude has caused the developers to separate the apartments, townhouses from the single family areas because of the marketing characteristics. (Peat: 6-7)

The expression homeowners most commonly use in land-use disputes to describe the effect renters and non-single-family-detached structures will have is, "They will lower our property values." The concern overwhelming all others in these texts is spatial proximity, therefore: apartments are all right, "but not *next door.*" There are often enough effects on the amenities of residential areas from higher density development widely regarded as negative, as well as effects on the amounts transacted in the real property market, but as often positive as negative, as I will discuss in Chapter Four. The text below is clear evidence of one organizing principle in American society: social categories must be kept quite distinct from one another, "so they don't really touch."

We got a fairly conventional developer who was willing to take, at that time, extraordinary risk and build one of these, which I think it was the first modern one in New Jersey. Radburn of course was the first. He had a hard time getting financed initially because the whole real estate idea was that—he had townhouses opposite apartments sharing the common parking facility, which we still do to this day because it makes a lot of sense. That was considered to be a problem because you don't mix uses, you don't get them that close together, if you do a PUD [Planned Unit Development]. You do single-family over here and apartments over there and townhouses somewhere else, but you keep them separated by green space buffers and some mechanism for making sure that they don't really touch. *Was this a difference, do you think, between the rental of the apartment and the ownership of the townhouse?* No, they were both rental. Treat them both the same, it wouldn't make any difference. (Ream: 8)

In light of there being, however, a singular and inevitable sequence of movement from one social category to another, the

52

movement itself needs to be better understood. Transition is also at the heart of life's natural evolution from stage to stage. Transition per se is a major factor in metropolitan areas, as people move in and people move out—movement that is in addition to the growth also often found.

Transition is a universal property of life, marked often by rites of passage. People traverse social time and social space by leaving one social category to enter another. In analyzing the structure of these rites in a wide variety of societies, van Gennep, an anthropologist writing in the early years of this century, found three major phases: separation from the category one is in, transition itself, and incorporation into a different category (1960: 10). The stages take on their significance in terms of a culturally defined contrast societies make between what I shall call the safe and the dangerous. Those considered safe are those who are settled, who have not changed categories in a while; they are in some taken-for-granted status. Those on the move, in the process of becoming one thing but not yet settled into it—the pregnant woman not yet in the new category of mother, the traveler out of reach of his social place, or the betrothed who intends to change categories but has not yet—their in-between status makes them dangerous. Transitional, they are endowed with powers, mysteries, or dangers, "disturbing the life of society and the individual" (1960: 13). Rites of passage are intended to reduce their socially harmful effects.

Distinctions between the dangerous and the safe also appear in American social thought. The life cycle is believed to consist of moving from a less safe to a more safe status: each stage is correspondingly manifested in land-use categories and each is evaluated by its proximity to the apex, the sacred and the most safe because there is no better status beyond it. (Sunday, the Lord's Day, I might note, is often reserved for newspaper advertising of "homes," directed to families; Saturday [Saturn's day] ads are more likely to specialize in apartments, directed largely to single people.)

No matter how orderly renters' progression through life may actually be, the opprobrium attached to them arises instead from their category itself, by definition one of transition in American axioms about the sequence of life.

The social homogeneity so often stressed in land-use arrangements, as I discuss further in the next chapter, is also a device for

53

maintaining the integrity of the owner category, that is, its level of safety: the block of all owners or all renters, all one category or another but not both together, separated by four streets, helps to assure owners that they are safe from the dangers of transition.

Furthermore, these dangers are introduced into a category once it stops being wholly and uniquely one single thing. A mixed *category* is, by definition, "transitional," no matter what the composition of the social groups in it. Then, once dangerous, any and all other dangerous categories become appropriate neighbors. Pope is quoting from a report on the prospects of locating sites for subsidized housing:

> "Site controversy is very possible because most appropriate locations are usually in transitional neighborhoods." I would add to that, transitional neighborhoods are most often characterized by the most rigid kinds of individuals living in them. They're frequently old established neighborhoods, very slowly being changed and you will find very long term residents, with very strongly held ideas, frequently heavy ethnic concentrations, very strong sense of community which feel threatened by the introduction of new or different kinds of housing. (Pope: 15)

Locales where other kinds of category-blurring are taking place become, then, "the most appropriate locations" for housing not produced by the natural workings of the market.

Indeed, red-for-danger is a basic symbol in the American system of land use: FHA insuring offices have long had the practice of "red-lining"—that is, outlining on a map in red—urban neighborhoods that are, by their technical definition, so *transitional* that no insurance is to be written for new buildings going up in them; these neighborhoods, fulfilling the prophecy perfectly, inevitably decay physically because investors then stop maintenance on the older stock. In Houston, the custom is to term the sleazy subdivisions of fly-by-night developers "red-flag subdivisions" as a warning that they are dangerous to buy in. "Red-light" districts are at the margins of social safety.

All this may sound familiar. We have not yet asked, "Why?" What are the dangers to those ensconced in safety? What do threats to their safety consist of? Van Gennep's analysis points to one answer: the dangerous are seen to have the power to redefine those now safe back to an unsettled status, no longer one that can be taken for granted. In order to equilibrate these socially disruptive effects and to bring about the final stage of social incorporation, thus reducing the harms of transition, rites of passage are performed. Van Gennep calls these states of danger and safety shifting "magic circles," for in passing "through the various positions of a lifetime," people will one day see as dangerous what before had been seen as safe, or the reverse (1960: 13). Among primitive groups changes in social categories may include changes in spatial location as well, such as changes in place of residence upon marriage or changes in the places people may use only upon reaching a particular age. These "territorial passages" bring together social time and physical space, physical transitions marked often by special ritual performances.

We, too, have rituals to "cushion the disturbance" wrought by changes of land uses: the commonplace hue and cry that a new apartment building nearby will lower property values or that its higher densities will wreak neighborhood social havoc.[2] Homeowners, even though once renters themselves, mobilize displays of block or neighborhood opposition in the face of the threat of an apartment building—the transitional land use category par excellence because, although people live in it, it is less "residential" if not, as the Supreme Court ruled, a business use. Renters threaten to redefine the neighborhood as a whole: the owner's address of "Windfield" is no longer such a "good address" because in the marketplace its social and monetary value will be lower. Thus do the "magic circles" of danger and safety pivot throughout the social time and space of American neighborhoods in city and suburb.

[2] With respect to both constitutional rights and the effects of higher density development on the social and physical environment, such arguments are without merit if put forward on principle alone. Constitutionally, property owners are free to develop, and to sell for development, within the bounds of locally legislated zoning laws whose function in the first place is to protect the rights of both owners and their neighbors. Case by case, requests for zoning changes or a relaxation of restrictions may be rightly challenged by neighbors and others who foresee their effects as negative beyond ordinary expectations, negative either to the community's objectives or to themselves next door. Technically, there are many remedies that can both maintain an owner's property rights and protect against negative effects of higher density—for example, well-designed off-street parking areas; secondary access roads; time-restrictions on lighting, deliveries, and trash removal; landscaping for visual and acoustic purposes; and other such legal and feasible stipulations.

Still, why? The owners once renters have, in accordance with the American Dream and the American Creed, negotiated life's hazards and passed through its less blessed stages toward salvation in a sacred home. But "the order of things" people have striven for can be changed, according to Dock. Lower-income people can redefine the category middle-income people are in. Staying on each rung of the ladder is not such a certain thing, then, in American society.

Traversing the ladder in harmony with "the natural and orderly processes of progress" requires that each rung be distinct from the previous one. Once on a rung, it is with two feet firmly planted, lest, as in the old spiritual, "Your foot might slip and your soul get lost." There is no use being in-between; it is unsafe; it is "insecure." In American parlance, the thing to do is "arrive" socially; that is, to have negotiated life's hazards and passed through its less blessed stages to *full membership* in the next social category —without question. Any rung spatially out of place represents a chronological misstep.

Renters double the problem transition presents. Their very category signifies the prospects of transition for, axiomatically, renters should change categories. They are supposed to be in transit, but in fact they might never cease being renters. They may never become safe and sacred owners of single-family-detached houses. They may never attain complete social personhood in the terms of the American Dream: Not "full-fledged citizens," they are socially marginal.

The force of the metaphor of life as a ladder to be mounted rung by rung toward salvation is brought home in the category of the townhouse or condominium owner: the owner of a single-family, but not detached, house. Case, in the text below, outlines this life script, matching marital status and children with the appropriate housing type. Notice that he does not use the term "renter" to characterize this couple living in an apartment. They have made the *choice* of not having the "bother" of a house. Once the children are grown, the couple says, "The heck with it, let's take an apartment," a way of putting it that I take to mean, "We've followed the timetable exactly, reached the apex of a single-family-detached house, and now we're entitled to make any choice we want." Their reward is the freedom now to choose any type of housing, any kind of tenure, with cultural impunity.

56

... the junior executives, executives that can afford it and most of them can afford, even the white collar workers, can afford it, would prefer a house if they have children. So the apartments are going to the *young* married couples to start out in an apartment, to a lot of people who move in and have no children that have always lived in an apartment and don't want the bother of a home, and to the older people whose children have grown and they say, "The heck with it, let's take an apartment, we can lock the door, we can take a trip, we don't have to worry about the yard man, we don't have to worry about this, that and the other." (Case: 6-8)

The townhouse and condominium category is seen to be a reward for having naturally progressed through life's competitive hazards and its many dangers. The special term for this privileged status is a metaphor recapitulating an entirely natural process: the empty-nester.

Where the American dream for the majority of people is probably still to have the traditional detached house and you might not be able to afford that when you first get married and you live in a compromised situation until you can achieve that step. And so if we looked at that average pattern today we will probably say that still is the majority dream or desire, and so you still have the, as young couples who can afford to, the move-up pattern, where they might go from an apartment to a better apartment to a house. Or from an apartment to a townhouse to a house. . . . Another thing which is very important today is the fact that a lot of builders are now merchandising to a specialized adult household. They started with just the plain retiree types but now you can look at several family profiles which are each kind of distinct and have their own needs. One we referred to is the empty-nester. By the time the last child is sixteen or seventeen or eighteen or gone then they would be able to go from this big four bedroom detached house down to a convenient townhouse and easily get away on weekends and don't worry about yards and all that type of thing. . . . (Goss Group: 29)

Empty-nesters are *entitled* to be free from the burdens of the lawns of their four yards and the repairs to their detached house. In no text is it said of the renter as it is said of the townhouse or apartment owner, who is also an empty-nester, that "he picks up the phone and calls the landlord" for repairs. The renter, not having progressed or upgraded, does not *deserve* those privileges:

> I think the popularity of the condominium-townhouse is a fairly clear indication that after you reach a certain progression from the young married, and garden apartments, through perhaps an intermediate townhouse into a single-family house and maybe upgrading once or twice or maybe you just haven't made a very good deal the first time around, but there is a point in time when you disinvest in real estate and go to a townhouse which is plush and all that sort of thing, and you've accumulated a lot of nice furniture by now, and then you do begin to spend money in other places. One possibility is recreation and recreation property. Another is extensive travel—boats, and a lot of recreational things. I think there is that kind of trend, and I still think there is a life cycle. (Ream: 13)

According to Moon, in the text below, the townhouse has two functions in life's proper chronology: as a "natural transition" in "moving from renting to owning" and as "the last stop." Moon is the same person who asked, "You mean character differences, moral differences?" when I asked whether there were differences in the owning and renting populations.

> So I think, really, the townhouse, it doesn't really compete with a single-family-detached house as far as what you can get in terms of square footage. It's the last stop that you're selling. It's not the dollar value. *What is the last stop?* Those people that are tired of the yard, that the children have left home, and maybe young couples who don't need a larger house yet are not quite ready for all the yard tools and the maintenance and those things. It's a lazy man's style and everyone wants to be lazy if they can afford it. So this is a poor man's way of living like the rich man, because he has the lawn taken care of, the swimming pool is there, he can use it and it's cleaned by someone else. The exterior of his house is maintained. The roof leaks, he picks up the phone. It's sort of a natural transition from being a tenant to a homeowner. Everyone ought to go through that stage, really, rather than. . . . Some people just aren't ready for homeownership. We've had many townhouses that will sit vacant in areas where the people should be buying them, the lower-income people when the Section 235 program [ownership subsidies for low-

and moderate-income groups]. They won't *take* that house, even with part of their mortgage payment paid. They want the single-family detached. Poor people seem to be more conservative than the moderate income people. Much more conservative, even though it was almost a gift, and I've had some builders fail selling townhouses to poor people, even with 235. (Moon: 6-7)

In these texts a tone of forgiveness and understanding comes through, one not used toward renters. The renter category, in contrast to the townhouse or condominium owner category, is one people are in without having chosen to be. Though not fulfilling the American Dream of the "white little house with the vines on the side and the white picket fence," and opting instead for freedom from yard chores, notice that in the text below, they are "overqualified" for their townhouse purchase: they could afford the single-family-detached house if they wanted it.

. . . more and more people are buying townhouses, the townhouse condominium or wherever as a residential solution. And the thing we find almost universally is that people who are buying into those residential units, shelters or whatever it is they are buying almost generally are overqualified financially for their purchase. Now you know the American syndrome has always been the white little house with the vines on the side and the white picket fence and you stretch like hell to get in there because this is the American ethnic—ethic. [Laughter] It's an American ethnic, too. And then, but that's no longer what people want to do with their money and their time anymore. They don't want to mow their lawn and take care of the flowers and so forth and so it is becoming an incredible bore and they recognize that's merely make-work and that's not really the important thing. (Goss Group: 46)

The cultural meanings of transition captured in the renter category ripple throughout the system of land use, and I will be elaborating them in the following chapter.

THE SOCIOLOGY OF TENURE: RELATIONS WITH BANKERS AND LANDLORDS

How is it that the ownership of a townhouse or an apartment escapes the opprobrium attached to "compromising" with the American Dream of the single-family-detached house? Why are there no "moral" differences associated with the townhouse dweller? Why do lower-income and black households shy away from townhouses?

(So commonly is "ownership" associated only with the single-family-detached house-type that most economic analysis estimating housing demand has "depicted the demand for owner-occupancy as a de facto demand for residence in one family homes" [James 1975b: 38]. *Not being a tenant* is an objective quite separate from that of occupying a single-family-detached house, an objective that nowadays can be realized by cooperative and condominium relationships and by buying a mobile home, for example. Owning a cooperative or a condominium unit or apartment puts one into a housing type termed "multifamily" or "attached single-family" [row house or townhouse]. The multifamily housing type has commonly connoted renting.)

Several facts about owning and renting provide important background to the discussion with which I answer those questions. One fact is the continuing economic research into the costs and benefits of owning and renting, and now, increasingly, questions about the equity of public policies favoring owning (James 1975a and b; Aaron 1972). Nevertheless, greater savings for households are possible through ownership as a consequence less of the actual cash outlays they make and more because of the tax credits they receive and renters do not—income tax deductions and avoidance of taxes on capital gains are the major, direct credits (Table 1). Those benefits depend, of course, on income level and enough other deductions. One definitive study has established that when occupancy for at least three years in the same house is possible, then owning is more favorable; renting is a better buy otherwise (Shelton 1968). But, of course, it always depends on particular circumstances, especially the total of other income tax deductions. Another fact is the continual appreciation of real estate values, which is the basis for regarding the house as a profitable investment—a real and widespread fact, in the face of inflation. Owning is now the predominant tenure form for all types of housing (Table 2).

Owner is the majority social category. And it is the category providing the "mark of quality of the person," with higher social value therefore—greater status—than the renter category; the greater status is also a function of the demonstrated intercorrelation of ownership with higher incomes. The higher the income, the greater the tax advantages of owning (Table 3). The proportion of single-family-detached housing available for rent has declined by twenty-four percentage points in the past thirty years: 42.5 percent of the total supply was rented in 1940, 27 percent in 1950, 22 percent in 1960, and only 18 percent in 1970. In general, about 10 percent fewer row houses and two family houses are rented now than were rented in 1940.

In all, then, the proportion of the total housing stock in non-multifamily or trailer units previously available for renting has declined by nearly one-third over the past forty years (Table 4). Although the proportions of the housing stock in the various structure types have remained quite constant over this period, the tenure forms have changed drastically. We have to allow for the possibility, then, that current presumptions about the correlation between renting and low income are a consequence of these particular historical changes in the socioeconomic system—a subject I will return to.

These social categories are freighted with many axioms about the kinds and desirability of the behavior expected of each. "Ownership" is widely believed to cause the valued behaviors associated with it: when a renter changes categories and owns, so too will his behavior change. The owner category, with its more valued behavior, has higher status than the renter category. Federal incentives for ownership and the promotions of the building industry stress these propositions, which have been a continuing feature of American politics since 1931 when President Herbert Hoover called a major national Conference on Home Building and Home Ownership. In 1968 the Kerner Commission on Civil Disorders incorporated the ideal into its recommendations: "The ambition to own one's home is shared by virtually all Americans, and we believe it is in the interests of the nation to permit all who share such a goal to realize it" (National Advisory Commission on Civil Disorders 1968: 261). In 1971, at the behest of Leonard Garment, a member of Richard M. Nixon's White House staff, the National Institute of Mental Health convened a "Working Conference on the Behavioral Effects of New Opportunities in Extended Property Ownership," asking whether, besides the behavioral attributes associated with being a renter, those associated with being poor might be expected to change upon becoming an owner. The group, made up of university researchers in sociology, anthropology, public health, and government administration found, of course, no reason to attribute behavioral changes to a single source, and preferred to put ownership into a larger context of "access to jobs, to credit, to education, to union membership, to particular neighborhoods. . . . The question of property ownership is neither conceptually or empirically separable from larger questions of access and opportunity" (National Institute of Mental Health 1971: 2). Nevertheless, the question was asked seriously by the then-political leadership.

Legal theory and practice have also defined behavioral constraints and opportunities through these tenure categories. The secondary status of tenants is perpetuated in the various anachronisms of real property law, especially in terms of landlords' minimal obligations and tenants' maximum liabilities. The basic value of owning is in the freedom from the landlord's right of entry to inspect his premises, as well as in freedom from the customary restrictions in leases against personalizing rented quarters.

History plays a part, too, in the experiences of immigrants or their ancestors raised in a lingering feudalism, landless themselves or the younger brothers of those inheriting the patrimony, so that the sting of limited rights and privileges in property relations remaining today so explicitly in lease forms may also account for the higher value on owning both house and land. Indeed, it is the greater personal power of the owner over the family's abode and the social identity, autonomy, and self-respect following from it that are supposed to be capable of transforming feudalized tenants.

Federal legislation had been enacted in 1968 to make homeownership feasible for the poor—with just such behavioral effects in mind—by subsidizing interest costs. In 1971 the results of one major reexamination of its implications began to appear. Peter Marcuse, a lawyer and planner, looked closely at the legal, financial, and economic consequences of the program and of possible changes in it. He observes:

> Indeed, what actually are the benefits of homeownership for which there is such a universal desire? It is surprising that the question has been so infrequently asked, let alone that there is no very adequate answer available. Neither in the literature nor in the public debates are the precise virtues of homeownership spelled out: phrases like "pride of ownership," "security," "inde-

pendence," a "good investment," a "stake in the community," "well-maintained homes," appear over and over, but their precise meaning is not clear. Nor is it easy to pin down. (1972a: 1)

Defining tenure not as a relationship between an object and a person, but as "a relationship among persons, subject to rules laid down by and enforced by society," Marcuse bases his analysis on the view that "both ownership and tenancy simply [are] different names often given to bundles of socially determined rights, powers, privileges, and immunities among individuals" (23). Marcuse thereby converts the current stipulations commonly associated with "owning" and "renting" into an output analysis of each tenure form, in terms of occupants' rights and duties. Instead of an a priori, abstract definition, he analyzes separately those legal rights, privileges, powers, and immunities present in both ownership and tenancy. There are indeed attributes common to each form, he finds, and furthermore, there are no impediments—in legal theory, judicial precedent, or the economic organization of housing production and management—to defining leasing arrangements having the most valued attributes of homeownership. Nor is there any reason why the more numerous citizenship rights of owners, in terms of their having standing to speak at public hearings or legal proceedings, cannot be extended to tenants (1971: 156). Marcuse therefore proposes a new form of the tenure relationship making use of the incompleteness inherent in ownership, termed "conditional ownership" or "guaranteed tenancy," a form that "might optimize the bundle of rights, privileges, powers and immunities that tenure can produce" (1971: iii).

More problematic are the particular combinations of outputs associated with the single-family-detached house, a house type that does indeed provide for the greatest degree of freedom from any social relationships involving the common use of facilities or space (the hallways, entrances, party walls, and recreation areas that are shared in clustered and multifamily development). So strongly is the ownership category held a desirable objective, however, that Marcuse suggests that any tenure relationship could readily include "the privilege of calling oneself owner," especially because he finds owning intrinsically incomplete, less so than tenancy, perhaps, but nevertheless, ambiguous (1971a: 168). Noyes comes to a similar conclusion, calling the search for total ownership "a game of blind man's bluff":

It is true that we in America more nearly approach the possibility of complete property in land. But even here . . . an undivided totality is not so common and the identification of anyone who may indisputably be called an "owner" is often more or less a game of blind man's bluff. (1936: 303)

But no matter: ownership is a category so socially valuable that the many conditions fragmenting its totality do not affect its import. These fragmenting conditions not only are legal—as in public laws of taxation, building codes, occupancy regulations, and the common law—but just as compellingly, they arise from the real estate market. It is in the resale market where the very benefits of ownership as an investment are to be realized, but too much personalization even of an owner-occupied dwelling can blunt its attractions to willing buyers. The costs of painting over an idiosyncratic color scheme, for example, or installing structural modifications that might appeal only to a narrow group of prospective customers are inhibiting to owners.

Nevertheless: despite their chafing at "interferences" with their "rights" to "private property" (interferences not so different from those renters experience, that is), for Americans "to own" anything less than the single-family-detached house (the townhouse or condominium) is, these texts say, a "compromise" with the American Dream.

So it is that widespread beliefs have little basis in fact and such facts as there are do not explain themselves. Why do the limits to the owner's autonomy have so little effect on the higher status of that category? Why is the status of owner higher? Why does legislation, both federal and state, provide direct tax incentives to owners and not to renters? My answer arises from the differences between the contractual (social) relationship of the tenant to the landlord and the "owner" to the lender, but not in those differences in freedom or security so widely believed to be significant. There are other dimensions of the higher value placed on "owning" that have consequences in both the social organization and social order of America as a complex social system.

It is not a detour to explain why I put "owning" in quotation marks: paid-up mortgages constitute only about 40 percent of all mortgages. The correct general term is homebuyer. Of all single-family houses still mortgaged, *80 percent of the principal owners are younger than fifty-five.* Of all single-family houses without

mortgages—only 30 percent of the total stock in 1970—71 percent of owners are older than fifty-five. Only 26 percent owning
outright are between fifty-five and sixty-four: 45 percent are sixty-
five and over. *Of all those between fifty-five and sixty-four, 55
percent have no mortgage, but a surprisingly high 45 percent still
do.* "Homeownership" is a lifelong process: only when "owners"
are over sixty-five have 85 percent paid off the mortgage (Tables
5 and 6).

To review first the contractual situation of each: commonly the
owner is seen to be immune from any other person's right to inter-
fere with the security of his occupancy. Unlike the tenant, whose
lease specifies a term, the owner's continued occupancy is perpetual. Once a lease ends, the landlord can decide unilaterally not
to renew it. Because there is, however, no legal limit on the term
a lease can specify, the landlord-tenant relationship need not inherently mean insecure occupancy: commercial leases running for
ninety-nine years (and regarded by the parties as "perpetual") are
not uncommon. Nevertheless, it is not the custom for residential
leases to run much beyond three years; the customary term is between one and three years. Additionally, besides the right to evict
during the lease term, the private landlord can force tenants to
move at the lease's end without their having breached any of its
provisions; lenders can take possession only if the owner fails to
make payments. In the landlord-tenant relationship there are provisions "for speedier action and greater likelihood of eviction for
the tenant falling behind in his payments, but a correspondingly
greater cost and potentially much greater loss to an owner in default" (Marcuse 1972b: 119, 134, 146-47).

There are many variations, and recently there have been many
efforts to improve the tenant's position, but one significant difference in the contractual relation, to which I will return, remains:
once the landlord or the tenant fails to renew the lease, or once
the landlord evicts the tenant, their relationship is ended; oppositely, once the owner defaults, "not only can his occupancy be
terminated, but his liability in the mortgage continues, and the
mortgagee also has as security against a defaulting owner whatever
equity there is in the house" (Marcuse 1972b: 147).

My thesis is, first, that the higher status of the owner is conferred
by the relationship with the banker. Through this relationship
accreditation for full membership in society is realized, accord-

65

ing to the correct chronology of life. For although the single-family house is itself a possession and an asset, often enough a concrete symbol of higher income, it is less that fact which confers the high status culturally and more the achievement of a social relationship with the banker. That is, the banker "qualifies" the homebuyer with a credit rating that is a major threshold of American social personhood crucial in the correct traversal of the ladder of life. Not having to so qualify brings, on the one hand, even higher status: inheriting property has the highest status of all, because, in effect, it is the original qualification that is inherited. On the other hand, qualifying through the category of poverty brings neither social honor nor its consequences in self-respect because it represents an artificial passing of the threshold, the opposite of the American Creed of "natural progression." Being "able to own" is a threshold criterion to social personhood that renters, by definition, do not meet; they partake of less citizenship and on that account have lower status.

A guide to American practices in mortgage lending, prepared by the Department of Housing and Urban Development to inform "the less developed countries of the world where experience in the analysis of credit risk and the servicing of delinquent mortgages is less extensive than in the more developed countries" (a cultural account of these American practices, in my terms), describes the role of the banker as unmistakably that of the gatekeeper to social personhood (Grezzo 1972: i).[3] Under the heading "Evaluating The Risk," American lenders rate the following characteristics either numerically (1, 2, 3 . . .) or adjectivally (excellent, good, fair . . .): "His employability and the stability of his income . . . management of his finances . . . financial capacity . . . motivation . . . family and social relationships. . . . The minimum acceptable rating [of each] of these considerations must be established by each lender":

[3] The Equal Credit Opportunity Act, singling out discrimination on account of sex and marital status, took effect October 28, 1975, and on March 23, 1977 it was amended to add the categories of race, color, religion, national origin, age, and receipt of income from public assistance programs. The Act is implemented by the Federal Reserve Board (Regulation B). The Fair Credit Reporting Act went into effect April 1971; it protects consumers from the adverse effects of credit reports and asserts their right to be informed of the basis for credit denial. But it does not set standards for the conduct of credit investigations, and efforts to amend it to do so have come to naught (Whiteside 1975).

The evaluation of the stability of a borrower's employment and income should take into account his employment history, his training and education and personality; his employer's regard for him, the character of his work and reputation; and his age and health. But a borrower's ability to manage his finances is usually indicated by his past record. ...

A borrower's relationship to his family and friends is a significant element of risk although it is difficult to rate. Evaluators usually consider whether a borrower has an established reputation, a harmonious home life, associates with good reputations, and if he is active in civic affairs or whether he has been dishonest and untruthful in the past, has a troubled family life, and associates of doubtful reputation. (Grezzo 1972: 13, 14)

A journalistic account of the practices of the credit-investigating industry reports:

The areas in which adverse information may be collected on consumers applying for insurance or for employment or for home mortgages include such obvious categories as habitual criminality, chronic drunkenness, and participation in particularly hazardous sports, like skydiving, scuba diving, and mountain climbing. But they also range far from these particular considerations. One Retail Credit [the largest investigative company in the country] checklist for the use of investigators contains this: "Personal: Describe marital status, domestic life, personal reputation, habits, morals, and type of associates. Careful attention to personal standing in the neighborhood and community: whether popular, well liked or disliked. Describe membership and extent of participation in any civic, social, or fraternal organzations. Cover other leisure time activities." (Whiteside 1975: 69)

The banker makes the judgment whether the next step to salvation may be taken. "If a lender must reject a borrower's application for a loan, he should explain his reasons fully and should tell the borrower what he should do in order to qualify in the future" (Grezzo: 14). That is, the lender can specify with particularity how the threshold can be crossed. Once having successfully negotiated for entrance in terms of the most personal and social details of his life, undergoing an evaluation of total selfhood, family, and friends, the category of owner takes on the character of an insignia of social worth: "the mark of quality of the person."

Having this power to bestow social honor, which also leads to the blessings of salvation at the top of the ladder, the banker exerts far greater social control than the landlord.

Next, because the social relationship with the banker is maintained by onerous sanctions, some of the owner's higher status results from avoiding them. Defaulting brings disgrace, in the loss not only of a local social reputation but of one's standing with all other current and future creditors. One's total social "character," as J. P. Morgan termed it, is also at stake (Wiebe 1967: 134). These heavy institutional sanctions spill over into the other categories of social personhood so that the loss of standing in the owner category entails changes in other social categories as well, most notably that of husband or wife. One crucial aspect of the kinship system of modern society is the balance it is called on to provide for impaired social placement and self-esteem—crucial because families often break down when faced with that task. In a study of single-family mortgage foreclosures, both lenders and owners ranked "curtailment of income" as the main reason and both viewed "marital difficulties" as being one highly significant factor (Herzog and Earley 1970: 36). Among defaulting debtors (on loans other than mortgages), divorce was reported for 9 percent and of continuing marriages, 34 percent reported quarrels. In this study, more significant was the relationship between the creditor's threat of the debtor's job and, through that, marriage: of 1,330 debtors in default, the 63 percent "who actually lost their jobs because of the debt problem experienced marital strain and 58 percent of those who were worried that they might lose their jobs did [lose them], compared with 40 percent of those whose jobs were not threatened" (Caplovitz 1974: 284-85). During the current recession, the speedy passage in 1975 of federal legislation to forestall foreclosure acknowledges the large homeowning constituency facing financial and social loss.

The social loss radiates because there is much more beyond this threshold of mortgage qualification: homeownership provides assets far in excess of shelter and hearth in that, throughout their lives, owners have a wealth position markedly better than those who never become owners. Homeownership is so valued a category because of the consequent opportunities to accumulate wealth it confers. What happens to people not in, or excluded from, the homeowner category can best be seen in the tenaciously discriminatory practices toward blacks in the housing market. In a study of the effects of homeownership on lifelong assets, Kain and Quigley conclude that the "reduced Negro opportunities for homeownership . . . is an important explanation of the smaller quantity of assets owned by Negro households at each income level." Once traversing that rung on the ladder, wealth position improves considerably: taking the example of a conservative increase in house value, the authors argue that "the typical FHA-financed homeowner by age fifty would have accumulated assets worth at least $16,000 [from an initial investment in 1949 of about $8,000], a considerable sum that he could use to reduce his housing costs, to borrow against for the college education of his children, or simply to hold for his retirement." That is, "under reasonable assumptions about the appreciation of single-family homes, a Negro household prevented from buying a home since 1950 would have out-of-pocket housing costs in 1970 more than twice as high as the costs which would have been incurred if the family could have purchased a home twenty years earlier" (1972: 273-74).

Taking the case of black households as but a special case of those Americans never owning, it is clear that ownership has reverberations far beyond simple possession. The social reputation conferred by the banker is an asset that can be invested.

The social relationship forged with the banker endows owners, then, with social honor and greater prestige. So prestigious and honorable is the relationship that it can negate the "moral" differences associated with the multifamily unit, as we have seen in the "natural progression" to the ownership of a non-single-family unit, in the form of the condominium "empty-nester."

Hale is an executive involved in civic and development enterprises:

> . . . there is a sort of homeowner's ethic that puts a very high value on you when you become an owner. That's sort of a step up the ladder of social as well as economic standing. I think I've observed that [in a previous involvement with the Model Cities program]. I observed that in the less affluent stage of the community, particularly in the black community, there's a great deal of pride even in the ownership of very modest dwellings, and people will go to great lengths to display to the public that they, in fact, own that house, even though it may not be much of a house. They'll put up fences and they'll plant flowers and they'll paint the front of the house even if they don't paint the rest of it in order to display the fact that they are independent,

they have reached a certain stage in their life where they can tell the world that this is theirs. (Hale: 6-7)

Here, among blacks, the significance of the social relationship between "owner" and banker is emphasized over and above simple asset value: "the fact that they own that house" and less the value of the house itself—"even though it may not be much of a house."[4] What is so intensely problematic for black Americans, their first-class citizenship, is problematic for all Americans. It is one problem that widespread homeownership, as so basic a feature of American society, has tried to solve.

STATUS AND STABILITY

Until 1940 most families paid no income tax and those who did paid at the rate of only 3.6 percent, with the result that although tax benefits were available to homeowners, they had little impact on the production of single-family housing, an industry highly responsive to tax changes that make more consumer dollars available—so much so that a 1 percent increase in subsidy generally results in a 1 to 1.5 percent increase in homebuying (James 1975a: 7). With the rise in personal income tax rates to finance World War II, the appeal of these incentives became immediately more widespread (exclusion from taxation of net imputed rent—the return on equity—and the deductability of mortgage interest and property taxes). The improvements in the availability of mortgage credit, beginning during the Depression and lasting through 1950, "made home ownership possible for millions of families who would have had to defer or forgo ownership under credit practices of an earlier age" (Aaron 1972: 276). Together, tax incentives and easier credit have created federal subsidies for private housing many times larger than subsidies for public housing.

But even so, the incentives are tied to higher family incomes ($10,000 and over), affecting low-income families "not at all," and middle-income families "negligibly" (Aaron 1972: 276). With-

---

4 Under the terms of "contract buying," a device mainly used in the black housing market, "buyers" are prevented from having a direct relationship to the banker, paying out to a middle-man who holds the mortgage. Nor do contract buyers have equity in the property throughout the length of the contract; if one payment is missed, the seller can keep all previous payments and reclaim the property.

out such subsidies, then, far fewer people would choose to own a single-family-detached house than to rent one. We do not know to what other uses—savings, investments, consumption—they would have put the money representing their downpayment and their equity over time. Nor do we know what housing types producers would have made available without the individual ownership incentives. Only in 1975 was federal legislation introduced, by House members in metropolitan areas having large renting populations, to provide for renters the same tax breaks as owners have been getting.[5] It was defeated in the Senate in 1976.

The ideology of homeownership—its strong sentimental appeal —may account for the political decisions of these last forty years to buttress some consumers' ability to realize the dream. There is no reason to doubt the strength of consumer preferences, given the incentives and the social significance of the housetype. Certainly fulfilling the dream is also good business, as the housing lobby often testifies: bankers, builders, real estate brokers, land owners, and lawyers benefit from the sheer volume of owner-occupied single units (39 million owner-occupied single-family units, each the subject of a complex set of individual negotiations, compared to 23 million units in non-single-family structures in 1970).[6] Simply as a residential environment, the single-family house may provide larger and well-arranged living spaces that have consequences for personal autonomy, ego enhancement, control

[5] "Thus what we have in our tax system is a clear discrimination in favor of homeowners and against those who rent their home. . . . Presumably, these tax breaks for homeowners were first designed to make the burden of owning a home somewhat lighter. But these days, when it is so difficult and expensive to find a decent apartment, we must take action, for purposes of equity and practicality, to equally lighten the burden of apartment living. . . . " (Koch 1973)

In New York State, a new "leasehold" tax to be paid by tenants—one that would be deductible—is proposed to "restore some measure of aggregate vertical and horizontal tax equity between tenants and homeowners" (Kee and Moan 1976: 531). Legislation titled "The Property Tax and Tenant Equality" has been introduced into the New York State Legislature.

[6] Chief Justice Warren E. Burger addressed the American Law Institute in May 1974 on the subject "Barnacles On Our Legal Practices," and singled out those "unduly complex and expensive" procedures and costs of transfers and titles ("initiation fees" or "hazing"?) associated with "the purchase of a home." "We see . . . that over the years what were once relatively simple legal tasks have become encrusted with excess procedural baggage that complicate legal processes and often add unreasonably to the costs" (6).

71

over the immediate environment, and competence, as I have discussed at length previously (Perin 1970, 1972, 1973, 1975). Owning, though, not the spatial advantages, is widely believed to make a more positive contribution to individual functioning than renting. The axiom has it that because owning represents freedom from the onerous and unequal contract inherent in renting, this freedom will raise the owner's sense of personal pride, and, by extension, greater interest in maintaining the family's property. To repeat: This enhancement of identity and autonomy is supposed to bring on changes in behavior; the lack of such pride is used to account for the undesirable—the unstable and transient—behavior of tenants.

Moreover, as I have been saying, the American ideal of homeownership is equally the ideal of perfected citizenship. Calvin Coolidge said: "No greater contribution could be made to the stability of the Nation, and the advancement of its ideals, than to make it a Nation of homeowning families." Franklin Roosevelt said: "A nation of home owners, of people who own a real share in their own land, is unconquerable" (Dean 1945: 40-41). President Hoover's Conference on Home Building and Home Ownership in 1931, where many of today's selective incentives began, termed homeownership a "birthright" and an "epochal event" in a family's life. The awful alternative was, to be "condemned," according to one realtor at the same conference, "to die in a rented house" (Gries and Ford 1932: 5, 15, 50). The Conference report concludes that "too much cannot be said about the value of stimulating home ownership because of its effect upon good citizenship and the strengthening of family ties" (1932: 1-2). Hoover himself put it that the "home has tentacles of sentiment as well as bonds of practical necessity that bind the occupant to it" (Gries and Ford 1932: ix).

Again, I pursue a sociological analysis centered on the relationship between owners and bankers, tenants and landlords, asking about the social functions served by the differences in these types of contractual relationships. I have accounted for the higher social status of the buyer compared to the renter in terms of achieving the threshold to social personhood signified by qualifying for a mortgage. Now I want to suggest that the social function of this higher status is found in the meaning of the length of the mortgage contract, one that puts the homebuyer in the position of per-

72

manent debtor, in contrast to the renter who is free from any obligations at the end of the lease term.

Mortgages commonly run between twenty and forty years; leases are customarily written to terminate at the end of one to three years. The tax laws exclude capital gains that are earned in the sale of a person's own house if within eighteen months they are reinvested in another owner-occupied house. The condition of permanent debtor is reinforced. A homebuyer wanting to pay up the mortgage more quickly than the term stipulated may pay a financial penalty, one that is highest during the first three years of the loan but that continues throughout its term (De Huszar 1972: 234-35). Shortening the term of the obligation can be negotiated, but it is not encouraged.

The function of long-term debt is, I suggest, to enhance predictability in the housing and banking industries, a kind of stability more usually couched, however, in personalistic terms: that the homebuyer has a long-term vested interest in the neighborhood, the community, and the maintenance of the household's own property and that of others—which indeed may all be the acted consequences of having put what are usually all of a household's savings into a downpayment. Oppositely, the social system provides no such ties as would positively integrate the renter into it: by throwing doubts on or disallowing the right to be heard on local issues, when standing is dependent on being a property owner and/or taxpayer, and by discriminating in the Internal Revenue Code, such that tenure denies renters the same rights of citizenship.

The opprobrium attaching to the renter therefore arises out of the uncertainties that the symmetrical relationship forces the system of housing production to deal with: a free agent in contracting for essential shelter the renter poses problems for producers in estimating demand that the tied-down owner does not. One mortgage banker I interviewed put it that houses for sale are his "bread and butter," and the system is designed to retain owners as owners when they move. But the renter may stay or go, may find a better price and give thirty or sixty days' notice, may rent or may buy the next abode: it is the uncertainty producers face in forecasting that becomes transferred to the renter as a social category.

The link between valuing one tenure form over the other and social stability hinges, then, on the permanence of the owner's indebtedness, a condition socially valued more highly than the com-

73

plete discharge of the contractual obligation, the distinctive characteristic of the lease agreement. Why should that be so? Where there is nothing owing, there is no occasion for contact, no social tie, according to Marshall Sahlins, a student of primitive economic systems:

> In so far as the things transferred are of different quality, it may be difficult ever to calculate that the sides are "even-steven." This is a social good. The exchange that is symmetrical or unequivocally equal carries some disadvantage . . . it cancels debts and thus opens the possibility of contracting out. If neither side is "owing" then the bond between them is comparatively fragile. But if accounts are not squared, then the relationship is maintained by virtue of "the shadow of indebtedness," and there will have to be further occasions of association, perhaps as occasions of further payment. (1965: 177-78)

While buyers remain under a "shadow of indebtedness"—and have an assured social relationship with the banker—tenants meet their obligations, and so finish with, polish off, and put an end to each contractual relationship: there is no asymmetry remaining.

Vacancy rates in rental properties hold terror for landlords, bankers, and would-be entrepreneurs. Vacancy rates are the index to risk, and the renter's perfect discharge of all obligations, paradoxically, presents the system with its greatest prospects of risk.

> . . . there are lending agencies and institutions and developers who have a philosophy about the type of client they wish to cater to and you just kind of move around town finding the developer or lending institution. Right now the push is particularly on single-family ownership, or on duplex type investment which six or eight months ago was a very highly acceptable risk for the mortgage houses. They will not lend unless it's owner-occupied now because of the tightness of money and they are looking for better interest rates on their investment and that sort of thing. They feel like with money being tight and unless the property is owner-occupied, they don't want to go into it. (Goss Group: 14-15)

The "philosophy about the type of client they wish to cater to" is—to clear away the personalism—hardly philosophical, but entirely practical. The risk of vacancies in a structure housing unpredictable renters is avoided once the builder sells directly to an occupant and gets his investment out of it. The homebuyer then has, according to Ream, "everything in his house"—not only savings, but social self as well. Compared to the renter on whom the banker depends once removed (if at all) these more direct and effective sanctions operating in the banker-buyer relationship reduce the risk of lower return on the investment or of its failure. Bankers will negotiate with larger-scale property owners when hard times befall them.

Apartment houses with five to forty-nine units are owned predominantly by individuals—74 percent compared to 12 percent owned by partnerships and 9 percent by real estate corporations (Table 7). And even those having fifty or more units are owned by a surprisingly high proportion of individuals—22 percent. The data reveal that the highest rate of loss from vacancies is felt by the individual owners of smaller apartment buildings—at a rate more than twice that of owners of the largest buildings. These overwhelmingly constitute the largest type of multifamily property —about 400,000 compared to 27,000 in fifty-plus units and 5,000 in the one-to-four units (Table 7).

As more an individualistic than a corporate industry, therefore, these entrepreneurs may lack access to sophisticated market forecasting and perhaps also lack professional expertise in property management, whose main task is to avoid vacancies. Rather than blaming themselves or the economy and demographic factors, for example, for their losses from vacancies, they personalize the blame and attach it to the renter. Structurally evident, "long swings" in vacancy rates also are culturally evident.[7]

And so a clear-cut distinction between the "freedom" inherent in each tenure form becomes further muddied. The relationship of the tenant to the capricious landlord—axiomatically, the major drawback of renting—provides more freedom and less social risk than the permanent tie of the buyer whose social status is embedded in and hardly separable from the mortgage contract.

What have we here? Can it be that it is the *lack* of debt that brings suspicion and lower status in American society? It may well be, as anyone who has tried to borrow for the first time can attest. The structure of the devices encouraging home buying and the fact that of Americans holding mortgages, 80 percent are in their

[7] A study of "long swings" (roughly between 1850 and 1940) finds that vacancy rates fluctuate about as much as residential building rates in urban areas (Gottlieb 1976: 22-24, 168-76, 187).

prime, lead unmistakably to the conclusion that indebtedness has become a social good. For mortgage holders debt is often enough a way to create wealth, thus also being a material good.

The term is "credit," and one's creditability as a fully social person is enhanced by the long-term obligation represented in home-ownership. The "homeowner's ethic that puts a very high value on you" and is a "step up the ladder of social as well as economic standing," as Hale put it, is a lifelong tie. These ties of indebtedness are also political, for in allowing access to debt there is created "a generalized gift not directly requited, compelling a loyalty" to the banker and to the public institutions whose rules and norms frame his (most often *his*) actions (Sahlins 1965: 160).

Bush, a developer, speaks from experience about the loss of the "simple meaning" of the landlord-tenant relationship, especially in the light of the recent attempts to redress its imbalance. He, too, seeks his own greater safety and certainty in "ownership."

Do you think that home ownership as a mechanism, as a way of getting shelter, is superior to rental? Oh, absolutely. Absolutely. Rental, even though we own and manage a lot of apartments, I think that ownership is the only way to go in this country. There is just no way around it because essentially, people have to have some sense of belonging and ownership has got to be the way we go. Another thing is the consumer [push on] laws that regulate the relationship between tenants and landlords. You become so one-sided in terms of the tenant, having been one-sided in terms of landlord, and nobody is going to be able to live with them on a realistic basis. It's impossible to evict somebody for nonpayment of rent. There's so many things you can't do, that normally have enforced the relationship—contractual relationship between a tenant and landlord that they really have no simple meaning anymore. So that increasingly, it is going to be difficult for people to manage to even make the economic necessities, make the economic decisions and collect the rent, and make the maintenance. (Bush: 7)

Thus it is that the American ideal of homeownership is actually the ideal of perfected citizenship. The transiency and instability of the renter—the distinctive features of that category—are in the tenure relationship itself. Being less under social control of the landlord than the owner is of the banker, the renter, lacking that tie, is not integrated into the wider system through the sanctions of foreclosure, the loss of property, lifesavings, and social worth, or the exercise of equal political rights.

CONCLUSION

Realizing the American Dream by arriving at the ownership of the single-family-detached house—and latterly, of any type of house—has been possible only through artifice. The actual opportunities for ownership possible from education and work are inadequate without public assistance, for the historical trend to widespread homeownership has come about not through some natural workings of the market, but only by means of an artificial set of incentives designed originally to stimulate the economy by increasing housing production (Table 8). The taxpayer-incentives are still being used in that way. One economist studying their effect on tenure choice concludes "that the structure of income taxes in the U.S. has worked powerfully to distort housing tenure choice by U.S. households" (James 1975a: 2–67). Another insists on terming these incentives federal housing "subsidies" to middle-income families, the largest such program, and one having "indefensible distributional consequences":

> Overwhelmingly the largest housing subsidy is favorable tax treatment of homeowners which, in 1966, left them with at least $7 billion more in disposable income than they would have retained if they were taxed as are other investors. . . . Only 8 percent of this subsidy accrues to taxpayers with incomes of less than $5,000. Taxpayers with incomes of more than $50,000 per year saved $487 million, slightly less than the total value of low rent public housing subsidies. . . . On equity grounds the rationale for existing housing programs is extremely weak. The largest program, income tax benefits for homeowners, has indefensible distributional consequences. (Aaron 1972: 163, 165)

Tenure and its social meanings are tied to the manipulable availability of capital, land, and purchasing power. The less-valued social category of renter is, then, also a product of this artifice: it is not a given and it is not inevitable.

At the same time, the single, coherent social meaning of "owner" will no longer be so clear, as more and more people similar to those who owned in the past cannot afford to own in the future. How, then, will a Secretary of Housing and Urban Development

77

characterize them? Here is part of a speech, replete with the American social geometry of tenure, delivered by Carla A. Hills to the American Bar Association in August 1975:

> All right, so where does all of that [energy conservation, high housing costs] leave us? It does suggest that maybe we should start looking at the old American dream through a pair of new American eye glasses. But, the real question is whether home-ownership is a national goal to be pursued or, to put it another way, what harm would come to our society if we were to become a nation of renters?
>
> To be selfish about it, as long as we own our own home, do we really care if the rest of the nation buys or rents? Yes, we do. The family who owns its own home, not only has an investment in a house, it has an incentive to take an active role in the decisions which shape its neighborhood, its community, its schools, and churches. Because the family has a real investment in a structure, it also has an investment in its environment.
>
> Those same family members as rental tenants might still classify as "good neighbors," but other than social pressure, they have no permanent incentive to be such. It is axiomatic that when neighborhoods turn from "owner" to "rental" properties, evidence of neglect begins to show almost immediately. The reverse is also true. A tool to improve the urban neighborhood is to encourage a core of homeowners.
>
> Homeownership provides a sense of identity, of roots and of security, which is the stuff from which neighborhoods are made and which protect against social alienation.
>
> Finally, homeowners have in effect a forced investment, and perhaps their only one. They also have a share in the nation's economic growth, and hence a hedge against inflation in the form of appreciation that homeownership has given middle America. . . .
>
> To sum up all of this, we do not intend to permit the dream of homeownership to end. But we will not mindlessly spark a massive subsidy of housing production that will defeat the very goals we have set out to accomplish. . . . This is after all the land where more homes of better quality are owned by a higher percentage of people than anywhere else in the world. We intend to keep it that way.

Many people will remain renters (and bad neighbors?) for much longer in the future, as energy, land, and capital shortages, and ever higher prices for shelter, new and used, continue. The rise of tenant self-consciousness among higher-income groups at a time when homebuying is so much less possible, even for them, is des-

78

tined to become a significant political and cultural fact. For if homeownership is no longer a feasible substitute for their full citizenship, demands for citizenship in other ways are likely to increase, as in demands by renters for income tax credits and in more tenant associations bent on equalizing landlord obligations.

In making it easy to become transformed from renter to owner, the American Dream materialized, at least along one dimension.

> How can you really say you've arrived? Everybody's out in the suburbs now. The guy who is the bank president as well as the guy who is the janitor who sweeps the floor, they're both in suburbs. (Gale: 7)

One study of 4,000 New Jersey households found that the 49 percent earning between $5,000 and $15,000 annually comprised 62 percent of owners of single-family housing costing about the same as apartments and townhouses (New Jersey County and Municipal Government Study Commission 1974: 57-58).

These last forty years of longer mortgage terms and easier credit may have to be regarded as a period in the history of an industrialized democracy when homeownership was converted into a major social solution to the unmistakable contradiction between actual social inequalities and an egalitarian ideology. A diversity of class groupings, otherwise marked by differences in income, education, and lifestyle, is reduced to the two status groups of owners and renters. Social conflict can be contained between "rental tenants" and "a core of homeowners," as Hills put it. A feature of American society tending to blur those other differences, homeownership has been one route to the apex of full citizenship for those whose earnings plateau is determined relatively early (Rosow 1971: 77; Sexton 1971: 54, 62). The house has been buying out the job, as it were.

Gale says that sharing the same timetable, more than the same socioeconomic status, makes people feel socially unified. The Goss Group commented that "even the price range doesn't seem to make much difference" for owners who have a "negative syndrome" toward renters. Henry Aaron, an economist, in discussing the merits of federal housing subsidies, cautions against programs that foster "leapfrogging," where families getting a subsidy are put in the position of being able to afford housing better—and sooner—than other families can afford on their own. The very term leapfrogging

79

captures the axiom of the correct chronology being manifested through a properly *gradual* improvement of people's housing quality. He regards leapfrogging as "unjust and is recognized as unjust," citing a "trickle of letters" to congressmen from irate citizens, certain to become heavier, he thinks (Aaron 1972: 578).

Americans appear to think in terms of the appropriate timing of rewards (Rainwater 1974). Their differences in tenure may play a more significant and symbolic part in conflict than their actual differences in income, education, and consumption habits. That is, a standardized timetable may be a fundamental cultural premise on which much of what observers label class conflict may actually rest. Its meanings being subject to the present facts of scarcity, tenure choice may come to be taken more for what it is—alternative ways of arranging for shelter.

Chapter Three

Domestic Tranquillity: The Sociology of Sprawl and Transition

In asking why the categories of renter and owner are culturally defined as they are, I have been pointing to *transition* as a major source of the distinction. I next address its meanings as imposed on other social categories similarly carved out of the juxtaposition of ideology and social practice. The American dream of hard work inevitably rewarded is idealized in a singular scenario for ascending the ladder of achievement, definitive movement from one social category and its status to the next, upward. These many transitions to the ideal are substantiated in both housing and neighborhoods; arrival is manifested in the single-family-detached house. Social time becomes social space. Along the way to arrival, transition between social categories is implicit: and yet, transitional categories of housing and people are believed dangerous. Social progress as social transition is warded off.

Suburban sprawl is widely believed to be a consequence of just such warding off—the flight to the suburbs, to escape central city dangers. There is, however, social flight *within* the suburbs as well: there is equally a sociology of sprawl. Often sprawl is faulted for its absence of community, in that spread-out, single-family-detached housing fails to provide people with that sense of belonging said to be aroused by a physical focus symbolizing their common interests. Both smaller-scale suburbs, perhaps with a central green, and the closer-grained single-family neighborhoods within the larger city are environments felt to be more socially and politically manageable. Here, still trying to explain not why people prefer their own house on its own land, but why they reject the prospect of anything different with such striking force, I ask about the will and capacity for belonging to and for including others in a community.

Pope finds that in market research, getting people to talk about their "real reasons" is difficult because housing is so "personal." In what ways is housing so "personal"? What are these "real reasons"? Ream finds that there is a "great reluctance in dealing with underlying social problems" on the part of "developer, town, and

81

planner—anyone you'd care to talk to." His psychological analysis, of a "pervasive anxiety," is one I address culturally in the last part of this chapter.

What is the response to giving up the homogeneity of the single-family suburb? Is that what these towns are reacting to? Is it the mixed housing types and the variety of densities? I doubt it. The economic arguments are, and the social reasons, but mainly the economic arguments for mixed housing, not mixed socially or economically, but mixed physically, are pretty persuasive. They satisfy a lot of *local* needs. Local teachers and policemen and firemen create a need that these towns are willing to satisfy. The effect on the tax base would be demonstrably better than the single-family subdivision that they were working with before. So our perception is that it is not a valid issue. The issue—I don't know that anybody has been able, one, to determine what the issue is, and two, if they were willing to talk about it. I find on everyone's part, developer, town, and planner, any one you'd care to talk to, a great reluctance in dealing with underlying social problems. They much prefer to talk about the peripheral thing, like traffic problems, sewer problems, and zoning problems, anything to avoid the heart of it.

Why do you think that is, and what do you think the heart is? I think the reason for it is that nobody knows what the heart of it is. My suspicion is that there is a difficult-to-define pervasive anxiety having to do with the rapidity of change, that people aren't able to cope with. The only way to deal with it. It is an anxiety, an anxiety in the sense that you can't determine what it is precisely, but you just feel badly or anxious. And one feels that way in an environment of change in which they can no longer identify in the sense of roots, belongingness, where they see things that they are familiar with changing overnight. When you're never sure who's going to move in next door whatever that means to you, when your kids are going to get mugged on their way to school, or your daughter raped or somebody trying to sell them dope, all this change which is taking place so quickly. The only way to cope with that is to try and stop it, stop the world I want to get off. And I think that most of the— I got a neighbor down the street that voted for Goldwater, he had no reason, he just said I want to drag my feet. And that's a very clear statement of a middle-class suburban attitude to how you deal with change, drag your feet. It's the only thing you can do if you can't understand it. You can't deal with it rationally, that's for sure. So you drag your feet. I think basically that's what's going on. (Ream: 3, 4, 5)

I have one comment about the texts of this chapter. They often report the opinions and reactions of others. Sorting out just who makes these correspondences between homogeneity and conflict, income and behavior, will continue to be an open question. Are they made by the producers and lenders I talked to, or do they reflect the assumptions of the consumers to whom they want to appeal? The confusion stems from our not really knowing whether producers lead or follow the demand said to express people's preferences and tastes. A question I raise in Chapter Four is whether producers and consumers, though both acting in the real estate market, behave on the basis of different criteria and principles.

CATEGORIES AND CONFLICT

Land-use regulations and their implications for population distribution are not only premised on a hierarchy of more-to-less valued land users, but they are a statement as well about people's capacity for getting along. Land-use compatibilities reflect what is believed about land users' compatibilities.

The texts strongly associate homogeneity with a lower probability of social conflict: among neighbors and in neighborhoods conflict will generally be avoided by not mixing income groups, housing types, tenure forms, or land-use activities. Beneath producers' maps of social structure are assumptions about the kinds and quality of social relationships to result from land-use relationships. Their investment strategies hinge on these details of physical arrangements of new developments. Much depends, then, on the social categories these land uses are thought to stand for, both the criteria for the categories and the behavior of people in them.

To those already settled in the suburbs, higher density signifies the "crime, disease, and all of the urban problems which they have just recently been able to afford to escape, so if it is not dense then those things of course can't happen," a reason for suburban opposition given skeptically by a developer of higher-density housing:

I think people respond adversely, economically, in response to density and in response to mix of uses which is the old zoning districts, buffer and all that sort of thing, compatibility. *What do they think is the consequence of density, in terms of their property values?* Crowding is an urban condition and that's what many people have escaped and the results of crowding by analogy are crime, disease, and all of the urban problems which they have just recently been able to afford to escape, so if it is not dense then those things of course can't happen. (Ream: 8, 9)

Lenders stay away from the "booby trap" of "mixture," and, as Pope put it, "lenders would be somewhat reluctant to see a mixture in the same identifiable project."

The analysis of renters and owners has established that one organizing principle of the system of land use is that social categories must be kept quite distinct from one another, "not really touch," and not "conflict." The social order will be disturbed if there are differences or category mixtures. A category not wholly homogeneous, both as it is defined and as it is actually filled by people, signals the dangers of social conflict. The texts propose that the best ways of avoiding conflict are by minimal contact— parking-lot buffers, yards—and by defining an unmixed social category—all renters, all owners, all single-family houses, all townhouses, all one density level.

Pope outlines a "family of complaints" arising from his proposal to develop a subdivision at a somewhat higher density than the surrounding single-family area, in two-story buildings having four individual units opening off a central, common foyer and staircase (a quadruplex), in which each unit is to be individually owned in a condominium arrangement. These "complaints" define as well the kinds of social situations that commonly raise the prospect that people will have to work out ways of dealing with, and possibly disagreeing with, one another, situations thought to be a consequence of differences in density levels.

We have since met with all the various homeowner groups out there, have showed them the plans and explained to them what we are doing and I think we have gotten most of them convinced that we are not going to downgrade the neighborhood, that it is going to be a very acceptable product. *Could you remember what kind of arguments they were throwing at you?*

84

Oh, we got in frequently to the second type of argument. People who live in $40 thousand housing are a different class people than people who live in $60 thousand. That we are going to be attracting more kids into the neighborhood. We were going to be flooding schools. We were going to be creating more traffic on the streets. Noise problems. Those represent sort of a family of kinds of complaints that you run into. (Pope: 3)

Social conflict is generally present in American society, and racial, class, and ethnic conflicts in both political and social arenas are but special instances of it. People living together who are "substantially" the same along one or several dimensions—age, education, religion—are not in fact conflict-free, but they are supposed to be—they are thought of as being—free of conflicting rules for resolving conflicts. People who "live among their own" or prefer to be among "like-minded people" are making use of strategies that can, sensibly, lessen the effort and time it takes to work out many intrinsic conflicts of social life. Absolute avoidance, spatial separation, and self-segregation are useful and widely used mechanisms in all societies. To keep peace, hiving-off occurs in many social systems when the group leaving can find land and subsistence elsewhere. People today can be expected to have friends within suburb and city in terms of shared interests and values, especially when, in industrial society, time is a scarce commodity and social relationships are to be established quickly and maintained with minimum investment.

The texts propose that unwanted social contact and the possibility of social conflict are best dealt with by the single-family-detached house in a socially homogeneous block. From this ideal of freedom from conflict, together with beliefs about homogeneity's being effective in reducing the prospect of it, stem the cultural artifacts "single-family-detached house" and "block." (The texts do not define the "street" across which houses face one another as the "block," but instead regard the block as being surrounded on all four sides by streets. The first is the linear definition consumers and residents ordinarily use; the second is axiomatic to developers and investors as they bound parcels by ownership in order to trade them. Maps and municipal ordinances governing both lot dimensions and street layouts reinforce this kind of boundary-making, in determining grids allowing for the access of fire equipment, garbage pickup, snow removal, and parking.)

The flight to the suburbs, widely regarded as a strategy for avoiding high crime rates, air pollution, low-quality schools and their implication of black, poorly-prepared students, is only one kind of step in the general process of social avoidance.[1] The single-family-detached house is itself another tactic.

Under conditions of sprawl, social relations are framed by the structure of spaces, with distance built in to avoid social conflict. Everywhere, the size of lots and the front, back, and side yard dimensions meticulously set forth in zoning ordinances translate as mechanisms for reducing the likelihood of intrusions into each homeowner's personal space. They are the envelope of private property rights. "Nuisance law" was the precursor of such fine points of zoning, as I discuss at greater length in the next chapter, and these latter-day regulations are intended to forestall social boundary violations as well as to protect each household's fair share of light and air, freedom from untoward noise and odors, and a guarantee of a modicum of visual order (in height, bulk, and density regulations).

Despite this cushion of explicit regulations, the potential of discord between neighbors is still anticipated. In the sociological models of the people I talked to, the categories delineating a social topography—primarily income, education, and race—are taken as indicia forecasting an expectable level of social orderliness. In these models only people homogeneous along any one of those dimensions are believed to be capable of maintaining an adequate level of it.

Moving to the suburbs signals "social arrival" to a lesser degree than it does "fleeing" from those central-city "poor" when even the "janitor" has joined the "bank president" in the suburbs:

> I frankly think the flight to the suburbs, and this is a bias, I can't prove it, but I frankly think flight to the suburbs that we've witnessed over the past twenty years now, has been more so

[1] One economic study of this process over a period of several years in St. Louis has concluded, however, that the so-called flight began well before inhospitable conditions existed. This conclusion is based largely on the fact that to buy new housing is more economically advantageous than to expend money on the maintenance of older housing (United States Senate Committee on Banking and Currency 1973: 3-4).

fleeing *from* the poor and disadvantaged than it is running to enjoy the greenery of the countryside. Because a lot of people have placed themselves in very difficult economic circumstance in order to get to the suburbs. The fear of rubbing elbows with the wrong people is far more persuasive as a reason for living in the suburbs than the attractiveness of the suburbs itself. How can you really say you've arrived? Everybody's out in the suburbs now. The guy who is the bank president as well as the guy who is the janitor who sweeps the floor, they're both in suburbs. It's essentially a racial thing, let's face it. (Gale: 6, 7)

When a developer is going to provide housing that is not single-family-detached, suburbanites see the city moving in:

See, you have to understand the fundamental feeling in suburbia is fear, let's face it. The basic emotional feeling is fear. Fear of blacks, fear of physical bodily harm, fear of their kids being subjected to drugs, which are identified as a black problem, fear of all of the urban ills. They feel like they've isolated effect, by moving to the suburbs they've run away from it, in fact, they haven't, but in reality they haven't, but in their own mind's eye they've moved away from that problem. They see us—they see non-large-lot developers—as bringing the problem back to them, and this scares the hell out of them. (Bush: 6)

The city and suburb contrast in the freedom to "avoid" people that each offers. Notice especially the way Able, a mortgage banker, describes his brother-in-law's neighbors. Despite all the detail in this text, they are not characterized as being in any way different from him, in income, race, or lifestyle.

I think people are probably—the neighborhood used to be extremely important and I think most people, frequently you'll find cases, again, in South Philadelphia where people are born, they grow up, they marry, they settle in that neighborhood, and they die in that neighborhood. I think people are more mobile and they are doing things. We had very close friends before we moved to where we live now. We see some of them. As a matter of fact one of them followed us out and bought a house near us. But we put our living environment before that, and we moved. As it turned out, it happens to be that we moved into a neighborhood where we have established new friends, very, very favorable and we're quite happy in that respect. But we didn't let the dependence on the neighborhood—where we live now it is a mile to the nearest store. Before, I could safely send my five-year-old daughter around the corner to a store, so we give up that convenience. Major shopping is farther away, I guess than it is now. Schools are further away, churches are farther away, houses are farther away, for that matter.

Even though we had very close friends where we lived before we liked the idea that we can now somewhat pick and choose your friends. If you have an acre and you want to live very privately, and not much in a hermit-like way, you can for all intents and purposes do that. If you want to be very, very dear friends with the neighbor next you can do that too.

When you are in a row home you cannot avoid your neighbor. As a matter of fact, this is the situation that drove my brother-in-law to move. He had a neighbor on either side of him, both of whom were very difficult to get along with. The people who subsequently bought his house lived there two years and they moved. So, it doesn't appear to have been my brother-in-law's fault and he gets along fine with his new neighbors, but that's a situation where he lives now in a single-family-detached home on I think three-quarters of an acre or something like that. If he doesn't want to frequent with his neighbor he doesn't have to, but where he lived before he had no choice. You have got to bump into these people and the odds are against being able to avoid them. (Able: 19)

Another person puts it that

in Philadelphia, next door really means next door, with party walls and row housing. One step and you're there. In Los Angeles, next door is what we would call a suburban situation. There's a guy maybe a half-acre away or a quarter of an acre. (Dock: 13)

The expectations of privacy are different in suburb and city:

I think what you're driving at is what's the difference between a block of row houses in the city and a block out in the suburbs? The difference is that somebody moves out of the city, even though they move to the same size house in the suburbs if the kid next door screams here in the city, they're accustomed to that, they kind of expect it, they don't care. It's just one other thing. Even though they move out of the same situation into the suburbs when that kid screams out there and keeps them awake at night they become offended because I think they have the feeling that they've moved out of the city to get away from that. (Able: 14)

Although privacy may be a universal objective that the single-family-detached house makes maximally possible, it is also a blanket term having other social meanings and implications. Privacy is not constantly valued; it is one aspect of a strategy for managing social interactions. At one end of a continuum of social contact, privacy is desirable only some of the time. Once leaving privacy and lack of contact behind, social interactions are also governed by norms or rules. Physical boundaries can represent and be a substitute for some rules of social interaction, as do the lot lines enclosing the four yards that surround the single-family-detached house and, analogously, the four streets by which interviewees define the block. People within these boundaries are believed to share and understand the rules; outside them or down the street the rules are thought of as different, foreign, or strange. In cities people living at closer quarters without much territorial insulation are less likely to be able to avoid one another or to choose the time when they will see one another, so they have to know more rules in order to handle the higher levels of actual and potential contact. Therefore, one basic contrast of urban living with suburban living is held to be the amount of outright avoidance possible. Beliefs about the stress associated with high-density living may be expressing instead the necessity of having to know and use a variety of social rules (for greeting people, waiting in lines, sharing public space) in the many social situations the heterogeneous and complex city affords. When avoidance is difficult, people have to be on the alert for signs in order to reach decisions about the interactions they do and do not want to engage in. I suggest that being adept at using and understanding many rules and signals accounts for the urban sophisticate or cosmopolite. Not knowing them accounts for social fears which are sometimes a result of ignorance of their meanings.

With the detached house, overt rules need be fewer in number. Four yards substitute for some of them. Fixed and visible territory,

89

they are not subject to social negotiations. Suburban townhouses —attached, row houses—on the other hand, have "party walls," which imply an unavoidable social relationship. Even though the number of neighbors may be fewer than in a city block of apartment buildings, the freedom from many rules is foregone. It is the necessarily greater number of rules families have to be mindful of that accounts for the lower price of higher density housing, insofar as it is lower priced.

Thus it is that anything other than the single-family-detached house represents a compromise with the American ideal of freedom—freedom from unwanted social contact and from the possibility of social conflict. That ideal couched as the American dream of homeownership is equally, then, the ideal of social peace and domestic tranquillity.

One interview occurred as a discussion with six executives of a large development firm who see this "compromise" in higher density housing:

What do you think homeowning means to middle-class people? You have spoken now of the frontier tradition, I guess of the homesteading tradition. What else is going on? Most people want to have some part of their life in their universe that they can make decisions about, and can implement. The best way for most people to do that, since they usually are employed by someone else or something, you know, the only place they can be boss is to own a home, you know. If you really examine it I think that's really what it amounts to but I think that's diminishing also, I think you know, apartment living and rental living is coming more and more accepted, and that's just a function of size and complexity of the city, you know, big cities get bigger, people find that they begin to make a compromise way back and don't expect too much. (Goss Group: 24-25)

This privacy afforded by the single-family-detached house also means that by avoiding and limiting social relations outside the solidary household—the family, whose primary, overriding ties and loyalties are to its members—the possibilities for social conflict are reduced. Within the house, even family ties are limited to the single family living in it. For each house must itself be homogeneous, to contain one family and not mixtures: households of unrelated individuals are not permitted.

90

In the case of *Village of Belle Terre* v. *Boraas*, there was this exchange during the oral argument (justices are not identified by name in the transcripts; Lawrence Sager is the attorney representing the opponents of the village ordinance prohibiting more than two unrelated persons from occupying single-family housing):

> Question: And you say that the Village, in this case at least, has no constitutional power to define the family, the way, at least the way they did?
> Mr. Sager: I think that's right.
> Question: And could not confine it to, what I think what sociologists now call a nuclear family. Is that it?
> Mr. Sager: . . . The familial bond which satisfies this [ordinance's] test can be a good deal more remote than the nuclear family. It can be, for example, a remote cousin, uncle, grandfather.
> Question: Well, tribal. They can't define it in tribal terms.
> Mr. Sager: Tribal terms may be more accurate, Your Honor.
> Question: Well, your clients do not form a family, do they?
> Question: By your definition, they do, don't they?
> Mr. Sager: They do not—I think we'd have to ask whose definition was being drawn on, Your Honor. By sociologists' definition, I'm not sure; by the Village of Belle Terre's, certainly not. By mine, they certainly formed a single housekeeping unit. As a practical matter, their dinner was—
> Question: My question was: Is it family—f-a-m-i-l-y?
> Mr. Sager: They are not what I would call a family, Your Honor.[2]

To this justice, the word once spelled carries a single, unmistakable meaning. A single-family house housing anything other than a "f-a-m-i-l-y" is a contradiction in terms.

Drafters of zoning ordinances are equally preoccupied with criteria that will maintain the "single-family character," as it is often put, of the dwelling itself and the neighborhood, a concern especially mobilized by the zoning category of "home occupation," for "home" and "work" are two distinct categories whose mixing requires the utmost forethought, when not entirely prohibited.

In addition to their many functions as physical artifacts, then, the single-family-detached house and the block are as well socially-defined or cultural artifacts of the American land-use system. As such, the house and the block provide two basic, cultural elements

---

[2] Transcript of oral argument in the Supreme Court of the United States, No. 73-191. *Village of Belle Terre et al., Appellants* v. *Bruce Boraas et al., Appellees.* 2:40 p.m. Tuesday, Feb. 19, 1974, and 10 a.m. Wednesday, Feb. 20, 1974, p. 30.

in producers' models of probable social relations in metropolitan areas because they are also used symbolically to define and value the types of social relations expected as a result of physical development.

The block is thought to serve functions similar to that of the house: it too is regarded as a unit of solidarity of both family and of a homogeneous nationality or ethnic group, and, equally, the ethnic group as signified by income group, as I will discuss shortly. Gale defines the inner city as a place "where a block is all Chinese, all Italian, or Irish, or white groups, or this or that" (7), compounding the likelihood of there being family ties as well among its many dwelling units. Pope says that blocks in new suburban developments must contain either all owners or all renters.

In the large-scale planning the Goss Group was engaged in, one idea was to provide block *services*—streets, utilities, parking—not in a gridded form but curvilinearly. But the government officials who eventually would have to approve this innovative plan could not "conceive of" blockless residential development:

> The next thing that will probably happen will be the city planning people [municipal employees and city planning board] are concerned about block links and really they just can't conceive of a community that has enclaves for residential that doesn't interconnect endlessly in this same block. [Our proposal for a] sort of a curvilinear system that has levels of access and identity built into it, structured so that you can really relate personally to it, seems not to be understood by our people in the city, so that as an issue that still continues and has to be dealt with but they're asking for a road through that site which would function to split it and segregate it even more. (Goss Group: 7)

To producers, "block" has conceptual force, signifying a social group that is homogeneous, undifferentiated, and solidary, in the design of new development—even though it may retain little strength as a locus for suburban social contact:

> *How much family-social life does happen in the neighborhood? The few blocks where people live, do people speak to that themselves, where neighboring is a goal they have? Not a goal anymore?* . . . they seem to relate now to the larger community than the neighborhood, generally, to a municipality which has a very strong political base. Whether they can relate to their own block,

they relate to their own block only in the sense of what's happening around the edges of it. I'm not sure that that isn't simply reacting to the erosion of the edges rather than a clear statement of this is our little thing, we don't want any intrusion. *That's interesting, yes.* Suburban people—you have a block party occasionally. It's not like South Philadelphia, North Philadelphia, *city* neighborhood, it's not like that at all. It's much more diffused. People travel much further. (Ream: 9, 11)

COMPATIBILITY AND INCOME

The presumption that social homogeneity is a consequence of income homogeneity follows those beliefs without pause. Income homogeneity is one organizing principle in the system of land use and is a basic principle, in turn, of social order in metropolitan space. An income-group is assumed to be homogeneous and permanent: all those in it, living in housing appropriate to it, will follow rules of behavior attached to it. An income-group so defined—a group with certain characteristics, moral concepts, and social categories indelibly associated with it—takes on properties commonly associated with ethnic groups.

American assumptions about how people do and should behave —the social order—are, in casual social analysis, commonly associated with their incomes. In the sociological models of those influential in metropolitan development this shorthand turns into a tight correspondence between people's expectable behavior and the neighborhoods and housing their income allows them to rent in or buy. Those physical objects signify the norms people will use in social relationships. Each income group is expected to behave on the basis of different norms distinctive to the income level, and each set of norms can in turn be deduced from the type of housing affordable.[3] These are folk correlations institutionalized in the system of land use.

[3] The United States Census of Housing provides household income breakdowns in its published tabulations with differences of from $2,000 to $9,999, compared to the Census of Population, which uses a $3,000 difference between categories up to $9,999. Above $10,000, the Housing Census uses a $2,499 difference up to $14,999, compared to the $4,999 difference in the Census of Population. These gradations serve the needs of the housing industry, in that they index the fact that income level responds to the tax advantages of homeownership provided by the Internal Revenue Code. As

Remarkably, occupation plays no part in the sociological models of these producers, as they estimate probable behavior, whereas politicians and social scientists, for example, would be at a loss without that social category as a prominent feature in their models. To interviewees, occupation provides no clue to housing consumption. If it did, their behavorial assumptions would have to do with those, not income, differences.

Housing types—single-family-detached, attached row houses, quadruplexes, garden apartments—are the products they merchandise, each at a price corresponding to a portion of total income the consumer will spend, a price influenced by the rules of federal programs or ascertained through "market research," which is, more often than not, a gross compilation of income groups, vacancy rates, and levels of current construction.

Do you think we know very much—this marketing study you did for the lower income groups—do you feel that in your work that we know enough about the middle class, so called, whatever that is? Have you ever run into any surprises? Yes, I was going to say. No, I don't think we know enough because we *do* run into surprises. I think we make some very broad assumptions about how people will react or do react and find quite frequently that those assumptions are wrong. I think part of it is attributable to our inability to test from a market research point of view the real, true desires of the people. We, e.g., in both of our projects, did extensive market research, extensive interviewing, and have a whole pile of data, and from that we have defined who we think our markets will be. But when you talk about, particularly housing, you get into—I think the single most complex decision that any individual or family ever makes. And market sampling techniques, I think are not either sophisticated enough let's just leave that sophisticated enough and let that cover all bases, to

---

income rises by the smaller differences, the tax advantages also rise, and people in these categories can be viewed as prospects for housing at a certain price, according to the rules of thumb in use. The Census of Housing is what it says: a survey of the characteristics of these products (including mortgages) and only incidentally a report of the characteristics of owners and renters. But the Census of Population, too, only incidentally reports the characteristics of owners and renters as well, and so there is a lacuna of systematic and basic data about the education and occupation of people by tenure and by the type of housing they live in.

adequately define the true reasons why people do things. I think we're at this point at the level in market research which we can identify reactions but not reasons. (Pope: 21)

Furthermore, Pope says, producers ask the wrong questions, misread preferences, or impose their own ideas without any basis in consumer demand.

> . . . A rental project on the West Coast—we were talking about swingles—I think we did get into this a little bit, about a project that they had designed—the apartment complex around a major recreation facility and they thought that all the singles were going to live near the recreation and all the older folks were going to live on the periphery, away from it. And it turned out just the reverse, that the singles wanted to be quiet when they get home and that the older folks wanted to be near where the action was because they took care of the grandchildren, because they wanted to *see*, they wanted vicariously to live this. (Pope: 22)

In setting off their products competitively, producers elaborate their own distinctions between income groups and their predictable behavior.

Producers are of course concerned with income because they have to estimate the levels of demand for housing and for shopping centers, customarily using as a rule of thumb a proportion of income consumers will allocate for housing and goods consumption, an amount that can be estimated reliably enough for the purposes of market research and comprehensive planning. Much more than economic behavior is estimated: what comes clear is that each income group is assumed to be governed by its own sets of norms for individual and social behavior that income level is used then to predict. Fare is a property appraiser and Pope is a developer:

When you're talking about the apartment in back of single-family development, is it just simply the structure or are people also thinking about the kinds of people that are living in the apartments versus the high income? That's a really good question. I think more than anything it's having that many people looking over your back fence. In a nice area, say, Sharpstown, you're highly unlikely to have apartments with low enough income which you should worry about the kind of people. The rent is going to be so high that you're not going to have any riffraffs so to speak. (Fare: 15)

I think there are two levels of reaction [to a proposal for a single building housing four condominium units]. Both of them are emotional. But one level has to do with what the structures look like, and the other level of reaction has to do with who is going to live in them and therefore the cost of them. For example, the quadruplexes that we are building in the $40 to $60 thousand price range adjoin property which has $60 thousand and up houses on it, and initially we got some very negative reaction from homeowners surrounding it that we were going to downgrade their neighborhood. By the mere fact of building quadruplexes, something other than a single-family house. . . . [They say] people who live in $40 thousand housing are a different class of people than people who live in $60 thousand . . . but I think in the vast majority of cases, we convinced people that people moving into our project weren't going to be substantially different from them either in social class, in income level or what have you, and were going to be sort of average human beings. (Pope: 2, 3)

Income differences and differences in the behavior of groups are found to be so closely related that "substantial differences" between people can be neutralized by high income—a "substantially higher income," as the phrase goes. That is, differences of race and religion, and the behaviors associated with them, can count not at all when the attribute of high income is also present. Gale, a black, is an insurance company executive:

. . . say you're in an area of Philadelphia where the homes are in the $40-60-70,000 range, and you have families that have incomes that can handle that kind of thing. Now for a guy to be excluded from that society because he happens to be Chinese that is utterly ridiculous because all—as far as I'm concerned, the tests of whether he is an appropriate member of that community has been satisfied when you consider what surrounds him at that socio-economic level; and that's the critical thing as far as I'm concerned. Now, when you talk about what church a guy goes to or—, that's ridiculous, totally irrelevant. (Gale: 10)

96

Residents, too, join in the belief that differences of income are also differences in the "substantial" characteristics of other "human beings," to such an extent that their future house value will be "downgraded." So it is that income level comes to stand for a primordial characteristic of persons, one perhaps more telling in the system of land use than sex, age, occupation, ethnicity, family. Income reveals more about social position and social behavior than any of those variables, in these sociological models. Ream recounts residents' beliefs:

> Well, the simplest way to put it is—when somebody makes as much money as you do then somehow there can't be a problem. Really that doesn't make any difference what color he is. Doesn't make a difference where he went to school or what his particular profession is or anything else. You can put up with all that. As long as his bank account is relatively the same as yours. And I think in translating that into housing type and density and that sort of thing, the perception is probably, is not altogether accurate nor altogether inaccurate, it's hard to measure. The perception is that more intense uses, different uses, from the single-family house which has to represent a high cost both public and privately, that's obvious affluence. But any deviation from that represents the possibility that that person is not in your economic rank and therefore is a problem to you, one way or the other. (Ream: 17)

The implication in the following text is that higher income people are sure to be "decent." Able is a mortgage banker:

> And I don't care how much you are an extreme ultra-liberal as far as low income housing, medium income housing—when you're talking in the mid-30's you're not talking low income housing: You're not talking *high* income housing, but you're certainly talking about decent people, usually. (Able: 2)

Furthermore, because residential location becomes a certain marker of income, house, norms, and income appear as a single configuration.

> Let's take the shopping center, for example. When you look at [an entrepreneur's] shopping center application [for a loan], you're looking·at the housing nearby because it speaks to the

97

income level, for the most part. I'm not saying that somebody didn't buy a house in a lower price neighborhood and he just happened to like it and that guy has now gone on to bigger and better things, but he likes it there, that happens. But generally, the quality of housing speaks to the income level of the people. You're going to predicate this upon the type of tenancy in your center. (Able: 7)

Race joins the configuration of variables—income, norms, and house:

Of course, if you look in the residential property you're looking for some different factors. Then you've got, I think, to a certain extent a built-in racism among the mortgage companies, the land developers that say automatically—if a neighborhood is predominantly minority it's automatically bad: they redletter it. Other problems result from that. *That happens in Houston?* Oh, yes. We have blockbusting—a lot of residential segregation, very severe problems with that. (Cole: 13)

Depreciating property—property having an expectably lower market value—and low-income minority populations is a correspondence the text below takes for granted. Again, high income changes the behavioral norms otherwise expected of a minority. Cole is a high-level municipal employee:

When you yourself think of depreciation of value, what kinds of factors do you think enter into that? One, of course, is age. The other is age accompanied by deterioration, and so on. Then of course there is the whole range of intangibles—quality of the neighborhood, quality of the area—a range of, is the neighborhood "declining?" *What do you think those words really are meaning, are you talking about the physical property, are you talking about the population?* Talking about the physical property. We have some neighborhoods with high income minority but not too many. (Cole: 13)

What these texts reveal is that stereotyping is just as common on grounds of income alone as on grounds of type of house or form of tenure, as we have seen already in the discussion of renters and owners. Low-income people follow norms resulting in behavior not certain to be "decent," and are considered to be "riff-raffs," or a "problem." A lower-income group is seen somehow to affect "me and my family" "adversely"—a proposition that implies that they will engage in behavior guided by norms not simply different but harmful. Nor are these ideas limited to an "amoral" lowest-income group. As we have read earlier, Americans living in $40,000 houses are seen to be substantially different from those in $60,000 houses, and Pope is put in the position of arguing that they are, nevertheless, "average human beings."

In general, nonwhites earn less than whites, occupation by occupation, but it is equally true that whites overwhelmingly constitute the majority of lower-income people.

Well, now this race thing is certainly a national thing, not just Texas. Leaving that aside—let's say that it is all whites, where it's the income differential. Is it your experience that the reactions are similar? Is that what you were saying or not? Um. I am really not sure that I have ever been confronted with a situation where they *were* totally separable. I think that there would still tend to be some reaction based on income levels alone, but they would certainly be much less intense. But I never have been in a situation where you could say, okay, we are going to bring in a white moderate-income subdivision and there will be no minority groups. (Pope: 4)

Here it is also assumed that every group of moderate-income people will include nonwhites or other minorities—that is, despite their considerably smaller numbers in the population, these minorities are expected to be present in every group able to afford housing of this kind.

These axioms about social behavior, housing types, and income clearly guide producers' actions. In the next chapter, I suggest that they guide consumers as well in their guise as investors in real property. But although consumers may also use such axioms in order to appraise quickly the interests and values they might expect to share upon moving next to new neighbors, once they have been suburbanites their own experiences—such as those Gans had in Levittown—might not fit the tight correspondences producers make so much of. For indeed, income masks many differences in occupation, in values, in living styles.[4] Gans found this diversity among households earning the same annual income:

[4] Anthropologists specializing in American kinship have recently argued that despite recognizable differences in social class, life style, and culture,

99

. . . class homogeneity is not as great as community-wide statistics would indicate. Of three families earning $7,000 a year, one might be a skilled worker at the peak of his earning power and dependent on union activity for further raises; another, a white collar worker with some hope for a higher income; and the third, a young executive or professional at the start of his career. Their occupational and educational differences express themselves in many variations in life style, and if they are neighbors, each is likely to look elsewhere for companionship. Perhaps the best way to demonstrate that Levittown's homogeneity is more statistical than real is to describe my own nearby neighbors. Two were Anglo-Saxon Protestant couples from small towns, the breadwinners employed as engineers; one an agnostic and a golf buff, the other a skeptical Methodist who wanted to be a teacher. Across the backyard lived a Baptist white collar worker from Philadelphia and his Polish-American wife, who had brought her foreign-born mother with her to Levittown; and an Italian-American tractor operator (whose ambition was to own a junkyard) and his upwardly mobile wife, who restricted their social life to a brother down the street and a host of relatives who came regularly every Sunday in a fleet of Cadillacs. One of my next-door neighbors was a religious fundamentalist couple from the Deep South whose life revolved around the church; another was an equally religious Catholic blue collar worker and his wife, he originally a Viennese Jew, she a rural Protestant, who were politically liberal and as skeptical about middle class ways as any intellectual. Across the street, there was another Polish-American couple, highly mobile and conflicted over their obligations to the extended family; another engineer; and a retired Army officer. (Gans 1967: 166)

This report of the variety among Gans's near neighbors—people living in housing costing the same—is evidence that although residents may make housing choices necessarily limited by their income, the homogeneous and compatible social characteristics it is said by producers to indicate do not necessarily register the same

---

there is but one American society with the same cultural conceptions available to all: ". . . cultural differences are not isolated from each other; they are available to all individuals. In general they are present in all individuals as potential means of constructing social reality, though the emphasis and mode of patterning varies in a systematic way between classes. . . . There are many poor people in America who are neither lower class nor working class. To equate the poor with the lower class gives rise to such old middle-class notions as the 'culture of poverty.' The cultural orientation of the lower class can be found among people who are quite well off, just as there are many genteel poor of undoubted middle-class orientation" (Schneider and Smith 1973: 29, 67).

significance for their daily lives. In this study, in fact, Gans concludes that "objective measures of class are not taken into account
in people's associations at all, partly because they do not identify
each other in these terms, but also because class differences are
not the only criterion for association" and that when people dis-
approve of one another, on grounds that he apparently would
consider to be class-based, they put their objections in terms of
"negative motives" rather than "class differences": "Class is a
taboo subject, and the taboo is so pervasive, and so unconscious,
that people rarely think in class terms" (Gans 1967: 167, 179).[5]

Homogeneity by income group is widely believed, even by social scientists, to be a means of preventing conflicts among neighboring households arising out of envy of possessions, of differences
in lifestyle as displayed by consumption patterns, of ideas about
child-rearing, and of prestige as defined by occupation and the
source of income.[6] Producers certainly use it and keep it going

[5] Of his statement that "class is a taboo subject," as a cultural anthropologist, I have my doubts in this sense: if class categories are not being
used in sorting out people, they are not used; there is no reason to call
them taboo unless it is shown that otherwise they are an inalterably basic
set of categories in a lexicon. See Chapter Five.

[6] "After all, social class or income is not merely a matter of snobbery
or an arbitrary taste for a particular style of life. There is a very real sense
in which social class and income do distinguish between people more or
less prone to violence and physical abuse. For whatever reasons, income
is a reliable sign of a neighbor's tendency to have children who fight, resist
school authorities, and meet in unsupervised settings" (Suttles 1972: 241).
Presumably, the author means "*low*" income is that sign. Another sociologist
"generalizes" about these same matters but, perhaps reflecting the state of research, from all directions: "Consequently, it may not be social homogeneity
so much as personal compatibility that proves to be the decisive intervening
variable between physical distance and sociability. Of course, the two generally go hand in hand. . . . Manual workers are not all alike, varying in
social background, current income, style of life, family composition, tastes,
and experiences. Some of these differences may be more significant for
neighboring and friendship than their overall similarities. The same holds
true for any other social category. Where these differences of class, status,
and style of life are neglected, we find friction, withdrawal, high rates of
out-movement, or continual strife among physically proximate residents. . . .
physical design as such . . . is significant primarily where social and personal
compatibility has prepared the ground for it. This compatibility may have
its source in social status or cultural similarity, shared attitudes, ideological
tolerance, or some sort of complementary rather than conflict-arousing differences" (Keller 1968: 83-5).

101

as an organizing principle of the social order of metropolitan areas for fear that the "stability" of their investments will be threatened if people do not get along, if they do not share norms of physical maintenance, or if there is turnover and apartments and houses stand vacant or unsalable because neighbors are unfriendly. Wing, a mortgage banker, finds that single-family-detached housing is his "bread and butter"—his preferred, assured, and safe investment whether occupied by Wasps or blacks:

Of course, we have dealt primarily with the standard, you might say, the bread-and-butter type, of a single-family and residential subdivision. *Yes.* We have dipped our toe into the water of PUDs, and I might say regrettably in some instances. *Oh, I would like to hear that.* All right. We have, of course, handled subdivisions, where there have been sales to of course not only the Anglo-Saxon, the Wasp, but we have handled a number of black subdivisions and very successfully, for the single-family types of operation. (Wing: 2)

But there are no guarantees of tranquil social order among people having similar incomes and spending the same for housing:

. . . children were likely to quarrel, and when this led to fights and childish violence, their quarrels involved the parents. Half the random sample had heard of quarrels among neighbors on their block, and 81 percent of these were over the children. Adults quarreled most often when childish misbehavior required punishment and parents disagreed about methods. . . . Of seventeen quarrels about which interview respondents were knowledgeable, nine had been concluded peacefully, but in the other eight cases, parents were still not talking to each other. In one case, two neighbors finally came to blows and had to be placed on a peace bond by the municipal court. (Gans 1967: 159)

Nor does having more education or income mean that people will not experience conflicts and share deficient means of working them out. The daughter of an upper-income family recounted a situation where the nine-year-old child of an equally upper-income next-door neighbor was abetted by his parents in calling for the police when, after her mother had repeatedly asked the child not to let his basketball bounce over into her tidy rock garden, she kept possession of the basketball. There is enmity between the neighbors now.

Because it is so tightly intercorrelated with race and education,

102

the income-level principle results mainly in the exclusion of blacks from those suburban resources claimed first by "homogeneously" middle-income groups. This one principle of the system of land use confronts other, and, as the courts are just now beginning to enunciate, higher principles of the larger social order.

SOCIAL AVOIDANCE AND SELF-GOVERNANCE

The sprawl of single-family-detached houses is fast approaching its end as the main peace-keeping technique of this plural, mobile, and growing society. If, in the period of energy and housing short-ages we face, people will have to adapt to living at closer quarters, it is possible, on the optimistic side, that racial, class, and ethnic conflicts will come to be ameliorated as people learn to be more adept at facing and resolving, rather than avoiding, social conflict as neighbors and as citizens sharing limited resources. But, in truth, other aspects of our social and cultural system retard these prospects of improvement, because, as I will discuss, I find quite opposite incentives embedded in the structure of our industrial system.

The dour neighbor of Robert Frost's "Mending Wall" (1914) is living in his dark ages, like a "savage armed," and he cannot be joshed out of relying not on fences but on himself:

> . . . .
> Oh, just another kind of outdoor game,
> One on a side. It comes to little more:
> There where it is we do not need the wall:
> He is all pine and I am apple orchard.
> My apple trees will never get across
> And eat the cones under his pines, I tell him.
> He only says, "Good fences make good neighbors."
> Spring is the mischief in me, and I wonder
> If I could put a notion in his head:
> "*Why* do they make good neighbors? Isn't it
> Where there are cows? But here there are no cows.
> Before I built a wall I'd ask to know
> What I was walling in or walling out,
> And to whom I was like to give offense.
> Something there is that doesn't love a wall,
> That wants it down." I could say "Elves" to him,
> But it's not elves exactly, and I'd rather
> He said it for himself. I see him there
> Bringing a stone grasped firmly by the top

103

In each hand, like an old-stone savage armed.
He moves in darkness as it seems to me,
Not of woods only and the shade of trees.
He will not go behind his father's saying
And he likes having thought of it so well
He says again, "Good fences make good neighbors."*

Java and Bali provide an illustration of the contrast Frost finds between "walling in or walling out." In each society, privacy is valued and obtained completely on the basis of differing conceptions of kinsmen, a cultural apparatus organizing much else in these societies. In Java, where territorial boundaries count for little, internal, psychological mechanisms are used. Inside houses there may not even be doors, and the houses themselves, made of bamboo, face the street without walls or fences. Outsiders can come indoors with hardly a warning, from front or back. As a result, "people speak softly, hide their feelings and even in the bosom of a Javanese family you have the feeling that you are in the public square and must behave with appropriate decorum. Javanese shut people out with a wall of etiquette (patterns of politeness are very highly developed), with emotional restraint, and with a general lack of candor in both speech and behavior" (Geertz quoted in Westin 1970: 16-17).

In Bali, where houseyards are surrounded by high stone walls, the families living in them consist of "one to a dozen" nuclear families, all of whose heads are related through their father. People who are not kin rarely come into the houseyard. The houseyard is entirely private space, and the public—nonkin—is walled out.

Those invisible social "walls" taking the form of negotiation and consensus that American self-governance requires have been underdeveloped partly as a result of being able to rely on and expecting to rely on physical and territorial boundaries. Animal territoriality is fascinating precisely because it is so inventive a system of signs in the absence of language. Human solutions should be even more imaginative, and where they do not exist, we have to ask why. The neighbors of Able's brother-in-law were not black, poor, or Croatian—they had, it will be recalled, no distinctive fea-

* From "Mending Wall" from *The Poetry of Robert Frost*, edited by Edward Connery Lathem. Copyright 1930, 1939, © 1969 by Holt, Rinehart, and Winston. Copyright © 1958 by Robert Frost. Copyright © 1967 by Lesley Frost Ballantine. Reprinted by permission of Holt, Rinehart, and Winston, Publishers.

tures he thought worth mentioning. They were simply people sharing a party wall, and all of them were unable to get along.

Our repertoire of mechanisms for getting along with one another—those more and less explicit—needs to be reexamined, especially in light of both the *time* negotiations take and the high levels of population mobility. The scarcity of time in industrialized society may account for overusing these mechanistic solutions of territory and boundary. Negotiation in good faith is becoming an art lost to the clock, in the customary circularity of our times: for men, especially, suburban sprawl means commuting, and that means time used; homeownership means sole responsibility for upkeep, and that means time invested inward by both men and women; suburbia means women's chauffeuring children and running long errands, putting in many hours every day behind the wheel.

Even where more formalized self-governance is part of the housing choice itself, as in Planned Unit Developments, the tasks are being professionalized because people are too busy to take them on. Now that there are about 22,000 Planned Unit Developments nationwide, consulting firms specializing in running civic associations are springing up (Oser 1976). I interviewed the owner of one firm that will train residents in organizing and running their association, as well as contract to provide the association with all essential services such as bookkeeping and maintenance of pools and parking lots. He got into the business because, in his former profession of landscape architect designing cluster developments, he observed how poorly prepared the residents were to take over from the developers—and make time for—the management and maintenance of their own common facilities.

One common manifestation of incompetent dispute settlement between neighbors is the spite fence. One property owner maliciously—perhaps after some other unresolved disagreement—puts up a fence obstructing a neighbor's light, air, or view. There are fourteen states with statutes forbidding spite fences. The Pennsylvania statute specifically applies to properties in suburban, not urban, areas, and a legal commentator on the constitutionality of that statute puzzles over this distinction.

> It is submitted that an argument could be made that spite fences are more common in suburban districts of cities and boroughs than in urban areas, and for this reason the legislature intended

105

to curtail the prime violators. A major objection to this argument
is that there is no legislative history to support it. (Pauline 1971:
300)

I speculate that suburbanites resort to spite fences because, unlike
city dwellers, they are accustomed to using walls but not rules.

In these last decades of population growth and industrial expansion, the form the suburbs have taken—suburban sprawl—is here
interpreted as one consequence of this singular strategy of insulation and social avoidance *within the suburbs themselves.* A strategy
embodied by suburbs now composed of single-family-detached
housing that brook no different housing types, it has become no
longer a matter of private choice, but one of constitutional concern. The strategy maximizes avoidance of those contacts believed
to lead to conflict, in contrast to a physical settlement strategy
bringing into play a diversity of social mechanisms for preventing
and settling disputes. That a very narrow range of mechanisms is
widely believed to be effective also erupts in public demands for
increasing police protection and the pervasive reliance on de jure
law as the means to a de facto social order.

Social conflict as an analytic category is usually reserved for
those pittings-against of interest groups, political parties, classes,
and power centers. But today's grave constitutional issues, themselves reflecting just such general conflicts, arise from *anticipating*
these seemingly trivial and commonplace frictions: not just criminal activities but also the necessity for facing up to social disagreements are anticipated, faintheartedly, at the prospect of a
hetereogenous population. The ready availability of physical avoidance having atrophied tactics of negotiation, mediation, and other
adjudicative mechanisms, social fright is heightened.

So it is that single-family-detached housing and the hopes for
domestic tranquillity vested in group homogeneity—defined by
income, ethnic, racial, age, and all other spurious criteria for presumed compatibility—remain the two significant principles of social structure and social order being used in the American system
of land use. We have been faulting suburban sprawl for everything
but its implications for authentic social order, that of *self*-govern-
ance.

The formal relationships introduced by restrictive covenants in
new towns and by the governing structure of condominiums are,

according to the reports below, problematic even for their higher-income, professional residents who appear to have little familiarity with techniques of dispute prevention and settlement. "Ironically," says a legal scholar, "we have better data about dispute processing in Indian villages, Mexican towns and East African tribes than we have about that process in American communities" (Felstiner 1974: 86).

> Don't put a television antenna on your home here. Don't plant a tree in your backyard unless The Committee says you can. Don't paint your house unless The Committee approves the color. And, if you don't mow your lawn, expect The Committee to order it done and send you a bill.
>
> The 14,000 people who live here, in a "new town" 40 miles north of Los Angeles, occupy a world of mandated conformity—of prescribed "good taste"—of a type that is beginning to spread across the country and affect the lives of increasing numbers of Americans. . . .
>
> In a development called Walden near Minneapolis, residents are forbidden to keep their garage doors open—except when cars are entering or leaving—so unsightly garage interiors cannot be seen from the street.
>
> In Columbia, Maryland, a Justice Department lawyer . . . is waging a battle with his village's architectural committee because he planted cherry trees and strawberry plants in his front yard. . . . In Palos Verdes Estates a well-dressed, middle-aged woman . . . silently attached a red cardboard tag. . . . When the new arrival asked what it was, the woman said that a railing design around the home's front porch had not been approved by the town Art Jury. . . .
>
> Critics say the rules breed informing and spying among neighbors. . . . Residents of several communities . . . conceded that the system leads to bickering and spying among neighbors. In at least one case . . . a neighbor's dispute came to the brink of gunplay. (*New York Times*, 25 August 1975, p. 1)

> The condominium apartment building I live in has a doorman, well-trimmed gardens, a garage door that opens electrically and four flagpoles, two each for the District and American flags. No one would ever guess what festers within.
>
> Casual obscenity, law suits, a lack of secret ballots, threats against small animals and an outrageous effort to remove my son's baby carriage—we've had them all. Although trying at times, perhaps it beats clipping the crabgrass at a cozy single family bungalow in Dale City. (*The Washington Post*, 31 July 1975, p. 1)

CULTURAL SOURCES OF SAFETY AND DANGER
IN SOCIAL SPACE AND SOCIAL TIME

Two fundamental properties of American social order, certainty and progress, stand in contradiction to one another: It must be possible to count on some things as stable, settled, and safe—but according to the American Dream and the American Creed, there is equally the imperative to improve, progress, change, and evolve from lower to higher forms of living. People in motion, though, are transient and dangerous. Moving upward and onward, yet standing still.

Those anticipations of conflict among heterogeneous groups in the suburbs express this same clash between the hope for certainty and the ideal of progress:

Now, when they [citizens of a suburb] are opposed to a "Planned Unit Development," let's say, are they in favor of additional single-family house development is that—do the two things go hand in hand? They favor the same. The fact that the continuation of what they have is driving them deeper in the hole [increased property taxes], which they know, doesn't seem to matter as long as that represents a lack of change. They're willing to pay any price to alleviate their anxiety of change.

So, the change—so, is it fair to say that the change is a change of housing type? Yes, and all of the things that go with it. *Like what?* You get different social groups, different economic groups, if you're offering apartments or townhouses they're going to be occupied by different people than single-family houses on acre lots. They're going to be older or younger, less children. *What do you find are the kinds of matchings up that people seem to do between housing type and social groups?* Obviously apartments, I say obviously from my point of view, obviously apartments are transitory, people are unstable who live in them and they're always moving in and out. By the way this is not true. We did a survey; we found the most stable housing type in the community are garden apartments. The single-family houses of the PUD had a much higher turnover rate than the garden apartments. I suspect this is not that untypical either. (Ream: 6, 7)

Ream's account attests to the force of beliefs about "transitory" and "unstable" categories—beliefs unsupported by the turnover

108

rates in apartments. Unmistakably, "anxiety" and social fright are widely associated with anticipated change and with heterogeneous populations. On the ground, in the actual arrangements of land uses, there are many stable situations of mixed uses, where single-family houses adjoin apartments and row houses, where offices are mixed with residential uses, and even where retailing still goes on on the ground floor and families live above the store. Only in single-family residential enclaves are any other land uses absent. These threats and dangers are, then, anticipated: less on the ground than in the mind are the fears of heterogeneity being revealed in these texts, which by and large express ideas for, and reactions to, accommodating growth in brand-new, self-contained, and large-scale developments being planned with the most up-to-date technical, functional, ecological, and aesthetic ideas there are.

The correct chronology of life is one major organizing principle in the system of land use that generates a cluster of propositions with which the people I talked to determine the social geometry of metropolitan development and new towns, expressed through housing types and land-use distinctions. The contradiction between certainty and progress is there resolved by putting the highest value on only the ultimate transition—single-family-detached homeownership.

That American ideology of progress is one of three cultural sources of conceptions of safety and danger in social space and social time. Each, I will try to show, creates its own version of "transition," with attendant associations of safety and danger because each has its own anomalous intervals, those spaces between clear-cut categories, in which category membership is unclear, indefinite, or incomplete. The second source is the legal domain, which postulates stages for becoming a recognized social person, by legal criteria (for attaining the right to vote, for example) and by relationships defined by a legal tie such as marriage. The third grows out of cultural conventions about the spatial separation of domestic production and reproduction—the family—from industrial production—the corporation. Each of these domains—the ideological, legal, and economic—overlaps with the other in American culture generally, but most visibly perhaps in the shape metropolitan development takes.

Rites of passage marking life crises, changes in social status, and seasonal changes are specific events in particular societies. Here I

109

suggest that there are also more general cultural conceptions about states of safety and danger to be found in other transitional events. The "passages" implicit in each of these domains are similar in structure and in their social force to the transitional phases common to ritual practice. The cultural criteria used to rank American social categories are influenced by these conceptions. No less here, I propose, in the heart of light and rationality, do similar public meanings attach to our own categories neither wholly one thing nor another. Our cultivation of "practical reason" still does not outwit culture (Sahlins 1976).

Since van Gennep's original contribution, anthropologists have observed many other concomitants of being between categories, especially in primitive cosmologies and their rituals. One of these concomitants is contamination. In *Purity and Danger: An Analysis of Concepts of Pollution and Taboo*, Mary Douglas analyzes a wide range of ethnographic reports and concludes that whatever is unclassifiable or whatever falls outside the boundaries of a category is regarded as socially polluting and dangerous: ". . . when moral rules are obscure or contradictory there is a tendency for pollution beliefs to simplify or clarify the point at issue" (1970 [1966]: 168). That is, when in doubt, people in these simple societies vilify.[7]

Its boundaries are the main characteristic of any category, and universally they are freighted with significance. Edmund Leach proposes that there is an "innate sacred-taboo quality of all boundaries which derives from their ambiguity," the same ambiguity that leads to pollution beliefs (1976:71).[8] The boundary

[7] Neat categories reduce uncertainty and ambiguity and are an aid to social and personal orientation. They resolve cognitive dissonance. Deviations from a mean identify populations displaying unaverage behavior. Those are psychological, sociological, and statistical concepts with which I have no good reason to disagree. The cultural question is why there is evidence of social fears of interstitial categories. For a discussion of personal relationships between "normals" and the "stigmatized" see Goffman 1963.

[8] Calling taboo "innate" does not, of course, explain it, and even though its many social functions can be described, its sources, whether psychological, biological, or social, remain a mystery. In the article on "Pollution," in the International Encyclopedia of the Social Sciences, Douglas provides some history of this concept in anthropological discussions of religion and primitive cosmology (1968: 336-41). In the same volume, Margaret Mead is the author of the article on "Incest" and the taboo always associated with

itself, in mediating between other clear-cut categories, necessarily partakes of their different qualities. Being "at the edge"—marginal —boundaries are themselves muddy, for in any ordered system, "dirt is matter out of place," (Douglas 1970 [1966]: 48). That is, boundaries and margins necessarily collect bits from either side. "Boundaries become dirty by definition and we devote a great deal of effort to keeping them clean, just so that we can preserve confidence in our category system" (Leach: 1976: 61).

"Archaeology and comparative ethnography alike show very clearly that, throughout history and throughout the world, human societies of all kinds have attached enormous ritual importance to thresholds and gateways. . . . it is essential for our *moral* security that [movement across them] should not lead to confusion about the difference between the inside and the outside. There must be a physical discontinuity, clean and portentous" (61).

Leach proposes a "general theory of taboo" applying to anomalous space and time. The simple fact of sharing attributes is what makes these margins and boundaries taboo. The markers of boundaries are endowed with special qualities, such that, in an apparent paradox, boundaries are also *sources* of power, secular and sacred. In a network of social categories (a social system) boundaries, in signifying that one category is different from the next, equally are interfaces. If all the "dirt" is removed from a boundary, then that property of interface is obscured. Without boundaries, categories have no force. Hence that paradox often noted in anthropological studies of *rites de passage* that people and objects in these intervals of being not quite one thing or another—i.e., in transit—exert special power.

In these rites this state of transition is made into one of timelessness. People are removed from the ordinary passage of time, as for example on honeymoons and in periods of mourning. Often enough, they are taken out of social space as well: initiates are kept separate from ordinary people or housed in a special place from which ordinary people are excluded. When in suspended time and space (intervals at the margin) the initiate or the new widow is "contaminated with holiness." Sacred, dangerous, and

---

it; the violation of the incest prohibition often implies social pollution (1968: 115-22). Incest is, conceptually speaking, the sexual combination of two social categories defined as unmixable.

"dirty"—all at once. "Consistent with this ideology, the rituals which bring the initiate back into normal life again nearly always include procedures, such as ritual washing, designed to remove the contamination" (Leach 1976: 78).[9]

The second concomitant of transition is the personification of dangers in spirits or gods representing a variety of beliefs about marginality and transition. In myths and folktales the world over, tricksters appear whenever there is change, transition, and trouble. Victor Turner summarizes their amoral traits:

> . . . destructive, creative, farcical, ironic, energetic, suffering, lecherous, submissive, defiant, but always unpredictable . . . the invincible child . . . [of] an uncertain sexual status. . . . Other traits . . . include aggression, vindictiveness, vanity, defiance of authority, willfulness, individualism, indeterminacy of stature (sometimes tall, sometimes dwarfish). These liminal [transitional] entities . . . behave as though there were no social or moral norms to guide them. Self-will, caprice, and lust impel them. . . . Yet though wholly other, they are perfectly familiar to mankind, even jocularly so, for they represent what everyone would secretly like to do. (Turner 1968: 580)

Tricksters are figures in which folklorists and specialists in literature have been interested for their representation of those "areas *between* categories, between what is animal and what is human, what is natural and what is cultural. Trickster and his tales exemplify this preoccupation, for at the center of his antinomian [contradictory] existence is the power derived from his ability to live interstitially, to confuse and to escape the structures of society

[9] In contrast to widespread *rites de passage*, both social and religious, where an in-between "polluted" status lasts only so long, the social order of some societies and groups is organized wholly by their pollution beliefs. In South Asian caste systems, their principles of pollution stem from religious ideas. Having the closest touch with the gods all worship, the Brahman caste is highest because immanent within each member is the most valuable, the most divine substance. All other castes are evaluated in terms of their distance from the substance of the gods. Because a less divine substance is believed to change the very nature of one more divine, rules govern which castes may exchange with one another. These beliefs about the transferability of divinity by touch are the basis for definitions of "purity and pollution" in caste relations (Marriott and Inden 1973). American Rom (Gypsies) order their moral universe and survive as a group on the basis of a system of sanctions for "pure and polluted" behaviors. Relationships outside as well as inside the group are governed by these principles, which also define the social and cultural categories each person belongs in and the rules of the behaviors each should follow (Sutherland 1975).

and the order of cultural things" (Babcock-Abrahams 1975: 147-48). Some see the trickster also as a "culture hero," in embodying as well the negation of conservative social codes, his acting-out being a kind of social control mechanism, as Babcock-Abrahams describes:

> No figure in literature, oral or written, baffles us quite as much as trickster. He is positively identified with creative powers, often bringing such defining features of culture as fire or basic food, and yet he constantly behaves in the most antisocial manner we can imagine. Although we laugh at him for his troubles and his foolishness and are embarrassed by his promiscuity, his creative cleverness amazes us and keeps alive the possibility of transcending the social restrictions we regularly encounter. (1975: 147)

One stereotype portrayed by American social thought is the "Sambo" figure of our folklore, only recently banned as a stock character of popular entertainments. One historian of "the national jester" finds that those traits ascribed to Sambo are also found in other societies where slavery—even that of whites—was institutionalized (Boskin 1972: 154). Human slaves are defined as nonhuman by their human masters. Robert Penn Warren's 1965 characterization sums up this American personification of the universal trickster:

> He was the supine, grateful, humble, irresponsible, unmanly, banjo-picking, servile, grinning, slack-jawed, docile, dependent, slow-witted, humorous, child-loving, childlike, watermelon-stealing, spiritual-singing, blamelessly fornicating, happy-go-lucky, hedonistic, faithful black servitor who sometimes might step out of character long enough to utter folk wisdom or bury the family silver to save it from the Yankees. (In Boskin 1972: 154.)

In the American ideological domain, the ideal route of life's passage maps social space. Technically, the developers' and planners' model uses these phases in order to estimate the housing supply, the amounts of land to be set aside for residential, industrial, commercial, and communal uses. The model simplifies by assuming that people will be following a lifetime script, moving from one housing type to another, each in neighborhoods having one character or another, following the jobs. These functional requirements for housing size, type, and location come also, as the texts tell us, to be translated into the occupants expected in each.[10]

---

[10] Chronology, as developmental time, is a principle having widespread social authority, of course, as in educational practice, criminal justice, and

Developers do not, of course, actually line up and match consumers in each stage to suitable housing and neighborhoods; consumers themselves make choices along these general lines to best meet their needs in each stage.

What matters is that transitional social categories are defined, and then they are subject to a subsidiary axiom: that all transitional categories should be collected together, for spreading such anomalies in space (and in social time) will be disturbing to social safety. Their contaminations are best contained by suspending them from "ordinary" space. Setting them apart assists in keeping other category boundaries clean, as Leach suggests. Pope cited a technical report recommending that subsidized housing should be located in "transitional neighborhoods." The term for neighborhoods at the edge of viable downtowns is "gray areas," neither one thing nor another, collecting the morally marginal—alcoholics, prostitutes, illegal businesses, porno shops, and criminals. A "combined black and white symbolism" is often associated with tricksters (Babcock-Abrahams 1975: 160). Jane Jacobs titles one of her chapters "The Curse Of Border Vacuums," and speaks of them in terms little different from those Leach uses:

> Massive single uses in cities have a quality in common with each other. They form borders, and borders in cities usually make destructive neighbors.
>
> A border—the perimeter of a single massive or stretched-out use of territory—forms the edge of an area of "ordinary" city. Often borders are thought of as passive objects, or matter-of-factly just as edges. However, a border exerts an active influence.
>
> Railroads tracks are the classic examples of borders, so much so that they came to stand, long ago, for social borders too— "the other side of the tracks"—a connotation, incidentally, associated with small towns rather than with big cities. . . . In the case of a railroad track, the district lying to one side may do better or worse than the district lying to the other side. But the places that do worst of all, physically, are typically the zones directly beside the track, on both sides. . . . (1961: 257-58)

---

in the seniority rules of many kinds of organizations. Nevertheless a recent reviewer of the literature on the life cycle finds that "Much more is known about culturally prescribed roles and about the scheduling of daily activities . . . than about social judgments on the appropriate timing of transitions, correlated sanctions, and informal networks of social control. . . . [T]he process by which age norms or timetables are constructed, transmitted, and learned remains largely unexplored territory" (Elder 1975: 176).

She continues this analysis for waterfronts, campuses, expressways, large parking areas, and large parks (257-69).

The second domain using similar cultural conceptions is the legal, in which social personhood defined formally is more highly valued than social position defined informally or voluntarily—as in specific criteria for citizenship and in some sort of legal tie to another person or to a corporate body (the bank, the firm, or the state). Renters, in having an impermanent legal tie ("tenancy-at-will" is common), axiomatically are also thought to be single, divorced, black, and elderly. The proposition again follows that those likely to be without a legal tie to any other person or who are incomplete social persons, according to legal criteria, are to be collected spatially.

Again, the tradition here is very strong for homeowners. You know, just as it's part of the American dream to have your own home, so is it here. Although fewer young people believe that, so you have these *huge* apartment complexes for special groups of people—singles and then you have apartment complexes for elderly—one of them was written up in the *Saturday Review*. A new single style of living—you have all types of apartment complexes: huge honeycomb type living arrangement. *How did that come about?* Developers build them for special groups and then they go out and recruit only certain types of people to live there, and some of them may have a hundred, some of them have 500 people in them, and they have their own swimming pool—it's their own little community. It's cellular-type development. But I think that's more of on the young people. The others are pushing for their little suburban home, two cars, that sort of thing. And I think the emphasis is still on that. (Cole: 7)

Being between formal social categories is similar symbolically to being between the rungs on the ladder up. Those at the "margins" of legal ties are equally in an in-between social category. Renters, like blacks and women, are not yet "adopted as being full-fledged citizens," witness the title of legislation introduced in 1975 in New York State, "The Property Tax and Tenant Equality," and the "Equal Rights Amendment" to the Constitution. Their legal ties to the state are not completely in place.

According to one Secretary of the United States Department of Housing and Urban Development, renters are lacking any "incentive" to be "good neighbors," that it is "axiomatic" that neighbor-hoods will be neglected by "renters" (not by their landlords), and that homeownership (the ultimate legal tie) protects against "social alienation." Like tricksters, then, renters "behave as though there were no social or moral norms to guide them" (Turner 1968: 580). The political plight of "central cities" stems also from their housing categories believed to be socially marginal, and so are themselves put in a "hands-off" cultural category.

The productive or economic domain is based on the distinction between social reproduction (the family) and industrial production (the firm): the separation of home and work. In the system of land use, the basic distinction is between "residential" land uses, at the apex of the land-use hierarchy, and all other uses. The gradations between these distinct categories of home and work are in the same sense "transitional," equally having moral implications. The single-family-detached house, the quintesssential symbol for the pedestalled "Home," may not also be a place of work: the right to "home occupations" is a ticklish subject in zoning laws. The majority of use violations—reported by one owner about another—in Houston subdivisions concerned home occupations (Siegan 1972: 31). Gradations of land uses combining features of home and work signal danger by confusing their difference: "There must be physical discontinuity, clean and portentous," as Leach put it.

In analyzing the American kinship system as a cultural system, David Schneider finds that Americans define the family by reference to the distinctive differences they see between "home" and "work":

> One of the most fundamental and yet specific ways in which kinship is distinguished from all other kinds of relations is in the physical separation of work and home. This separation is seen most vividly in those special cases where, for some reason, work and home are in very close physical proximity. Where a shop is run by a family with living quarters in the rear, or upstairs, or where a doctor or lawyer has consulting rooms in his house or apartment, the line between the two is very sharply drawn. It may be nothing but a curtain or a door, but the boundary is treated with the utmost respect. . . .
> Work is productive, its outcome a product of some kind. Whether this is an object like a pair of shoes, a service like legal counsel, or entertainment like a theater does not matter [according to American concepts]. Work has an objective or goal which

116

is clear, explicit, and unitary. . . . Home has no such specific, explicit, unitary objective or goal. The outcome of home is not a single product, a specific form of entertainment, or a special service.

Home is not kept for money and, of those things related to home and family, it is said that there are some things that money can't buy! The formula in regard to work is exactly reversed at home: What is done is done for love, not for money! And it is love, of course, that money can't buy. (Schneider 1968: 45-6)

The suburbs, by definition, establish the greatest distance between home and work, for the suburb is primarily defined by its lack of resemblance to the city, the place where people "go in to work." The physical dissimilarity expresses the principle of separation and the spatial distance signifies social and moral contrast, and in also signifying social arrival, a primary sign of being at the top of the ladder of life, the suburbs thus combine the ideological domain with the economic. Separation from the profanities of work and commerce enhances the sacred aura of the family and its bonds of love in its single-family-detached house.

Greenpoint, a part of Brooklyn just off the Williamsburg Bridge, is an industrial section where residents live cheek-by-jowl among the factories where they work. A few years ago one plant was expanding, and, although that would add jobs, it would also remove thirty or forty houses that, under the zoning law, could not be replaced, for housing in industrial areas is commonly forbidden by zoning ordinances. That housing, long since in Greenpoint, constitutes a "nonconforming use." Residents, not only those displaced, took up the fight to change the zoning, demanding that the lost houses be replaced. They won. I spoke to a young woman who had grown up in the neighborhood, and whose mother and father had always worked there and are residents still. She and her husband live and work there now. But not her brothers who, scattered earlier in the suburbs, fulfilled their parents' ideas about the mark of their children's success: that they would *be* successful only if they they "got out" of Greenpoint and went to live in the suburbs. How to keep in the close touch they valued posed a great problem for parents and their sons. In her mid-twenties, she declared she would never live anywhere else but Greenpoint.

Arrival is "making out," the safe and stable thing to do, symbolized by the house and the white picket fence. Less valuable is "making do," represented in the "mixed use" of a single category,

117

as in home occupations or living behind the store. These category blurrings spell trouble and the danger of contamination for those staking a claim to having arrived.

The apartment building especially signifies this confusion: deemed a business by the United States Supreme Court, it is also a place where people make their home. But it cannot be profitable and sacred, all at once. A mixed category and by definition dangerous, apartments are used to mark off "suspended space:"

> Like many courts, the Maryland court accepts the principle that apartments may and should be used as buffers between single family residential development and the more intensive and supposedly less desirable nonresidential users. (Mandelker 1971: 92)

In New Jersey, a variance was approved "*on the grounds* that the proposed apartments were in an undesirable area, and that apartments in that location would serve as a buffer between nearby single family homes and a noxious industrial tract" (New Jersey County and Municipal Government Study Commission 1974: 114; my italics). As Gale put it, apartment houses are not considered to be "very residential." The Goss Group finds that "transient type people always create unrest," and another person spoke of the mixing of renters and owners as "planting a booby trap." Renters are likely "to pick up in the middle of the night and steal away."

Fare, an appraiser, discusses the differences among apartment developments:

> As a matter of fact there are even divisions down to swinging singles, young adults, family, old adults, you know in some of the larger projects. That is a common occurrence in Houston. Almost all the new projects have a family section and an adult section, not many of them are breaking down in the singles and adults, except like they put all the one-bedroom units in one place. . . . *And that seems to work?* Oh yes, it works better. If you're a—say a retired couple stays around the house all the time he doesn't particularly want to have the little kids around in the front yard screaming and yelling. If you're a swinging single who likes to pick up whatever happens to be laying around the pool you don't want little Johnny Crawford stepping on your stomach just as you're trying to do something real suave. (Fare: 27, 28)

Mythical tales attribute to tricksters the same sort of out-of-bounds sexuality (a metaphor for their danger to social order) so commonly attributed to blacks, "swinging singles," gay divorcees, and merry widows.

The apartment building and the motel (abodes for the trickster's "caprice and lust") are consigned to spatial limbo because they accommodate those categories believed to be in social and chronological limbo. In *The Zoning Game*, Richard Babcock reports a case in which a Chicago suburb had denied a developer the right to build a motel in a zoning district where hotels are permitted:

> Motel is such a dirty word that the phrases "Motor Hotel" and "Motor Inn" have made their appearance partly as a response to the rather unimaginative attempts of communities to segregate motels from inns and hotels. The truth, as any college sophomore knows, is that illicit sex is just as rampant in hotels and probably more delectable at inns than in motels, but most suburbs do not have hotels and an inn has a connotation of snug respectability. . . .

One witness for the village was the president of the board of education of the local high school:

> The Witness: My opinion is that this would have a deleterious effect on the morals of the young people who are going to be required—
> The Court: On what do you base your opinion?
> The Witness: On the fact that this, or any motel or hotel, has a lot of transient trade which cannot be controlled. . . .
> The Court: How would that affect the students, is what I am trying to find out, if there is a motel there and the transients stop there. How will that affect the morals of the students?
> The Witness: Because I feel these youngsters could be enticed into this motel.
> The Court: Enticed by whom?
> The Witness: By transient people.
> The Court: Yes, go ahead. You mean the boys or the girls?
> The Witness: I think both, yes.
> The Court: Both. And you think that strangers or transients will stand at the door and say, "Come on in little girl?" [sic].
> The Witness: Yes, I do. (Babcock 1966: 33-34)

The distinction between sacred house and mundane apartment does not end with those two. People who live in trailers, housing having a temporary location most often on the "outskirts" of town, are in an even less valued category than renters. They also have no legal address from which they vote or from which they can be

119

summoned to jury duty. Upgraded recently (in the face of the low-income housing shortage) to "mobile home owners," permanently parked, still they retain an in-between, and less valued, status. Owners of mobile home parks in most states have the right to evict without cause, which often means the forced sale of the unit; the threat of financial loss maintains the landlords' arbitrary power. Nor do mobile home buyers get mortgages because these homes are regarded not as permanent objects destined to last for twenty, thirty, or forty years, but as consumption objects, and like cars, they are subject to the same installment buying terms.

Legal minors—children, adolescents—are a dangerous category par excellence. As minors—not yet socially recognized persons—children are growing, changing, and dangerously uncategorizable for very long, stage by stage. They are quintessentially on the move and even in the residential environment where one might think they have a rightful home, they are a lightning rod for social friction. The segregation of families with children from adult households is common in Houston apartment developments, for example, and retirement communities may prohibit sales to families with children.

I asked the editor of the local newspaper in the new town of Columbia, Maryland, what kinds of disagreements seemed to arise most frequently among neighbors and at local civic meetings, and she fairly shouted, "Tot Lots. I don't care if I never hear another word about Tot Lots. The minute they come up, there is sure to be a quarrel at civic meetings." It seems that not only do children make noise while playing, but on their way to and from the spaces set aside for them, they may cross lawns, use others' backyards, and be intrusive, as adults see it. Of course these same families want to live in Columbia because its neighborhoods are planned around children's activities. Tricksters often appear in folktales as "the invincible child."

Bush, a developer, was experienced in managing suburban higher density, multifamily housing:

Just one last thing. What's your experience with density, high density in an apartment complex like this one? If you were the scientist making the report of the variables that lead to problems in a high density setting, what out of your experience would you point to? I would say that the density problems are

120

directly proportional to the number of children. This community, which has very few children, there are very few problems in high density. In a community with lots of children, high densities are murder, because children require space, children make noise, children dig up things, children annoy other people. Children are by definition, you know, children, so that—it's the comfort level.

Density is directly related, in my opinion, to the numbers of children, of all ages that you put on the site. So that you better cut the densities when you increase the number of kids to have happy people. Here we have fifty units to the acre so there're no real problems, because they're all an older group of people, very few kids, a handful of kids, no problems. The few we have do, at times create problems—nothing malicious but they're kids.

So that you don't put children in highrise, families with children in highrise, we learned that in public housing, well, that's true. That's a truism. If you want people to be happy, the more kids you have, the lower the density should be. I don't know what the break point is, but I would think that when you get round about five, six units to the acre, if you have sufficient recreational facilities, if you have reasonably good access to the walks, if you have schools that they can walk to or playgrounds, if you have easy access, with bicycle paths, and you have outlets for kids, it could be an idyllic kind of a thing. There are a lot of intangibles that relate to the ratio, but I think there's a direct relationship—the number of kids and the—I think it would be the sensitivity point of density. (Bush: 12-13)

The lower densities of developments of single-family-detached houses keep down the total child population, and the privacy of each backyard is also a means of reducing the frictions that, as Bush says, children, being children, produce.

A niche at the legal margins all too often becomes a permanent status. Teenagers, betwixt and between maturationally as well, are not expected, by definition, to be up to much good. Circularly, then, there is no clear-cut work opportunity for them, no spots where they might make a socially useful and recognized contribution. Juvenile delinquency, better entrenched institutionally than juvenile development, reflects the unsettling behavior

121

that the *adult* world makes the most of. That there are few if any
workable channels for adolescents' social contribution is due in
part to these cultural meanings.

In American social thought, not only children signify the dis-
turbances of transition: the segregation of the elderly (whose
loss of a partner also signifies the absence of a legal tie) is one
social response to the mysteries of the final transition to death.
Funeral homes are one of two land uses raising the most neigh-
borly objections; in the twenties and thirties they generated the
greatest volume of nuisance cases, together with gas stations, that
other singular symbol of transition (Ellickson 1973: 721).

> Relief [is] often provided against the operation of funeral parlors
> in residential areas, even where no invasion of fumes can be de-
> tected; many courts conclude that funeral homes inevitably remind
> people of death, cause consequent feelings of depression, and thus
> are sufficiently damaging to constitute a nuisance. (734)

Using the terms of this cultural logic helps to frame quite differently the issue of denial of social justice to blacks and other
groups being discriminated against. Blacks are the most "dangerous," because, in being positioned marginally to nearly all valued
American social categories (of which "white race" is primary),
they are also inevitably chronologically out of step. Not fully
positioned on one rung or another—education, equal pay, homeownership—they are always "slipping" and always at the margin
of achieving the next category. In their in-between status, poised
for movement, they are perceived as presenting the dangerous
prospect of socially redefining others. When their membership in
the next and more highly valued social category is unmistakable,
they are no longer feared, as in settled interracial neighborhoods
where incomes and education are generally the same (Hamilton
1971: 135-38).

The fundamental social issue for blacks has seemed to be their
constitutional rights. Once full citizenship is theirs, they will be
inside, not outside, basic legal categories, and desegregation, equal
opportunity, and voting rights are of course significant gains. But
in the terms of the fullest statement of citizenship—as criteria are
culturally rated—the social creditability that homeownership confers is still not allowed to blacks as freely as it is to whites. One
less-than-reliable, but fascinating, survey done in 1935 by *Fortune*

magazine (whose categories all too well reflect those times) reports these figures:

According to a *Fortune* survey the per cent of home ownership in the various socio-economic classes in 1935 was as follows:

Well-to-do	77.0
Upper middle class	59.9
Lower middle class	45.9
Irregularly employed or unemployed	30.1
Negroes	24.1

Class	% of owners who would rather rent	% of renters who would rather own
Well-to-do	12.2	45.3
Upper middle class	16.6	41.9
Lower middle class	15.4	49.0
Irregularly employed or unemployed	19.2	59.1
Negroes	7.5	74.0
All groups	15.6	51.4

(Dean 1945: 5, 6, 92.)

I interpret this great overrepresentation of blacks wanting to own rather than rent to express then as now their transformation of homeownership and its ties of debt into fictional citizenship: their rejection of townhouses and preference for a free-standing house today, as commented on earlier by Moon, express these same understandings of first-class citizenship. Being "condemned to die in a rented house" means not having become a fully social person in one's lifetime.

The overrepresentation of minorities in general, but especially of blacks, among all who make use of credit has been found in a recent study but could not be explained by income or occupation (Caplovitz 1974: 20, 24). I suggest that the "conspicuous consumption" of cars, clothes, and vacations is equally a heightened participation in those kinds of social relationships that signify social placement otherwise unavailable. A "good credit rating" is in itself a legal tie into, and recognition by, the wider society attainable few other ways under conditions of unemployment and underemployment, for example.

Under the spell of the American dream of progress, lower-income people of any race or national origin signify, like renters, a transitional or permanently transitional category (they are going to move up, or they do not but should). The persistence of national-origin neighborhoods—ethnic neighborhoods—may be a result of these same social meanings: in remaining solidary on the nationality dimension at least, a group fills its own category and decreases its social marginality in the wider society. By the very fact that to observers it is a settled and intact category, going nowhere, its members' vulnerability to these cultural meanings and the discriminations which accompany them are reduced.

CONCLUSION

My point is not that actually being outside of or marginal to particular categories matters, for that will always be. Nor will the "achieving society" give up its abundance of rationalized steps and hurdles; some people will not "qualify" as members of valued categories. What does matter is the sub rosa institutionalization of contamination beliefs and opprobrious trickster stereotypes, against which, as social categorization multiplies and produces its inevitable reciprocal, marginality, we need all the more to be on guard.[11]

Whether the hurdles and criteria of qualification are defined fairly is not the issue here. Rather, the fact that there is this social bent to clarify ambiguous statuses by social beliefs about their polluting powers needs to be recognized. Experiments have shown that simply by dividing individuals into groups and identifying them with labels, systematic "discrimination" is produced against the out-group. Further, that once there is an in- and out-group

[11] In a different vein, the observation is made that because there are fewer rites of passage in contemporary society, people experience life transitions without their having the social experience of being reintegrated into society (Douglas 1970 [1966]: 117-18; Kimball 1960: xvii). Turner extrapolates the in-between or liminal phase of rites of passage into a more or less permanent state of "communitas" shared by particular groups of people who "fall in the interstices of social structure . . . are on its margins . . . or occupy its lowest rungs" (1968: 125). From the point of view of the members, he defines communitas as the celebration of a "spontaneous" social bond among them, as opposed to a bond imposed by "the norm-governed, institutionalized, abstract nature of social structure" (1968: 127).

distinction (when there is also direct competition and rivalry), the out-group will be the target of hostility and negative attitudes and behavior. These destructive attitudes and actions subsequently become general norms (Williams 1976: 661).

Often a "pariah" people are in an interstitial social position and gain their cultural category from that fact. Prohibited from full membership according to the rules in place, middlemen groups are conceived as dangerous, amoral, tricksters. Put in the middle, necessarily playing both ends against it, they are an interface, implicated in the powers and dangers of those social boundaries—and, on that account, stigmatized. For example, in West Africa, where Lebanese immigrants have settled primarily as traders over a long period, they "often used to refer to themselves as the 'hyphen' between the Africans and the Europeans. . . . [Despite the fact that now] the Lebanese have a somewhat clearer and more dignified social position . . . they remain an isolated and exposed minority and make excellent whipping boys" (Winder 1967: 105, 141).

Thus are social categories *made* to be culturally problematic. Women are not members of the more valued gender—the only other gender—and, in being apart from it, are endowed with powers, mysteries, and dangers. Homosexuality is regarded as "intermediate" to each gender category, and it, too, is subject to social stigma and discrimination. The handicapped are "marginal" in not being wholly intact physical human beings—and they, too, struggle for equal rights. Halfway houses, for people formerly in jail or mental hospitals, are always a cause for neighborhood alarm. Why does society create these meanings? To an anthropologist, the subject has to be the entire system. Each state of transition and marginality exists within, not outside of, the very same social system defining the valued, settled, and intact categories. Both the less and the more valued are cut from the same cloth.

Once having created both negative and positive meanings, what does society do with them? The low cultural rating bequeathed to renters, minors, women, blacks, and central cities sharpens the definitive achievements of their opposites and makes more crisp the attainments of the categories owner, adult, male, white, and suburb, sweetening the struggle to achieve in so categorizing a world. I find it a culturally interesting fact that only within the last several years has there been recognized a chronology of adult development, that adults, too, (like children!) keep on changing throughout life, displaying marked regularity in their patterns of behavior and concerns, age group by age group (Gould 1972). Adults, having polarized and protected themselves from the less valued status of minors, remained blind to their own evolutionary stages that, by definition, have marginality. Adulthood, too, signified the social safety of arrival, with no question about it.

A related possibility is that marginal social persons, their cultural significance, and the way they are treated are cautionary tales told to maintain the status quo. Ritual practices in simpler societies often include the complete overthrow of all acknowledged social categories: inversions of sex, tasks, dress, mating rules all take place within a stylized, repetitive—and temporary—framework. Not a spontaneous "rebellion," however, it is one completely legitimated within the society—morality plays put on by the authorities. They provide an orderly place for disapproved behavior, inserted regularly in communal life perhaps as cautions that anything other than the existing social order is mysterious and dangerous. So do stereotypes—abusive linguistic rituals—and the demeaning treatment of people "at the margin" serve as institutional cautions against the awful consequences of being outside the rules.

The rules as they are need to be called into question. They are the invisible girders for the social structure as it is. In *A Theory of Justice*, John Rawls declares: "The primary subject of justice . . . is the basic structure of society. The reason for this is that its effects are so profound and pervasive, and present from birth" (Rawls 1971: 96). Perhaps, Rawls says, compared to a person's social position at birth and its relationship to wealth and talent, the "most important primary good is that of self-respect . . . a person's sense of his own value, his secure conviction that his conception of his . . . plan of life . . . is worth carrying out. And . . . self-respect implies a confidence in one's ability, so far as it is within one's power, to fulfill one's intentions. When we feel that our plans are of little value, we cannot pursue them with pleasure or take delight in their execution. Nor plagued by failure and self-doubt can we continue in our endeavors. It is clear then why self-respect is a primary good. Without it nothing may seem worth doing, or if some things have value for us, we lack the will to strive for them. All desire and activity becomes empty and vain, and we sink into apathy and cynicism" (440).

The natural distribution [of talent] is neither just nor unjust; nor is it unjust that men are born into society at some particular [wealth] position. These are simply natural facts. What is just and unjust is the way that institutions deal with these facts. Aristocratic and caste societies are unjust because they make these contingencies the ascriptive basis for belonging to more or less enclosed and privileged social classes. The basic structure of these societies incorporates the arbitrariness found in nature. But there is no necessity for men to resign themselves to these contingencies. The social system is not an unchangeable order beyond human control but a pattern of human action. (102)

But the "social" system is as well a cultural system. Its patterns of human action reproduce patterns of social thought. Real differences among people convey no information until the particular *meanings* of those differences are explained. Real differences among people, those created by their talents and those indexed by their place in the social, economic, and natural order, are also socially interpreted. The actual fact of being a minor, woman, black, divorced, or a renter is without social significance until we know also what meanings—socially circulating, publicly available —crystallize in each. For it is not the fact of having a particular status, but the social meanings attaching to it. In our society, negative meanings become rules and norms of institutions that assail and assault self-respect and "plague" those categories with prophecies, often enough self-fulfilling, of "failure and self-doubt." Therefore, the institutional position, as Rawls puts it, of people from birth and throughout life is equally a cultural position.

In pointing to some of the symbols expressing American conceptions of in-between categories, it is obvious that they are not social thoughts only but social practices as well. Renters and women, blacks and browns, the divorced and the single, children and the elderly and all that stands for them, in cities, buildings, and spaces, convey their constituted meaning of being neither here nor there, neither one thing nor another. We invent confusion even as we do order. Interstices are as much created and charged with significance as they are simply there. Nothing prevents us from putting a higher value on them.

Our attentions, then, should not be on social categories as given, but on what gives meanings to them. We shape our culture, and it shapes us. One mold is the organization of the housing industry so overwhelmingly toward the sale of housing, which

127

leaves out of symbolic account other valued principles of American society—those of learning, growing, maturing, becoming. Another is the legal lens through which relationships are so ubiquitously evaluated. Its monopoly devitalizes a customary social order of mutual respect built on the individual's felt sense of social duty. The atrophy of social competences in the everyday role of neighbor is a casualty of so paramount a value on formally prescribed rules. The sharp distinction between domestic and industrial organization symbolically deprives the family as a whole of its productive contribution, keeping women and teenagers especially from broader social participation and the social esteem and self-respect that goes with it.

Chapter Four

Many Wagons, Many Stars: The Uses of Land, Zoning, and Houses

The sanctity of family love is signalled by its home, and the profanity of trafficking in money by a place of work far distant. The texts tell another story, however, for America's most widespread cottage industry is the house itself as small business, the household's credit rating providing for each generation's economic well-being, the location for the children's public education, and its eventual resale and profit-taking for the parents' future. Not being a "nation of shopkeepers," America is one of homeowners, busily investing in plant maintenance and expansion with both money and time, keeping the product attractive for use and for sale. Up and down the social ladder, the janitor and the bank president, as Gale said, are both involved in homeownership, as lifestyle and as occupation: managing the patrimony, taking time for and investing in painting, repairing, and extending.

I propose that we cannot fathom American land-use practices until we come to terms with the fact that housing consumers are also housing producers. When they sell, they produce the used housing on which the total supply is so dependent. Annually, brand-new housing accounts for only about 1.5 percent of the total supply. The National Association of Realtors estimated for 1976 that 3 million existing single-family units would be bought and sold for a total of $125 billion, compared to 1 million new single-family houses having a total value of $55 billion. The used-property market represents 70 percent of housing activity, and in volume about three times that of the new-property market (1976: 1).

Opposition to anything that may "lower property values" echoes in today's disputes in settled suburbs and neighborhoods over the prospect of higher density and differing forms of housing, for whenever homebuyers move and whenever they think of selling for any reason, they expect to recoup their equity in order to use it in buying the next house, they expect the sale to cover the costs of the transaction, and always, they hope to realize some profit or a fair return on their investment.

129

In sharing the same hearth, sentiment and materialism themselves confuse categories of American thought. The confusion is
the backdrop to the major social contradiction of today: American ideals of liberty and justice for all subverted by constraints
on each household's freedom to choose where it lives. Obstacles
are placed in the way of blacks, lower-income people, and others
defined as marginal to valued categories, such as single-women
homeowners or unrelated groups living in single-family-detached
houses. For households with children, the location of residence
also implies their educational preparation for college and for better jobs. In terms of social esteem and self-respect, a lesser share
is denoted by the patently inferior necessities and amenities of de-
valued central cities and the black neighborhoods of so many
towns. Now even the fruits long available only to the favored
have begun to sour as a generation of white, middle-class Americans turns up who cannot themselves afford the suburban residence of their own childhoods.

They also may not be able to get in on the ground floor of a sure
thing. A full-page newspaper advertisement by the "Washington
Area Buy A House Now Association" claims: "Historically, the
housing market outperforms the stock market," and it spells out in
detail "The Great American Dream" quoted on the page opposite.

Other options for investments as certain to appreciate or that
people believe to be as certain appear to be limited. Because there
are significantly more homebuyers than tenants in the population—about 64 percent of American families—and because almost one-third of our national wealth is in the residential environment, the operations of the residential property market display
most of the population's lifelong wealth strategies (Kaiser Committee 1969: 114). Their current decisions are made in terms of
future expectations of income and expenditure (what economists
term permanent income). No doubt any other asset playing a similarly important role would have other kinds of consequences, not
necessarily all socially beneficial.

Hale finds that social and occupational mobility reinforces neighborhood homogeneity, because the sellers believe that "the next
buyer will be more willing to move in":

> . . . But at least in our work we have observed that this is a
> buyer preference and— . . . *Where do you think it comes from,
> this preference?* I think there is a presumption on the part of

130

THINK OF A HOME AS AN INVESTMENT!

The purchase of a home is one of the most prudent ways you can invest money. A look at the chart tells you why. Over the past 10 years, a home has provided a steadier and greater appreciation than savings accounts or the average stock market investments.

HOW NOT TO PLAY THE MARKET AND LOSE

Playing it "safe" and waiting in the housing market could cost you. Look at it this way: A $30,000 home today could cost you $33,000 next year or $36,300 in just two years. The point is that a home is today's best buy so it makes sense to buy now.

THERE ARE PLENTY OF HOMES AVAILABLE NOW

All kinds. High rise condominiums, multiplexes, townhouses, single family homes—new and resale homes. There's almost certainly a home available that will fill your needs and fit your budget requirements.

MORTGAGE MONEY IS ABUNDANT NOW

Federal Home Loan Mortgage Corporation, FHA, VA and conventional sources have mortgage money to lend now. And new laws make it easier to qualify: The income of both the husband and wife can count. Even singles can now qualify for mortgage loans.

DON'T FORGET THE TAX BENEFITS

Your property taxes and the interest you pay on your mortgage are tax deductible. Ask any homeowner how his interest deductions help him at income tax time.

PLAY THE HOME MARKET AND WIN

Remember, a home is about the only thing you can buy today, use and enjoy for years, and sell for more than you paid. And if you're concerned about recession, remember that Washington is virtually recession-proof thanks to the solid base of Federal employment.

How typical assets have appreciated in 10 year period from 1964 to 1973*

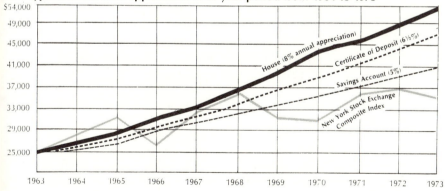

* Assuming an investment of $25,000 on December 31, 1963, the chart shows asset values at end of each succeeding year.

What are you waiting for? The Great American Dream is alive and well in the Washington area. (*The Washington Post*, 1 May 1975.)

the typical middle-class buyer that his property values—well, typically, these people are very mobile, as you would expect, and therefore, they are very concerned that when they have to sell their property that they will be able to realize at least what they paid for it so they'll have equity to put into their new home, wherever that may be, whether they're upgrading from their own choice or relocating by force of necessity. So there's a presumption on their part that, in most cases, by having "high neighborhood standards," which I translate to be a homogeneous, sort of middle-class neighborhood that the next buyer will be more willing to move into that. Now that presumes a mind set, I think, on the part of this economical class of people that says it's a high value to be in a homogeneous area. I don't know that that presumption is correct. In other words, I don't know that the developer couldn't promote nonhomogeneous neighborhoods as a given and find market acceptance for it. There has been some effort to do that in new towns, as you know. And we're doing that in some of our developments. But not in the sense that you sort of mix everybody up, but in the sense of structuring neighborhoods that appeal to various economic levels which . . . and then juxtaposing them in such a way that geographically you can identify the separateness, but in fact they are part of a larger community you might say. Now, but putting a $25,000 house next to a $45,000 house or apartments next to residences, or townhouses and apartments and single family dwellings all in some sort of collage—we've not found that to be acceptable and have been a little reluctant to try to force it as a marketing technique. (Hale: 1-2)

Gale speaks of the house as "the greatest single asset" in dollar terms that some people have:

The same argument that you get even in the inner city where a block is all Chinese, all Italian or Irish, or white group or this or that, the reason that they become so upset when a Puerto Rican moves in or the black moves in is that the housing value is going to come down, because everybody is going to move, this depresses the prices. And for most people we do have to admit that the biggest single investment that they have, and the asset value that is the home, is the largest single asset that most people have. If they have a little $14,000–$15,000 row house with maybe a mortgage outstanding at $6,000; that $9,000 bucks, that is the greatest single asset that they have. It's more than anything they've got in the bank; it's more than the cash value of their life insurance policy, it's more than the value of the automobile that they drive. . . . The lower the so-cial economic status of the people involved, the bigger the is-sue. *Why is that?* I don't know, but that has been a fascinating thing to observe. You have these frictions, the farther down you go in the social economic ladder, the bigger that issue be-comes. The higher up you go, the less it becomes. Senator Hugh Scott lives next door to my best friend [who is black] in Chest-nut Hill; there's no problem for them. (Gale: 8-9)

Savings, insurance, cars—but there is no mention of stocks, other real estate, or any such diversity in their assets. One would indeed have to be the Dr. Sax Engels quoted to call them capitalists.

For some families, homeownership is their most certain route to material security. For others, whose assets cover a wider range their house becomes a marker of these other resources—their oc-cupation, inheritance, and investments. For people whose occu-pational and income plateaus are reached early, the house is less a symbol and more a tangible source of future income, especially as monthly payments decrease and housing costs take a lesser share of a fixed income. Many kinds of wagons are hitched to many kinds of stars in metropolitan areas. The dreams have dif-ferent scenarios, and houses, land, and zoning take different parts in them.

THE CONSUMER AS THE PRODUCER OF USED HOUSING

The texts of this chapter speak to a basic home truth: that the homebuyer as a small-scale trader is important to understand-ing the lack of support for regional planning as well as the potency of exclusionary stances. Those "unplanned" and "chaotic" land-use patterns of metropolitan areas, where hunks and chinks of land are put into development without regard for coordinated facilities or services—these represent as well the gamble inherent in homeownership as a readily accessible speculative investment. The small-time investor is the market for the big-time speculator who subdivides and moves on.

One journalist, writing in the muckraking tradition, calls suburban sprawl "profitopolis":

> Many homebuyers themselves, by insisting on bigger houses on more ground in increasingly exclusive neighborhoods because these homes bring bigger resale profits, encourage the waste of land, reinforce patterns of segregation, and help push home prices beyond the reach of a growing number of the less affluent. (Downie 1974: 3-4)

A British sociologist studying American suburbs outside of Columbus, Ohio, found that "a number of the older families . . . had made a practice of moving every two or three years . . . in part to take a profit on the transaction. With their profit they were able to make the downpayment on a better house. One American, an artisan living on one of the most expensive subdivisions, had moved seven times in sixteen years. . . . Both he and his wife expressed themselves ready to move again if they found a better house or a better lot. . . . Another, a garage foreman, also living on one of the higher priced subdivisions . . . 'never bought a home with the idea of remaining indefinitely.' They had moved ten times already, each time within a radius of ten miles of the husband's place of employment which had not changed during the period" (Bracey 1964: 23).

The homebuyer may be getting a larger house and lot at the same time, of course, but because the house is the family's major capital resource it is in the eye of the storm over open housing. Homebuyers are on guard against whatever they, and their bankers, believe will lower property values—not "values," however, *but prices in the resale market*. Though the public is persuaded by the homebuilding industry, as the advertisement reproduced illustrates, that they can do better by investing in a house than in the stock market, they receive those benefits *only if they sell*. The homebuyer's preoccupation is with that day.

Within twenty years, Dole reported, he bought and sold three houses "and made a profit on every one of them." The appreciation of house value is regarded as a "right" that is, Peat finds, "religiously defended in *all* income-levels" against the "specter of decreasing home values":

One of the developers down there wanted to buy some property down there and get into one of these low-income housing developments, and there were so many problems raised by the local people that he abandoned that. Didn't do it. It was, you

134

know, "It'll lower our housing values," and all this kind of stuff. There was this furor about it. So there are pretty strong feelings about the federal requirements for mixing the income levels and thereby raising the specter of decreasing home values because the idea that you can buy a house here and it is going to increase in value and if you get transferred and move some-place you can sell it for more than you paid for it is kind of treated as a *right* here rather than just something that happens. And people defend it pretty vigorously, pretty religiously, in *all* income levels are pretty strong about that. *If you were to just talk about income, and not race, which is in my view not a Texas problem but a national problem, is that what we're also hearing? It's simply income levels?* I think so, probably more that than the race situation now. Ten, fifteen years ago, I think it would have been essentially a race situation, regardless of income levels, but I think we're getting more and more toward the income level situation and not quite as significant as far as the race is concerned. I think the race situation is hovering there in the background. The feeling that the blacks have lower in-come than the whites in this area certainly—but I think really we're leaning more towards the income level as a basis for it rather than just strictly the race thing like it used to be. (Peat: 12-13)

Ream says that when people buy a house in the suburbs they have their "whole world in that move":

Right now everybody is perceiving the energy crisis as a great tragedy which it was for a lot of people, an abrupt adjustment, probably a part of this problem of change and anxiety which people are instinctively reacting against. If we go to all this trouble to move to suburbia to buy a house on an empty lot, if you got your whole world in that move, and to put a garden apartment project near you and jeopardize that possibility is more than anybody can take. But in fact what is happening is that's going to be jeopardized in ways that people won't have any control over—you know—energy. (Ream: 14, 15)

People may buy more house than they can afford. They are so overcommitted to meeting their monthly mortgage payments that their houses stand unfurnished:

For twenty-five years now the economy has been going up. Income level has been going up, salaries have been going up, everything has been improving. So people say, "I'll buy all the house I can possibly afford now because five years from now, I'll be able to afford it without any problem. I don't want to buy a house now and then sell it again within two years when I can afford a better house." Of course, they end up doing that, they end up buying all the house that they can afford *now*, and then five years from now why they sell that and buy a bigger one because they can afford more, but I don't think that's their. . . . I know out there where we live, went to visit some friend's house out there—neighbors, weren't particularly friends—find them living in $40,000 houses and only have three rooms of furniture, and the other rooms don't have any or very little, so they buy the *house*. . . . It's astonishing to me the way my house is worth almost twice today what it was eight years ago when I bought it. I don't know that I could afford to buy it today. Actually, we probably could have bought more house many years ago than we bought, because we did want to put nice furniture in it, that sort of thing. It is amazing, you find people with $60 and $70,000 houses that will have half the house unfurnished. (Peat: 23-24)

Cole knows of the same kind of case:

What is your sense of the level to which people are house poor? In the sense they are spending a larger proportion of income on ownership than they might in fact be able to afford? I don't really have a good feel for that. I have heard stories and talked with people who were spending 30, 40 percent of their income on house notes. Part of that is just ambitious people who want a big home even though they don't have furniture for it, and stuff like that. (Cole: 8)

The same tight-money situation exists among lower-income suburbanites:

But I think it's a similar situation where you have people buying homes. And perhaps FHA and VA are too liberal in their underwriting and they let the guy buy more house than he can justify. So, that at the end of the month if he has made his mortgage payment, by the time he puts food on the table, and clothes on his family's back, he doesn't have the money left over to maintain his house, or because of educational failures he doesn't have the ability to maintain it himself. He has never been schooled in maintaining a house, because he has never owned one before himself. (Able: 10)

Gale sees financial hardship as an unspoken sidelight to the "flight to the suburbs":

... a lot of people have placed themselves in very difficult economic circumstance in order to get to the suburbs. *Do you think they are overspending?* Oh yes! When you consider that a person moves ten, fifteen miles out of Philadelphia and they have the expense of getting to and from work, and don't forget that most of us still are working in Philadelphia, when they have a tax load that can become burdensome because new fledgling communities don't have any industry to speak of to lighten the tax load. . . . Now, their salary didn't adjust just to take care of this. They've got to be in a bind. If they're not in a bind they are, at least, in poorer economic circumstances than they would have been had they stayed in the city. But they put up with this. (Gale: 6)

Hand, the executive director of a public-interest, private, development association, thinks people are living "on a very thin margin in suburban America":

Neighborhood-education-occupation? And how these factors affect their personal measure of self-esteem and success? I would, I think, say it is probably the job that is the most important consideration and that it begins—I'd stop right there. I think education is tool toward job and I think neighborhood is manifestation of status born from job. And I think a little evidence of that is clearly seen in the highly marginal circumstances under which so *many* Philadelphians and others push themselves in order to get to a neighborhood that squares with their concept which, I think, they sometimes (maybe I'm contradicting myself) use to kind of compensate for a work status situation. But I honestly think occupation is the most important. *Are you saying that your experience is that there are people who are house poor?* Oh yes, I think without any question. House-poor in the sense that they're extraordinarily

137

over-extended. I think that's a particular phenomenon of the ascending black in the city and of the white one step removed —probably living on a very thin margin in suburban America in the development house. It's picked up, I think, in the two workers in the family, the kind of sideways rationalization for day-care that often crops up. I think those are very strong and very pronounced forces that we have tended to underestimate. (Hand: 7)

Both Gale and Pope find that people with lower incomes react more strongly to heterogeneous housing types and the people they will presumably house than do those with higher incomes because, Gale says, their house "is the largest single asset they have."

To people "down in the scale" there is greater risk in an unconventional house-type as a neighbor.

But nevertheless, there *was* the issue raised [by a quadruplex structure] on the emotional plane, this stuff is *like* an apartment and it looks *like* an apartment, and therefore it's bad. So you have to deal with that issue number one, and then the secondary issue was, in many cases, particularly as you get down in the scale, this becomes a primary issue, how much are they going to sell for, therefore how much are people who are going to live in the units will they be making. Are they equivalent in social class, and there is obviously a racist bias in that question, at least here in Houston. *Meaning black and white races or Chicano or do you mean just class?* White, in parenthesis, redneck versus either black or Chicano. And it has been my experience that you get a much, much stronger reaction the lower down you go income-wise into the white populus. (Pope: 3)

Dock, a black, identifies the uncertainties faced by those who have arrived:

I think property value is the superficial argument. I happen to think that it's a deeper psychological motivation. Middle class today is, in many instances, particularly black middle class, is first-generation middle class. A lot of the white ethnic middle class is first generation middle class and they grew up in families where the *whole purpose* of the family was to make the children middle class. They were taught this. And they were given an idea which became a fixation as to what that was going to be. And they want that dream to come true. They don't want it to be diluted in any way. And so they worked— and many of them worked their way through school and struggled to get to a position which, about which they had a preconception as to what it was going to be like. And then when they get there somebody says "Well, no it is not going to be like that anymore. It's going to be different from that, we're going to have an economic mixture. We're going to have you living across the street from". . . . And they say, "Oh, no we don't want that." It can work, this economic mixture. I lived for seven years in a neighborhood in North Philadelphia which was re-developed called York Town, which I guess was what you would call middle to lower-middle-class neighborhood. When I bought there the houses—the highest house was about $15,000, now they're up to maybe about $25,000. But they were surrounded by public housing projects. Yet, this neighborhood worked perfectly well. And there was harmony with the people in the public housing and there wasn't any problem. But I think that part of it is a psychological reaction as to what a middle-class neighborhood could be. A part of it, of course, are some of the myths about what poor people do. We have this myth that poor people are responsible for crime, that poor people are responsible for poor schools; that poor people are responsible for filth and all other things, so that they are unstable, they need mental health, that they need all this. And I think that's part of it. I think it's a class thing. And people who are first-generation middle class are probably more threatened because their status is not that secure. (Dock: 2-3)

Architecturally innovative housing is said to be unsuccessful among the majority of housing consumers—but that is because they are looking ahead to being producers. They are on the lookout for prospective buyers, when that time comes. Those wealthy consumers who commission "Falling Waters" and "Glass Boxes" as well as those buying less opulent but still avant-garde housing have other assets to rely on and are able to wait out the search for a buyer from their narrower market. Further, the range of assets a household commands as lifelong income will be related systematically not only to housing choices, but to patterns of voting on zoning and tax issues as well. The expected yield of each asset (house, savings, education, job, and children) is calculated for both present and future, and the one horizon affects the other.

Compounding the threat that their major asset will turn out to be a disappointing investment is their overcommitment to it. Foregoing liquid savings and reducing consumption of other things, "house poor" homebuyers are precariously situated on their rung. They are all too ready to be socially redefined, barely hanging on. They know themselves to be renters-in-disguise, all the more intent to put social distance between their fictional selves and the meanings renters carry.

PROPERTY VALUES, APPRECIATION, AND UNCERTAINTY

A study of prospective house buyers in large-scale single-family house developments found that about 20 percent of them thought it "very likely" that their home values would increase $2,000 annually over the next five years, about 50 percent thought that increase was "likely," and about 30 percent thought it "unlikely" (Werthman, Mandel, Dienstfrey 1965: 135). In Houston, where deed restrictions engage fate in more closely controlled ways, subdivision covenants may be written at the *request* of single-family homebuyers to include the option of selling out to higher-density uses should the new-property market look their way (Siegan 1972: 44). Blockbusting works on just the same principle: people are willing to sell in order to realize a return in line with their expectations.

Homebuyers not ready to sell persist in the common belief that lower-income and higher-density housing will lower their property "value"—but the chances are it will instead be raised (Rupnow and Clarke 1972; Maser, Riker, and Rossett 1975).[1] These property owners do not, at the present time, want the neighbors that such development implies, although they may be glad to realize the higher appreciation when they sell in the future. In Atlanta, when developers show an interest in vacant lots they consider ready to be developed, the neighborhood becomes di-

---

[1] In a study of the prices of and assessments on single-family houses in Chicago, it was found that housing "prices are greater the higher the income level of the neighborhood (a clear status effect) and the greater the proportion of apartments (presumably reflecting land use competition)" (Berry and Bednarz 1975: 29).

vided into those who do and who do not want the zoning changed. Developers do not find a united front among adjacent property owners: some refuse to consider the zoning change at all, but are not willing to buy the vacant land; others, looking to their permanent wealth positions, are willing to permit a zoning change

> ... if they, too can participate in any profits that arise from the changed market for their land. They may attempt to sell their land to the developer. They may offer to appear at the Aldermanic Zoning Committee hearing in support of the application. However, this is unlikely because, despite the difference in their view of the zoning change and the views of other APOs [adjacent property owners], they realize that they must continue to live in the neighborhood at least for several months to come. Therefore, they may be reluctant to appear to be actively supporting the application.

> There have been instances where commercial interests have made an offer to purchase property at a large profit to the owner if the zoning can be changed to permit the desired use. It may be that up to the time of this offer, the property owner looked at zoning as a protection, but now it is a hindrance. The reluctance of the aldermen to readily agree to this change of view is difficult for the owner to accept. (As 89 percent of the APOs stated during their interviews, the APOs' views of zoning change when personal interests are involved.) ... In addition to being angry at the aldermen, the property owner will be infuriated at his neighbors who oppose the change. (Rupnow and Clarke 1972: 121-22)

Single-family property owners often enough *want* to sell to developers of higher density uses, whether they are residential or commercial. The same study of zoning change hearings in Atlanta asked whether large developers dominated over single-property owners in rezoning requests. The data show that owners are even slightly more active, with seventy-eight of 152 applications (or 51 percent) from owners and seventy-four applications from agents representing developers, in the course of one year. Of 154 applications filed, 67 percent were to reclassify residential uses, of which only 10 percent requested a less intensive use. Of all changes requested to the apartment classification, 71 percent are low density residential uses, 7 percent apartment uses, 4 percent commercial, and 12 percent industrial uses (Rupnow and Clarke 1972: 15).

Peat spoke of having an apartment house built down the street from the single-family subdivision in which he lives. His neighbors objected strenuously on the grounds that their houses' "values" would go down:

I don't know if they realize—I am sure that they are aware that their values haven't gone down because the houses are still selling for more than they were last year, more than they were three or four years ago. But I don't know that anybody has stopped and said to themselves, "You know we really didn't know what we were talking about." I doubt that anyone has done that. Not too much self-examination on that score. *Has the environment, as you live in it, actually shown signs of change?* No, there is little more traffic on the street, but from the subdivision standpoint, the people that bought the property donated some land across the street from the apartments for a city park. When the street was extended, the city has developed a park, so our subdivision has *gained* substantially as far park and open space is concerned by having it there. And all the people's kids go down there and play ball in the park and all the rest of it, but whether they ever get through their head that those bad apartment people were responsible for us having this good—I doubt it. I seriously doubt it. I seriously doubt that there's that much introspection going on. (Peat: 16, 17)

Ream reports the homeowner's "perception" of the apartment in these terms. The house appreciates because "you got everything in it and you're taking care of it," in comparison to the apartment, which is "diminishing":

That's a rental property—simply for the purpose of making a lot of money for some guy [people will say]. And it isn't going to be kept up any more than it has to be and therefore it will visually deteriorate the neighborhood as well as, you know, visual pollution. And that the people who progressively over time will come to accept that kind of house will be of less and less economic stability compared to yours. You see your property *increasing* because you got everything in it and you're taking care of it. You see that property diminishing every time, and the gulf getting greater. How much truth is there in that perception? There are obvious examples, you know, where it's happened. I guess the thing you have to question is the premise. Because somebody makes less money than I do, does that mean I can't live with him, or shouldn't, or don't want to? I

142

mean somehow they're going to adversely affect me or affect me and my family. You see, that question is never raised. It is the underlying premises which are never discussed. (Ream: 16-18)

But Able maintains that low-income housing at higher density will inevitably "affect values":

How do you match that with the protecting property values, that is, isn't that what we always hear, that the single-family homeowner when he hears about high density occurring nearby, or whatever, speaks of the effect on his property value, I guess he means it's going to lower it? I think, again, it's the uninformed. There are estates off of Montgomery Avenue that have had (Montgomery is out here on the Main Line) where there have been multi-family developments nearby, and I'm sure that they haven't lost a nickel of value. It depends on the nature of the development, and regardless of what the liberal psychologists will say about low-income housing and so forth, if you put low-income housing into a higher class neighborhood it's going to affect values. (Able: 9)

Lower income housing nearby is believed to lower the resale price of single-family housing because, I suggest, of a fear that the *rate* of appreciation will be slowed down. The threat to the homebuyer's permanent income strategies is the possibility that the house investment will take more time to earn less. Publicly owned housing—about which there is the greatest amount of outcry by homeowners—*never* appreciates because its market value is never tested. Because it provides no rising value to influence the properties nearby, neighborhoods of owners oppose it. This static characteristic of public housing (occupied as well by a permanently transitional category of people) is what makes neighborhoods of both black and white homebuyers so inimical to it.

For example, the "most important recommendation" in a compromise to resolve a heated dispute over providing new moderate- and low-income housing in Newton, a high-income, inner suburb of Boston, was to devise a new zoning category, a Public Residence Zone intended "to make land available for low-income, multiple-dwelling units without opening land to commercial apartment development," even though the actual sites so zoned might

143

be within existing residential zones (Haar and Iatridis 1974: 107). In my terms, this new zone will insulate the rate of appreciation of neighboring properties from the retarding influence of public housing. In effect, each zoning district is a separate market. A seven-year study by the Federal Home Loan Bank Board found that from 1966 to 1973 the average sales price of used housing increased about 60 percent (from $21,000 to $33,700), compared to a 43 percent increase in the average sales price of new houses ($26,900 to $38,400) (National Association of Homebuilders 1973: 1). On an annual basis, prices of single-family houses sold in the used-property market increased 8.6 percent: That becomes an approximate standard against which the house investment, compared to other possibilities, is measured.

Still, while homebuyers are living in their houses, their short-range wealth strategies are quite different: as a house appreciates in value so could property taxes, and they resist that mightily. A political resolution of that particular paradox is for assessed valuations to lag well behind market value, one "bad practice" that is not a mistake.

Zoning and Three Property Markets: New, Used, and Old

In following my particular interest in the kinds of social relationships that might distinguish homebuyers as closet business-people from entrepreneurs, I have concluded that rather than there being a single property market, it is useful to consider that there are three, each having different actors and incentives. Home-buyers' lifelong wealth strategies, however, tend to mirror—necessarily mirror—the beliefs framing the national capital market. These beliefs are enshrined in zoning regulations designed more to protect *new* ventures than to enhance the liveability of development once in place.

New, used, and old: three property markets operate, but most legal and economic analyses of land-use issues concentrate mainly on the institutional contexts of the first market and the kinds of social relationships and forms that define it. Because of that emphasis on the "new," the used-property market is consistently understudied, and the differing social and economic meanings of zoning or other forms of land-use control in each have not been acknowledged.

144

Undeveloped land—usually agricultural—coming into urbanized development makes up the "new property" market, whose buildings and acreage immediately enter the second market upon occupancy. The "used-property" market consists of property currently in use, being maintained, and available for eventual resale. The "old-property," or obsolescent-property, market exists where developed land occupied by buildings or by uses no longer viable is ripe for redevelopment, and thereupon reenters the new-property market. All kinds of land uses belong in each of these markets—industrial, commercial, residential, open space, agricultural. But each market operates on the basis of different amounts and availabilities of land and capital, each has a different set of actors, incentives, and outcomes, and each works from a different view of time and risk.

In the new-property market, land-use regulations reduce investment uncertainty: effective ahead of development, they are designed wholly to protect and recapture monetary and social values. Municipal adoption of a zoning map (the "official map"), in transferring some of the risk from the individual investor to the collectivity, expresses what has become an accepted public obligation to protect individual property rights from the possibility of harm from other land uses. Deed restrictions and other private covenants are still other ways of insuring this kind of perfection for new beginnings, and they can be added to zoning. Basic to the operations of the new-property market are the dual assumptions that risks to investment are foreseeable in terms of land-use relationships and that these land-use regulations will forestall and reduce them. (In Appendix 3, excerpts from the Baltimore Zoning Ordinance provide one example of how detailed this assumption is.)

Having been a widespread social mechanism only since the 1920s, zoning regulations applying to an entire city are, historically, adopted after a land-use pattern, usually having pervasive inefficiences and disharmonies according to some lights, is established. These "nonconforming uses," preexisting the zoning legislation, remain under both constitutional and political protection.

In the used-property market, zoning regulations reduce the uncertainty of existing owners that the new-property market (new development next to them) will cause them to forfeit their properties' accrued values. But zoning does not hold the same kind of

145

promise in this situation where development is in place and being used as it is seen to hold in the new-property market, of beneficial (planned for) relationships among uses. Many kinds of uses, within any one general class of uses, can settle down next door.

The used-property market is studied less than the new-property and old-property markets, in a literature devoted far more to new towns and redeveloped city centers. Perhaps we regard it as a more naturally operating market, the one we are all in twelve times yearly, writing our checks to bankers or landlords. It is apparently less problematic than the other two that so often call the great resources and powers of governments into use and into question. "The new" is also a strong American theme, and certainly capital will seek out the new as long as investors benefit from accelerated depreciation schedules on their income taxes. As a competitor for capital investment, the housing industry must assure investors that the demand for new units is high and that their return will be guaranteed. Growth gets the spotlight, therefore, and new development once in place is all but ignored in research and policy until it is old (Citizens League Report 1973). Rehabilitation, the one federal housing program directed to the used-property market, has been a disappointing source of low- and moderate-income housing in the quantity needed. A major problem remains that of retaining used-property neighborhoods and their lower-priced housing supply without their either becoming unlivable (obsolescent and ripe for new development) or priced out of reach by speculative rehabilitation. Even the goal of the new town of Columbia, Maryland to be a regional source of moderate-income housing is eroded by the very financial model on which it was based. As the city has grown, prices have risen, in line with the model's predictions (and hopes), and there are many original younger families who have traded-up and moved several times, so that the moderately priced houses they sold at appreciated prices cannot any longer be bought by younger families. In addition to trading-up, some Columbia homebuyers have also kept their first houses, in order to rent them.

The reasons behind the fact that zoning has become the major social mechanism for regulating the use of land are important in these distinctions among the three property markets.

"Given the huge amounts at stake, it is not surprising that special influence problems have plagued zoning from its inception," says a contemporary legal scholar (Ellickson 1973: 701). Far from "plaguing!" Special influences initiated it, and they will keep it going. In 1914, before zoning had been adopted widely, an observer commented:

> The tendency of districting is to convert interests in land—which in undistricted cities have proved to be of uncertain and fluctuating value—from speculative into conservative investments. It is like changing a somewhat risky 10 percent bond or stock into a conservative one. The result is an increase of fully 50 percent in its value, with no lack of buyers. (Williams 1914: 115-16)

Seymour Toll, a legal historian, describes the role of investors in New York City between 1912 and 1915, before the first comprehensive zoning ordinance was adopted anywhere in the United States. The Equitable Office Building, opened in 1915, was then "the world's largest office building, the equivalent of some forty city blocks piled upon the one it would occupy at 120 Broadway":

> It is clear that during this period whatever public concern may have touched the investor or the builder was never more than a rare twinge. . . . Many of the objections to the Equitable Building came from men of great wealth who owned adjoining properties. They were as indifferent to larger public concerns as those who built Equitable. They feared that Equitable would so oversupply office space that it would ruin many of their own skyscraper investments in lower Manhattan. . . .
> Practically all of the surrounding owners got reductions in their assessed valuations when they proved a loss of rents because of the light and air stolen by the massive new building. Its noon shadow enveloped some six times its own area. . . . (Toll 1969: 71)

Even earlier, competition for the grandeurs of Fifth Avenue was keen among the retail merchants, the owners of its elaborate mansions, and the garment industry. The garment industry lost, and its lofts were banished. "In the development of American zoning the conduct of the Fifth Avenue Association and of the avenue's retail merchants was an urban episode in creating and applying private power to private ends," an episode that, repeated throughout the maneuverings and debates giving birth to the 1916 Zoning Ordinance, today keeps on being repeated (Toll 1969: 109-10). A comment still apt, sixty years later:

> . . . the exhaustive factual material developed by the [Heights of Buildings] commissioners sometimes so militated in favor of cer-

147

tain regulations that it seemed to mock the very conclusions which were finally drawn, conclusions dominated by the commissioners' overriding concern for private real estate values. (Toll 1969: 164)

Real estate interests had been the original regulators of themselves, and, no less important, of their competition.

The Standard State Zoning Enabling Act was a model law developed in 1924 under Herbert Hoover's direction when he was Secretary of Commerce. It stemmed from the New York City zoning ordinance and experience, but soon became "a national law," one which "blitzed through one state legislature after another" in those years (Haar 1959: 350). "That such a swift spread of law could occur despite the intricate processes of many state legislatures and hundreds of local governments is at least statistically extraordinary" (Toll 1969: 193). Never could that have come about if zoning were not also much to the advantage of investors.

Zoning is no less a product of the industrialization of its time, a streamlining of the ever-present process of trading in land and property, mass-producing parcels for ready appraisal, pricing, and exchange. The sociologist Everett C. Hughes studied the Chicago Real Estate Board just after zoning had become widespread:

> Subjection of a tradition to modification in the interests of making real estate a commodity, such as is apparent throughout the movement for zoning, furnishes us one of our best cases of the process which we have called secularization. Sentiment has been taken from the notion of individual property rights and added to a new definition of the rights of the community. The dealers in the commodity affected have played the part of heralds of the newly defined rights. . . . The trader is he who would make all values economic. He makes secular that which has been sacred. He is a revolutionary in relation to his own commodity, although he may call himself a conservative in other aspects of life. (Hughes 1928: 340-42)

Toll documents zoning's historically consistent split from the rationalistic ideas of comprehensive, long-range planning. Even to its most convinced champions, zoning has never been a reliable mechanism for deliberatively limiting and channeling growth. In fact, just the opposite is true: it is a major piece of industrial equipment, quickly tooled, I am suggesting, to produce the latest models favored by the capital market, national and regional.

148

Planning in the civil service has been accepted only in its guise of technical neutrality, and rarely is it a match for the dynamic and demanding forces in all three real estate markets. Long-range comprehensive planning—the primary concept of planning—has been, historically, all too often an obsessive exercise, rarely coming to closure in municipal zoning regulations and capital improvement schedules at once technically, pragmatically, and socially appropriate (Perin 1967). It is no mistake that planning is so often inconclusive. Not only does its failure often enough serve the interests of local realtors and developers, but, as I have been saying, the interests of homebuyers as small-scale traders in real estate as well. No matter how conceptually and technically impeccable the ideas of planners are, they meet the resistance of these ordinary citizens who also want little interference in the market for their singular and often greatest asset. Elected representatives in city councils and state and federal legislatures understand these interests well, and when they are slow to support the reasoned reforms planners advocate, their positions reflect a clearly mandated social choice. Planning and zoning have certainly accomplished many good deeds for the general welfare and they have often been powerful in braking licentious practices, but all the same, zoning has been legislated widely due to the support primarily of real estate interests and secondarily of municipal reformers.

To understand why investors could be dragged into a net restricting their private property rights, one they still rail against, to be sure, it is necessary to look back at what zoning replaced. The common law of nuisance had been the main avenue of redress for mediating property owners' disputes over the harm one might cause another (smoke, soot, noise, deprivations of light, or air, for example). Each complaint had to be heard, case by case. What *facts* will courts take into account in judging wrongs and assigning damages? How much chance is there of winning? One legal scholar puts it that the nuisance remedy is valid only if it can be "based on externally applied objective criteria which do not have a base in value preferences" (Mandelker 1971: 32). But the courts had displayed enough capriciousness, "lulling vagueness," and variation that some better form of risk-reduction was needed if investors were to dam the seas of uncertainty in which they operate.[2]

[2] "Long before the modern era of comprehensive zoning, courts in the hit

149

With zoning, an investor could expect a stable and unchallenged return from any use within the law, no matter how sensitive or irascible its present and future neighbors. That is, whatever the costs of complying with zoning ordinances—reducing rentable space to comply with density requirements, for example—these would be less than the costs envisaged from a future neighbor whose nuisance of a business might drive tenants away. Further, zoning restrictions were a surer hedge against loss than going to court against a detrimental neighbor without winning the case, or as the plaintiff being taken to court, deprived of the right to continue without being compensated for loss.

> The role of the developer is also that of risk bearer. His tie-up of capital and labor subject him to interest rate risk, and the project in which he has his capital and labor committed is subject to business risk (failure of the undertaking) and market risk (the possibility that the project will decline in value). In most cases the financial risk associated with borrowed funds will also be incurred. The developer must know and understand these risks and be prepared to accept some, avoid some, and pass some along to insurers. (Smith, Tschappat, and Racster 1973: 279)

As an "insurer," zoning is part and parcel of what people buy and sell in all three property markets.

Paradoxically, the risk-reduction that zoning regulations provide often is an impediment to the wealth maximization strategies of used-property owners wanting to sell. Thus it is that zoning amendments or variances permitting redevelopment to prohibited uses or densities are commonplace. These changes are often regarded as subverting good planning; they are also perceived as changes wrought by bribery or other kinds of corruption.

In another sense, the time horizon is a determining fact, for the developer, in contrast to the occupant-owner of an already built-

---

and miss, haphazard fashion of our case law and through loose standards of private and public nuisance were attempting to mitigate against the worst effects of unplanned, topsy-like land development in English and American communities. Thousands of discordant land uses have been reviewed by the courts since the law of 'nuisance' began to take wobbly shape soon after the Norman Conquest. The judge-made criteria for the resolution of such land-use disputes show just the sort of vagueness, and resultant flexibility one would expect, . . . over and over [American] judges have quoted the Latin maxim, lulling in its vagueness: 'Sic utere tuo ut alienum no laedas'—so use your own as not to injure others" (Beuscher and Morrison 1955: 442-43).

up parcel, is a *prospective* property owner. As a result each of these three property markets differs significantly in contemplating the meanings of deleterious neighbors, present and future.

Gale suggests that zoning will become even "tougher" once homeowners (formerly renters?) make their investment:

Do you think that the house in the suburbs is—or as you were talking earlier these other neighborhoods in the city, does everybody expect to sell their house for a lot more than they paid for it, is there this basic assumption, operating assumption that's made? I think that's a fair statement. One of the things that have responded very steadily and proportionate to inflation has been housing and given a neighborhood that does not show prospects of declining, yes, there will be an increase in housing and in the value of the house. Whether or not it's a *real* increase, is questionable, but there will be a value in the value of the house. *Do you connect that expectation with the using of zoning to protect, is that what is being protected, the investment in the house?* That's what people will claim, that—they will insist upon their right to the protection afforded by zoning laws even to the extent of trying to make the zoning tougher after they're once in there because it's their right to protect their investment and to do all that they can to assure that there is no deterioration in that investment. (Gale: 7-8)

In the used-property market, once settled into an investment, damage to its market value that could be wreaked by neighboring uses and users can be remedied by persuasion to desist, using perhaps the "good manners" advocated by one legal analyst in favor of a return to a more privatized regulatory system (Ellickson 1973: 762). If a lot next door or around the corner is being redeveloped or if a building is changing its use, owners and occupants can insist, as Gale has said, that all ordinances and codes are being complied with by inquiring of and complaining to the appropriate municipal bureaus. All that failing, nuisance law provides just the right remedy, after the fact; before the fact, threatening suit might be effective. In the used-property market, investors have at hand many avenues of protection and redress. The stakes may not be any lower in this market, but the assaults are actual and the remedies are calculable. Being in the middle of what is actually going on, and not fretting over taking the plunge, leads to distinctly different operating assumptions from those used in contemplating investment in the brand new-property market.

There, all those ordinary possibilities are perceived and anticipated quite differently: they are prospective harms piled upon what is already an undertaking fraught with unknowns. Zoning regulations are a major "insurer" to which some of the risk is passed along, and, as I have said, it is that function that accounts for the decisions of bankers and investors to accept zoning, and, through their influence, Chambers of Commerce and city councils. New-property ventures are financed by commercial banks whose rates of interest are higher than those of the savings and loan institutions that cater to the house-mortgage market and, by definition, the used-property market. That is, developers of new housing are purchasing construction loans from commercial banks at rates two to four percent higher than rates at which homebuyers get their mortgages through savings and loan institutions.

A British observer of American land-use practices finds that developers support zoning because it makes development less hazardous and it protects investment without the cost of ownership in the adjoining property, a situation quite unlike that in Britain. American zoning, he finds, emphasizes the distinctions between land uses, rather than their relationships, thus accounting for our less cohesive, more fragmented development (Delafons 1962: 83). Competition in the capital market, where investors use zoning insurance to help attract money into their ventures at the lowest possible cost, accounts, I suggest, for these insulating fine points of difference.

In this light, zoning regulations are probably the single most significant incentive on behalf of development.[3] Therefore, to change zoning, there is bribery and the corruption of community-wide objectives already legislated. "Getting the zoning"—changing the zoning usually from a less to a more intensive, and profitable, use—simultaneously means "insuring my investment" against future drop in market value, and, equally, guaranteeing the recapture of the new value it creates. One study of active investors

[3] That self-interest in the new-property market is more enhanced than abrogated by zoning is a viewpoint different from the vast literature on private property rights and public interferences with them. See Bryant 1972 for a concise restatement of the ways these arguments have been made and his analysis of mechanisms for public controls besides zoning to meet contemporary conditions.

found that only "4 percent used the discounted rate of return, which gives less weight to earnings in future years and more weight to early earnings. This result is surprising in view of the emphasis given to present value concepts in real estate and financial investment courses."

> Among the factors considered in making a decision to commit funds to a real estate investment [one study] found that investors and other participants regard market value appreciation, safety of investment funds, and a high rate of return on equity as first, second, and third in importance. *Loan terms were generally more important than characteristics of the property in decisions to commit funds.* (Smith, Tschappat, and Racster 1973: 110) (Italics supplied.)

Bankers set these "loan terms" which define the level of risk by the rate of interest they charge. One major role of zoning is to augment the borrower's argument on behalf of minimum risk and a "good deal."

Risk-reduction is no small contribution in the risk-prone development business, a proneness that is often enough also self-made. An experienced developer in Houston told me that, even there, where the residential market has been strong for so long, the failures he knew well were not attributable to unpopular housing design, location, or an otherwise unacceptable product, but rested in the structure and organization of the business and the experience of the entrepreneur. All the more reason for grasping at any straw believed to share the gambles.

Zoning regulations have, then, a quite different significance for anxious entrepreneurs on the verge of venturing their own and others' capital. Zoning soothes the trials of investors as the soothsayer of a beneficent future that all face equally blindly. It maps the entrails and provides an augury available nowhere else. In their classic guide to real estate investment, Ring and North make it culturally official with the basic axiom: "Controls, generally, are designed to direct real estate use and development in the interest of the community at large, and to protect the investment of real estate owners from exploitation or misuse of neighboring lands" (1967: 43). For even though the details, fine points, and precision of zoning regulations are two-edged (they govern the new investment itself) they backstop the "great care" that investors must take in reading the future:

153

. . . an average of eight to ten years' gross income must be ag-
gregated for invested capital to "turn over" once. Such slow capital turnover calls for great care in the analysis of the real estate
market particularly in forecasting the certainty, quantity, and
quality of future property rights to come. (37).

So far, the fact that zoning is primarily prospective, functioning
as a system of nuisance prevention, remains a strong attraction.[4]
That is not to say that bankers and investors have not lost in the
bargain the freedom to develop with the fewest restrictions on *their*
project as possible, which as poor losers they keep trying to re-
gain.

Zoning insurance is worthless, however, unless backed by the
currency of investment. We know now, finally, that "neighborhood
decay" is often another mask over a process far from natural:
decay may be the consequence of bankers' decisions to engage in
redlining, to cease making loans for improvements, resales, or new
investment in a neighborhood, usually one that is older and that
has some black and lower-income households. Redlined neighborhoods then become the turf for the new-property market that,
insisting so on different uses "not really touching" and assuming
many a "booby trap," wants to work its will on large land assemblies
instead of investing in the specific pockets and scattered parcels
that have actually reached obsolescence. Redlining ripens "transitional" neighborhoods for the total redevelopment whose function
is to insure against investment failure by guaranteeing "compatible" neighboring land uses in advance.[5]

[4] Ellickson's analysis founders on his fundamental supposition that "neighbors" will negotiate things out based on a system of fines for the nuisances
they may each call the other to account for: but they are not permanently
neighbors. Each successive use would have to be exactly the same on both
sides of the property line, and when different, reassessments of their spill-
over effects would have to be made. People would spend more time in court
than in the backyard. Unaware, he is speaking only of the used-property
market, for which I agree the nuisance remedy is useful. In calling zoning
"weak" because it is "prospective," his analysis entirely ignores the new-
property market, investors' view of incentives, and the private benefits
accruing from public regulation (Ellickson 1973: 706).

[5] Jane Jacobs distinguishes between "cataclysmic" and "gradual" investment funds—in my terms, these are the different premises underlying risk
reduction in the new- and used-property markets. My reinterpretation of
her position is that she objects to the use of Garden City-like, predigested
compatibilities to insure against the "dangers" lurking in the "lively, di-

CRITERIA FOR RISK

Now the question is: by whose lights are homebuyers' resale prices endangered? Do the criteria for safe investment by entrepreneurs "thinking big" in the new-property market apply equally to individual investors in the used-property market who tend to "think small"? Are the financial criteria of bankers, appraisers, and investors the same as the criteria and interests of people as they experience their daily lives in the residential environment, in those days, months, and years when resale is not on their minds?

What criteria do new-property market investors use? The personal "gut feelings" of developers are significant sources of "good" land-use relationships:

> . . . I mean there are certain things that we are saying [in laying out a large development] that are just good design planning and gut feeling . . . we don't want that there, we do want it here —we don't know *why* we want, we haven't really established the wants. . . . All the principles are there intuitively through land-use planning, through education. Every one of the staff comes to the drawing board with a multiple background of degrees and exposure and what have you and a consensus of experience that we're pretty much able to see what has worked and what hasn't. (Goss Group: 13-14)

Mortgage bankers do not sit idly by when development proposals come in for financing:

> *You didn't tell me you were an architect.* I'm not an architect. That [certificate] was given to me at a party. See the numbers 000, that was given to me because every set of plans that came in, I redesign 'em. Frustrated architect, and they come in and I say, this is wrong, this is wrong, and this is wrong. So my clients and friends and everything had a party for me and they presented me with the "architects' certificate." (Case: 19)

An appraiser immediately associates growth with "congestion":

> *Well, how about the mixture of density? You were saying earlier that the mixture of tenure types wouldn't come under [FHA cri-*

---

versified city, capable of continual, close-grained improvement and change" (1961: 314).

teria for] health or safety perhaps. No, they don't come under health and safety. It's just the fact that considering your appraisal of the area of the neighborhood. You appraise the house but you also appraise the neighborhood. *So what about a multi-family project coming in contiguous to a single-family subdivision? What would be your response to something like that?* It lowers the amenities of homeownership in the area. *It does?* Certainly it does. It's a form of congestion, traffic, congestion of people, additional demands on the local area in the way of schools, shopping centers, and very frequently simply disrupts the neighborhood's peace and quiet, which may be desirable for some and not for others. Generalities are a nuisance to deal with, very inadequate. (Dole: 11-12)

> While many land use incompatibilities are a product of physical damage flowing from close proximity, in many cases the conflict is predicated solely on matters of taste and preference rather than on observable physical effect. . . . Not only did the [U.S.] Supreme Court borrow explicitly from nuisance analogies in upholding the [Euclid] zoning ordinance . . . but it recognized at least implicitly that zoning distinctions were founded ultimately on taste and value preferences. (Mandelker 1971: 32-33)

Judicial or quasi-judicial decisions about the nature and extent of harms are, according to Mandelker, "matters of taste and preference" and not based on their observable effects, according to his analysis of about fifty cases in the Maryland Court of Appeals dealing with apartments adjacent to single-family housing.

Only when a sale is in prospect are appraisals made, and this text by an elected official, who is also in real estate, describes what Bean himself calls the "human evaluation," "the way that he feels, the way that he sees things." Prices in this largest of all housing markets are established and anticipated on such grounds.

You hear it said that car-tinkering around home depreciates values. Now where does that come from? I think that what happens is that, let's say that a person is having his house appraised and one of the things that you want to do when you are having something appraised is you want to make sure that everything is in its best light. The house is freshly painted, the grass well manicured, the floors are nice and clean, the place smells good, the whole works. 'Cause you have got to understand that what you are dealing with is an individual [the appraiser], who goes in and what he is basing his opinion on, in addition to facts, is the way that he feels, the way that he sees things. So he goes into an area and lo and behold there is a guy next door, a poor fellow who can't buy a car but who's scraped enough money to take an engine out of one and put it into another. He's got it up on some kind of lift. That man will see those things and in his mind, that appraiser will subtract some value from that. That's a situation, unfortunately, where *that* human evaluation comes in too. *I'm* an appraiser and unfortunately for me if I go through an area I try and think in terms of the fact that this house, because it's in a specific price range, that it will serve a specific need, it'll get a guy who maybe wouldn't be able to do anything else but rent. And then when I'm trying to wind up with all my figures, I'll ride through the area, and if it looks like all the people in the community are trying, in terms of keeping their properties painted, the glasses [windows] in and the yards up and the like, that helps me, maybe I'll be a little *high* in my evaluations. I drive through this *same* neighborhood and I see trash cans all over, and I see four or five little cars parked in front with license plates three and four and five years old, I see an old car on a lift, I see grease and oil all over that driveway apron, when I get back to that office and I'm starting to put down, when I finish and I write in my value the man could suffer three or four hundred dollars because of what I have seen and how I have related to that. (Bean: 18-19)

One study of Pittsburgh's zoning asked whether people actively trading in property markets use the same criteria as are reflected in the ordinance (Crecine, Davis, and Jackson 1967). It found that they do not. The harmful effects implied in the land-use categories and district classifications were translated into the expected effects on prices, and these were compared with actual market prices between 1956 and 1963. For example, by separating them, the regulations implicitly declare that two-family dwellings, row houses, and apartment houses will be financially harmful to single-family dwellings. Similarly, buildings with relatively small lots and yards should have a negative influence on the prices of those nearby residences with larger lots and yards. Tall buildings should have a similarly depreciating influence on relatively shorter ones. The authors argue that these are a matter of the "taste" of the drafters of zoning regulations, for there is "no physical or technological reason why, say, apartment houses and single family dwellings should not exist side by side." Thus, supposing that people generally have the same tastes as those drafting zoning regulations, the record of prices in a competitive urban property market will reflect these "undesirable aspects of neighborhoods" (1967: 82).

In my terms, they tested for the difference not in tastes but in the viewpoints I have outlined between new-property market beliefs and used-property market practices. They have asked whether the general welfare reflected by the market is the same as that defined in the preconditions, designed to protect venture capital, that zoning sets up. Overall, they found that the prices established in the market tended to ignore these predictions of bad influence established by the zoning ordinance. More specifically, they found that the use that negatively affects prices in one district might be beneficial in another (92). Their evidence points to a good deal more independence of uses from one another in the urban property market than zoning ordinances suppose, and it shows that the proximity of different and supposedly incompatible uses do not have the negative effect on prices predicted by zoning regulations. They draw the conclusion that zoning ordinances overspecify details in district regulations.

If you're building a new town and you were able to maximize your value that you expressed earlier, of what you called a healthy attitude about diversity of mixed land use and such, what do you think in terms of—what do you think it would take to bring that about, given the way people tend to think—I could be wrong about this—about how their investment is protected? I think that you have to build communities in areas with diversity *planned* into it. You couldn't do it the way we've been doing now. The way we do it now is whatever happens to the neighborhood as it grows—I think you couldn't do it that way. You'd plan it from the beginning. And you'd be tough about it. And you build circles around areas, and you'd give deeds for certain lands for certain purposes in perpetuity; I don't mean just green-belts, whole wildlife areas, flood plain areas, recreation areas. (Cole: 16)

Why is it that brand-new, future development cannot, as Cole sees it, reproduce the process that has led historically to the urban diversity he personally values? What makes it necessary to have "tough" regulations? My answer has been the differing relationships to risk of those already invested compared to those venturing.

People trading in the used-property market may, then, sort themselves out differently from the way land-use controls, designed primarily to protect new-property investment, would have them. Indigenous ideas about the compatibility of land users are demonstrably different from those ideas of investors in new development. The axioms and propositions underlying zoning are by and large those of new-property market investors. The used-property market operates out of another geometry, one necessarily influenced by the first, but having axioms unique to it.

Together, the dual private-property market (one for blacks, one for whites) and new-property land-use regulations lay down a social geometry that more often than not prevents people from working out their own social order. Not only does zoning abet patterns of racial and income segregation, but the physical surroundings themselves symbolically categorize people. For example, in Douglas Park, a redeveloped neighborhood in Chicago, "at least three attempts to start a community organization to represent the entire area" came to naught because the builder provided "an intact residential identity" so that "people are almost uniformly identified by the developments they come from." These axiomatic identifications inhibit social exchange:

> This fragmentation of the area has made it difficult for community groups to identify themselves in such a way that they can bargain for the entire area. Most generally, community groups emerge within a particular development and then find it difficult to enter into broader confederations because their interests are so narrowly associated with their own living quarters. . . . Thus, where consensus may exist it is often precluded by the ecological legibility of income and racial differences and the general presumption that their differences outweigh their similarities. . . . This stereotypic view of the way community groups operate is not entirely due to the economic and racial distinctiveness of each development, but it is a large part of the visual contrasts in the community which give credence to such a point of view and help structure the community organizations which have emerged in the area. (Suttles 1972: 100-01)

In the used-property market, zoning is quite the wrong target for people who want to insure that their property appreciates, in contrast to ensuring safety from undue risk. As the Pittsburgh study of market prices shows, district-wide regulations may have little effect on them, and what one section of the city finds will lower prices, another does not, even though it is similarly zoned. Something else must be at work, something other than the social geometry laid out by new-property investors seeking the protections and enhancements of zoning.

That something else is, I suggest, the major source of property appreciation: how well all owners in an area maintain their properties and, perhaps even more significantly, whether the municipality does its part in street repair, garbage collection, lighting, planting, and public facilities. Private maintenance and continuous public investment are the two most significant factors contributing to keeping up prices in the used-property market. Cities abound with carefully tended nonconforming uses that do not necessarily or inevitably lower prices, especially when maintenance and public investment are also going on. Not only do bankers redline: municipal governments do, too. The "stability" of a neighborhood (not that of its residents) is determined by the regularity with which public services are provided.

But a major consequence of widespread homeownership has been the creation, de facto, of what amounts to a national "system" of property maintenance: an individualistic, handcraft industry, single owner by single owner, investing time and money as each sees fit, but each still utterly dependent on others in their block, for resale prices.

The block, as one organizing principle in the system of land use, is therefore an important economic, not social, device in the used-property market. In Levittown, the "block was a social unit only to assure a modicum of house and lawn care, beyond which there was no obligation for neighbors to associate":

> Given the boundaries within which neighboring takes place, the significant social unit in the community (at least in one like Levittown) is the sub-block—which is not a physical unit. . . . Conforming and copying occur more frequently than competition, mostly to secure the proper appearance of the block to impress strangers. A pervasive system of social control develops to enforce standards of appearance on the block, mainly concerning lawn care . . . the prime cause of both competition and conformity is home ownership and the mutual need to preserve property and status values. . . . What, then, accounts for the critics' preoccupation with suburban conformity, and their tendency to see status competition as a dominant theme in suburban life? For one thing, many of these critics live in city apartments, where the concern

160

for block status preservation is minimal. (Gans 1967: 156, 173, 176, 179)

After twenty years, house prices in Levittown doubled, paid, perhaps, by the "strangers" Gans speaks of.

CONCLUSION

We do not know what alternative national system of property maintenance might have resulted from a supply more balanced between ownership and rental housing (whether single- or multi-family). An industrialized, professional, and economically efficient system of maintenance might have arisen in order to serve housing that is not owner-occupied. Instead, the "neighborhood effect" so influential in setting prices—that sum of private and public influences on prices in an area—is now in the hands of each owner whose self-interest may be high enough to keep on fixing the plumbing and weeding the crab grass, but whose life events may prevent spending money and time that way (Winger 1973).

No matter how much pride or pleasure each individual household takes in maintaining its property, the sale price will depend on what the neighbors do and have done and how attentive to the public plant city departments have been. This same interest in neighborhood effects spurs the formation of homeowner associations. Even so, no matter what the social sanctions and pressures, each family is on its own time plan, and resale is farther away for some than for others. Citizen groups today, trying to preserve older neighborhoods from being "rehab-ed" by speculators, are rent by the dissension caused by those households, hitching other wagons to other stars, wanting to sell.

For most families, current income is the major problem they address daily, and a constant shortfall is the source of their resistance to anything that raises their property tax bill. Newcomers, especially, will cost them money, in the American idiom. In the longer run, if their taxes rise, the prices they can expect for their houses will fall. Socially exclusionary practices thus become inseparable from the fate bestowed on the house as a speculative and singular asset for most American families.

It is often said that lenders and developers mirror people's social tastes, and I do not doubt that that is often enough the case. But it is not often enough the case that homebuyers are free of producers' conceptions of social organization and social order. How else can we understand the fact that redlining is being fought by people living in redlined neighborhoods? They want to remain and they *want* to refinance their mortgages and make further investments in their property even as their neighborhood changes—but are denied loans. They are no less investors. The difference is that they live amid those arenas where social order is acted out and not merely contemplated, while lenders live close to their accountants' advice, far removed from the substance of social exchange.

Nor do lenders make it easy for blacks and whites to live as neighbors. The dual housing market uses the premise of social safety in homogeneity, either all white or all black neighborhoods. Yet, once the barriers are down, those categories are not on people's minds. "Most studies of racially mixed suburban neighborhoods agree in reporting that characteristics of housing services and physical surrounds were more important to both blacks and whites than whether the area was racially integrated" (Williams 1975: 139).

Furthermore, once housing is racially integrated there are signs that educational integration as its natural result is objected to far less than is busing:

> The willingness of whites to accept Black neighbors includes an acceptance of integrated schools. That is, in 1974 only 5 percent of the white respondents in a national sample also conducted by the National Opinion Research Center said they would object to sending their children to a school where a few of the children were Black, and only 28 percent objected to a school where half the students were Black. The majority of whites oppose busing for integration but apparently do not object to public schools which have large Black enrollments. (Farley 1976: 23)

Here, too, the difference rests with living out social order rather than contemplating its possibilities.

Chapter Five

A Place for Everyone: Negotiating Social Space and Social Order

Throughout I have been drawing attention to the contradictions between ideals and practices manifested in today's metropolitan areas, taking a tack quite the opposite of others dominating social science research and public policy analysis. Those will often pose an ideal distribution of powers among each level of government, or diagram a correct hierarchy of decision-making, or model some inevitable set of utilities, and then evaluate current practice in light of those theoretical—ideal as well as normative—representations. Whatever deviates is termed a "public problem."

But these "imperfections"—the economist's term for conditions not fitting models of ideal market behavior—*are* the American land-use system in action. The good practices and the bad: the system consists of both. The bad practices are not mistakes, accidents, or conspiracies. Their regular appearance is generated from similar regularities in the structure of the system itself.

Only by understanding where the incentives lie, both rewards and missing sanctions, can they be rearranged with the sticks and carrots of public policy. Incentives are not, often enough, readily apparent. Moreover, their revelation can lead to explanations more theoretically expansive than those stopping at "prejudice," "greed," "conservatism," or "market failure," for example. These, too, are consequences even as they are causes.

In metropolitan development, chaotic patterns and the waste of energy and land; in zoning, procedural confusion, costly delays, and the bribery more often suspected than proved; in the suburbs, the monotony of speculators' subdivisions and the injustice of suburban exclusion; along the highways, the ugliness and physical dangers of strip development—all of these, in being cultural artifacts of the land-use system, have to be explained by reference to it. Labelling them "public problems" does not state the facts, and the only conspiracy is that which we enter into when we fail to look for the system-wide sources of their manufacture, stamping them out of unchanging molds. The molds will remain as they are until we change the questions we ask. One question is why we *continue* to have land-use regulations and taxing policies that redound to the social, economic, and enviromental hurt of so many.

One response is that these social practices are sustained by the social meanings of homeownership as I have just been proposing, and by persistently local zoning control, whose origins and import are the subjects of this chapter. Why is zoning, having so major an influence on educational and housing discrimination, both popular and scorned?

> The discovery that it is practical by city zoning to carry out reasonable neighborly agreements as to the use of land has made an almost instant appeal to the American people. (Hoover 1924: xv)

> No one is enthusiastic about zoning except the people. The non-people—the professionals—hope it gets lost. . . . Yet thousands of local officials regard zoning as the greatest municipal achievement since the perfection of public sanitary systems. (Babcock 1966: 15)

> The problems just illustrated have not won zoning many friends other than the 9,000 governments that employ it. (Ellickson 1973: 705)

The local definition of the scale used to value resources of many kinds is what local control over zoning per se stands for. As communities grow, the scale adjusts. Those local interpretations of the meanings of neighborhood and social and political position express American adaptations to the spreading industrialization we are still experiencing. It rests with zoning to be the social mechanism—the popular mechanism—for defining this scale formally, and it is local control over that which is vigorously guarded. Local control over land-use policies and over the actual directions of development is but a manifestation of this more fundamental social process of defining one's place in the scheme of things lying closest to hand.

Along the expanding suburban frontier the distinction between newcomers and old-timers dominates. An entire society built of newcomers which today treats them so badly—of what is this contradiction built? American conceptions of newcomers influence today's premises about their unwelcome impact on the municipal treasury. For example, specialists in law, economics, and political science find that persistently local and parochial land-use control represents underlying issues of taxation and school financing. The social exclusions implicit in suburban zoning and building codes are only a by-product because, these studies say, communities are really resisting the added costs of newcomers, especially those who are lower-income and by definition higher cost (Ellman 1976). There are better remedies: less reliance on local property taxes through the initiation of state-wide school financing, support of federal and state revenue sharing, and promotion of other forms of tax redistribution. These, experts say, are more effective levers, and once used, no longer will localities use zoning to exclude blacks and lower-income households. Indeed, these analyses find that zoning regulations have far less impact on local-level land use compared to the greater influence of regional transportation systems, industrial development, and large-scale public facilities (Gaffney 1973).

There is, however, convincing evidence that neither reductions in tax burdens nor the full knowledge of fiscal impact will ameliorate those exclusionary practices. Measures of the actual fiscal impact on 175 suburban New Jersey communities where lower-cost housing has been built show that over a 10-year period tax rates simply have not only not gone up, but they have not changed, even with a population growth rate of 100 to 200 percent. Despite these facts, still there is "fierce opposition" to lower-cost housing:

> Small apartments are often a fiscal asset to local communities, because apartment residents usually have few children and put less strain on public schools. Local planners sometimes know this. Yet construction of new apartments often encounters fierce opposition in suburbs. . . .
>
> . . . the most expensive homes may be no bargain for the municipality that must foot the bill for educating the children who move in. A community's desire for social exclusiveness does not always match its real fiscal interests. (James and Windsor 1976: 132-34)

These are communities practicing exclusionary zoning, ostensibly with fiscal well-being in mind. They are also the communities subject to the path-breaking Mt. Laurel decision in 1975, requiring the regionalization of the lower-cost housing supply; their representatives in 1976 introduced state legislation to overturn that decision.

Nevertheless, however wise the arguments for lessening local reliance on the property tax may be in the long run, and no matter

1970 Municipal and School Effective Property Tax Rates, by Population Size and Growth Rate 1960-1970[a] (New Jersey) *

1960 Population	Population growth rate: 1960-1970 (percent)						
	Less than zero	Zero to 19.9	20.0 to 49.9	50.0 to 99.9	100.0 to 199.9	200.0 or more	Total
Less than 1,000	2.8[b] (6)	2.6 (33)	2.6 (34)	2.6 (29)	2.6 (15)	2.8 (3)	2.6 (120)
10,000-24,999	3.0 (1)	2.6 (17)	2.8 (13)	2.7 (11)	3.0 (3)	—	2.7 (45)
25,000-49,999	—	3.2 (4)	2.6 (2)	—	2.7 (1)	—	3.0 (7)
50,000 or more	—	—	2.4 (1)	—	—	—	2.4 (1)
Total	2.9 (7)	2.7 (54)	2.6 (50)	2.6 (40)	2.6 (19)	2.7 (3)	2.6 (173)

[a] Property taxes are expressed as a percentage of estimated true market values of properties. Property tax rates are the sum of rates applied to finance schools and the municipal budget. Figures in parentheses report the numbers of municipalities in the classification.

[b] Data were unavailable for the two municipalities in this classification.

Source: CUPR Municipal Finance Data File

(James and Windsor 1976: Table 7, p. 138)

* Reprinted with permission, © 1976 Journal of the American Institute of Planners.

how generally true the lack of impact of lower-cost housing on tax rates, it remains the case that citizens perpetuate the mandate of local leaders who do not act on such findings. Neither regional land-use control nor more welcoming local zoning ordinances are enacted. No matter what kinds of mechanisms regulating taxation and land use are proposed, they will be defeated by the same underlying factors that now produce these exclusionary policies of suburban constituencies, their lack of support for regional planning, and resistance to increased taxes that represent a fairer assessment for regional costs and benefits. One of these factors is the leitmotif of marginality, both social and temporal, running all through exclusionary practices.

Another is the social process accompanying growth, taking the form of local control over land use. This chapter provides a perspective on metropolitan development as a social process making use of a particular set of cultural conceptions to distinguish be-

ZONING, HOUSING VALUE AND FISCAL ADVANTAGE IN BERGEN COUNTY, NEW JERSEY 1970*

| | | Type of unit | | | |
| | | Single-family units on specified lot sizes | | | |
Housing unit characteristic	Multifamily units	Less than .25 acre	.25-.49 acre	.50-.99 acre	1.00 acre or more
Housing value per unit	$24,100	$51,700	$60,200	$72,300	$91,700
School-age children per unit	.31	1.21	1.50	1.70	1.71
Persons per unit	2.42	4.05	4.35	4.63	4.63
Housing value per school-age child	$77,800	$42,600	$40,100	$42,600	$53,700
Housing value per household resident	$10,000	$12,800	$13,800	$15,600	$19,800

(James and Windsor 1976: Table 1, p. 133)

* Reprinted with permission, © 1976 Journal of the American Institute of Planners.

tween newcomers and old-timers. Local control over zoning is one social form used to renegotiate social status in the face of newcomers who change its local meanings, and as such is equally one of the symbolic ways in which a plural, democratic society adjusts to growth.

SOCIAL SPACE, SOCIAL STRUCTURE, AND SOCIAL NEGOTIATION

There are two ways of thinking about social status: from the outside looking in, and from the inside looking out. There are the social pigeonholes people are defined to belong in, and there are the social principles with which they negotiate their relationships with one another. The ways social scientists, lawyers, journalists, and civic leaders observe and define social placement and the ways lay people do are different, and are of more than academic interest. This is not shoptalk, but a discussion of cultural conceptions that may help to explain important aspects of the kinds of social exclusion found in metropolitan areas.

Social scientists' maps of and terminology for social structure have become a widespread vocabulary that is used quite generally in describing and analyzing social position and life characteristics (Packard 1959). Commonly social class is defined by some combination of education and income levels with the type of occupation. Social status is generally regarded as a quantity of prestige or social reputation or power not necessarily causally related to degree of wealth. Using these terms, social stratification studies delineate, usually quantitatively, the American class structure. Social mobility is usually defined as the change of population in the categories up and down the groupings of income level and scales of occupational prestige, sometimes analyzed generation by generation.

From the inside looking out, the data consist of how and when such attributes as education, tenure, race, and income come to matter to one and to one's fellows in the social relationships generated by the situations of life: in the family, in the neighborhood, at work, in school, at church. I provide an example later of one study organized around and analyzing such self-reports.

The quantitative studies objectively document the differentiation of industrial society. Often they are used to estimate political iden-

168

tifications and to test one or another hypothesis about the relationship between class position and ideology. They are sometimes complemented by organizational studies, usually in the community-studies tradition of both sociology and anthropology in which investigators, sometimes in field studies, examine the mechanisms and principles by which smaller units such as neighborhoods and towns are tied into the larger society—for example, by newspapers, work, religion, politics, and markets. These studies often share the general theoretical question of how a highly differentiated, industrialized society coheres.

Descriptions of patterns of metropolitan population distribution, patterns largely created from census data, do not explain from the inside looking out how the patterns have come to be as they are. They do not speak to the principles people are using in ordering their relationships. A major study comes to the conclusion that although choices of housing and neighborhood can be said to be made on the basis of a "small number of differentiating properties" discovered through factorial analysis, such as "socio-economic status, familism, ethnicity, and mobility," "direct evidence for this proposition is minimal" because "very little material is available on residential aspirations and preferences" (Timms 1971: 97). What describes does not explain. Patterns are not processes, but are the results of them.[1]

That groups sharing some modal characteristics, of income or race, are a statistical majority in one area and not in another does not, then, explain either that predominance or its significance to the group itself. Neighborhoods appearing in census data to "belong" to one ethnic or income group are, when observed, diverse. In Boston's West End, for example, "there was little ethnic clustering within buildings or streets and, despite some social class differentiation of subneighborhoods, a considerable dispersion of people from different status positions throughout" (Fried 1973: 75).

Urban "subareas" are described as having internal "consistency" and a distinctive "character" by virtue of certain features clustering

---

[1] Muth's signal reexamination of metropolitan area population distribution, showing how economic variables in their historic context can account for suburbanization, is one example from economics of processual explanation (Muth 1969). Firey, a sociologist, taking issue with the ecologists' model of "natural" succession, demonstrated that the social and symbolic value of Beacon Hill in Boston (before its landmark designation) prevented land-use changes (Firey 1947).

169

around a statistical mean, such that one study of Seattle concludes that rental values identify spatial units "limited by natural boundaries and enclosing a population with a characteristic moral order" (Herbert 1973: 130). But another has found that when sub-areas are defined by different criteria they had "few common features," for example, as ecological areas based on natural barriers, land use, land values and race, as demographic areas based on population uniformity, and as "socially intimate areas" based on "levels of local interactions" (Herbert 1973: 133-34).

People like to live among their own kind, one axiom puts it. Which attributes make them similar, as they see it? The import of shared ethnicity for friendships is far less significant than shared religious preference: in a statistically drawn sample of about 1,000 native white men in Detroit, of their three closest friends about 70 percent share their broad religious preference (Protestant, Catholic, or Jewish) and only about 25 percent have two or all three friends drawn from their same ethnic group. Friendship on the basis of occupation showed an even greater dissimilarity from oneself. The average man's social networks are more heterogeneous than homogeneous (Laumann 1973: 51, 82, 93).

Socioeconomic indices delineating the familiar six-class groupings (upper, middle, and lower, each divided into an upper and a lower range) more often describe statistical than social groups. That is not to say that people cannot also classify themselves in these terms, *when that is what they are asked to do*. In the United States, Australia, and Great Britain, for example, when people are asked in national surveys what class they are in, 95 percent in Britain, 40 percent in the United States, and about 50 percent in Australia put themselves into the middle class and the remainder put themselves into the working class. The two-class division is a common response in industrialized societies (Broom, Jones, Zubrzycki 1968: 220). But those studies only reveal that when investigators ask about "social class" that is what they find out about—and not anything else. W. Lloyd Warner, the anthropologist who devised the six-class hierarchy in his study of Newburyport, Massachusetts, in the 1930s, chose research subjects to make status judgments because they already did: "A good judge is ordinarily someone who has been in the community all of his life, who

170

thinks about the people in his town in status terms, and who has a vocation that relates to all social levels" (1960: 68).

The conceptions of the people I talked to also reflect the structures of their corporate and political careers. One study of so-called "status discriminators" found that those "who identify themselves as upper, upper-middle, or middle class are more likely to be high on the index of status discrimination than men who identify themselves as upper-working or working class (who are likely to be lower on the index of status discrimination). . . . A particularly interesting finding is that men who thought that beliefs and feelings were the basis of class membership were much more likely to be low status discriminators, whereas men who thought that occupation, education, income, or family background was the basis of class membership were high status discriminators" (Laumann 1966: 109, 118).

> Generally speaking, the upper classes tended to have a much more differentiated picture of the occupational structure than the lower classes, who tended to blur distinctions between adjacent groupings [in a study of subjectively defined class structure]. Whereas the upper class had only 21 nonsignificant comparisons, the working class had 40 such comparisons. This enhanced status sensitivity of higher-status persons has been noted in a number of community studies of prestige and class (59).

Neither Warner's schema nor the social maps of bankers, developers, and planners are distortions—they are simply incomplete. The highly differentiated status hierarchy they find is one kind of social map. It has also often enough been the kind that social scientists, themselves perhaps more, rather than less, status conscious especially vis-à-vis natural scientists, have uncritically accepted because it fits their own (Huber and Form 1973: 15-43; Goldschmidt 1955).

The people providing these socioeconomic indices and statistical categories are not, however, analytically concerned with social organization as it takes place or with social order as it is negotiated. Sociologists and economists are formalizing the operations of social and economic systems at some remove from the arenas of daily life where such substantive principles matter most. Nevertheless, they have been just about the only social and cultural indices social science and public policy have had to go on. Many of the social geometries used in mapping populations in land use

171

(and education, law enforcement, and health systems, for example) often use no other data. Inferences about behaviors are drawn from these indicia all too often in terms of analysts' personal experiences. There are just too few ethnographic or journalistic reports of what people in their neighborhoods and in their social choices are about. Personalized, scatter-shot, or picturesque vignettes are simply inadequate background to the interpretive problems a large-scale system presents. They are insufficient if we are ever to comprehend the social processes creating those patterns clicking out of computers at high speed.

There is, therefore, a fundamental weakness not only to *this* discussion of residential exclusion, but to most other discussions as well.[2] The data I would like to have here do not exist, for the trend in substantive sociology and "urban" anthropology has been to a literature about lower-income and excluded groups—but almost no analyses are made of those with higher incomes doing the discriminating and the excluding. Although Anthony Downs's *Opening Up The Suburbs* is directed to higher-income groups, both blaming them for and informing them about the social consequences of their suburban monopoly, it provides little analysis of their behavior. Instead, Downs argues his own position in favor of greater economic diversity in the suburbs, asking for changes in residents' attitudes to bring it about (1973: 133, 135, 185). Twenty years ago Robert C. Wood put his finger on what continued to be the contradictory social implications of suburban politics (1958). Herbert Gans's *The Levittowners* and Bennett Berger's *Working Class Suburb*, now over a dozen years old, are still singular studies of American social relations in the suburbs.

These are the data now missing that, by their absence, *explain* metropolitan social organization and social order. Lacking objective, qualitative, systematic, and credible information about how people negotiate their differences, social frights are perpetuated, and segregation by race and by income is the social tranquilizer. Calling for more data in this case amplifies, not apologizes for, the adequacy of this theoretical approach to metropolitan social structure.

Although many more whites and blacks are living as neigh-

---

[2] A comprehensive discussion of *The Politics of Exclusion* as being practiced across the country by interest groups and governments is Danielson 1976.

172

bors today, there are no significantly large-scale trends toward the breakdown of rigid institutional barriers for blacks in their quests for access to jobs and housing. There are a few findings, however, that social differences of many kinds are generally accepted as negotiable. One study, designed to weed out the sources of distortion and bias of national samples not distinguishing between southern and nonsouthern populations compared working class and middle class attitudes toward civil rights for blacks, finding not only that on a national level each do not differ as much as popularly thought, but that in fact "the blue-collar group is slightly more favorably disposed to equality than the upper middle class" on three of four questions (Hamilton 1971). And a comparison of studies on these topics conducted in 1942, 1956, 1963, 1965, and 1968 indicates a consistent trend toward more favorable attitudes on equal rights and equal protection.

Producers may well share a tendency to exaggerate *others'* intolerant attitudes, a finding of this same study. Outside the South, just one respondent in ten favored pure segregation (in both middle class and blue-collar groups), but when the same people were asked how they thought "most people" in their area felt, about two-fifths thought that others favored strict segregation (1971: 134, 149).

A study of the way people rank themselves socially found that there is a great range of voluntary between-class contacts among friends, relatives, and neighbors that, in turn, also affects self-assessment to a greater extent than do education and family income, the traditional indicators of class location. "A person's own class identification depends as much on who he knows as on where he is in the class structure" (Hodge and Treiman 1968: 547). People mix themselves up, using a social logic about which we should know more than we do.

Geography, sociology, and economics have provided ecological models perhaps the most influential in limning our understanding of social negotiation in metropolitan areas. In mapping population distributions over time and in space in terms of socioeconomic characteristics (those asked about in the U.S. Census), these models often transform the "natural systems" analogy into a social geometry. The terms "invasion," "succession," "competition," and "selective survival" are used analogously in explaining social processes that actually have to do with changes

173

in income, education, land-use regulations, and opportunity structures. The biological analogy gives the impression that, as may occur with flora and fauna, these are autonomous and naturally occurring events, not behaviors responding to objective, widespread economic and social conditions.

No matter how useful they are to temporal models of population patterns, these Darwinian terms are culturally loaded, carrying frightening implications of human invasions and threatened survival, especially as they also ostensibly describe long-term residential patterns of urban neighborhoods, but in fact totally leave out the historical record. Social scientists are themselves, then, not immune to American cultural conceptions in having chosen this vocabulary of "danger" in which to discuss transitions.

Land-use regulations themselves should be added to the list of decisively influential man-made factors. They represent an exercise of social choice through the legislative and administrative branches of local and state governments. Those socioeconomic morphologies are their result, not their source. Guided by the premises underlying them, the regulations set up relations of workplace, home, shopping, and recreation. Patterns of population distribution cannot be viewed outside of this framework simply as the consequences of an ideal and purely rational market in houses and neighborhoods, or as the consequence of natural social flocking. As I have been saying, that market's formal operations are determined by cultural premises and social rules governing densities, adjacencies, and separations of land uses and land users. The general finding that physical and social regions exist cognitively is evidence, for example, of a common cultural apparatus used in defining land-use categories and relationships (Lynch 1960; Lowenthal 1972).

Those "inside-looking-out" social categories now missing from analysis take on even greater significance in the social organization of industrial society once we consider American residential neighborhoods as but the residuals of that social geometry embedded in land-use regulations. The social "membership" provided by living in a residential area is largely artificial and only partly voluntary. It is imposed by school districting practices, for example, or by community newspapers whose function is largely to *define* a commonality of interests by bounding areas, but often as retail shopping markets (Janowitz 1967). The common finding that people do not make friends with their next-door neighbors is an expression of this very artificiality, and not, I believe, of anomie or alienation. On the contrary, ever since the advent of cheap, public transportation and the telephone, it would be more anomic to exercise only one substantive choice in social relations and be bound to people simply by reason of proximity.

The social map drawn from the inside looking out is entirely different from the one based on inquiries made in terms of social class and status. Its raw materials consist of valued (including negatively valued) attributes of self and others. These enter into the social exchanges of particular situations that are structured by neighborhood, work, friendship, career, and family. Perhaps only at first may these evaluations use that map of purportedly objective classifications; after a social first-sort in terms of income, race, and ethnicity, other attributes come into play. They matter more to the character of the relationship and the forms it takes socially, economically, and politically.

As in every social relationship, something is transacted between the parties, but, I am saying, the media of this exchange are not the same coin as race or levels of wealth. By definition, the participants in each particular situation come to an agreement about what value to put on the media of their exchange—money can be one medium, certainly, but there are others, such as reputation, goodwill, loyalty, advice, appreciation, help, prestige, and opportunities—and all their negatives. Somewhat different media and criteria may be employed in each kind of situation. The situations are likely to be repetitive and widespread, so that research could proceed from a taxonomy of types. Once having evidence for these exchanges, the media used, and the criteria of value, not only the structure but the meanings of many kinds of behavior—voting, consumption, moving, and other choices—would become clearer.

The lot, the block, and the neighborhood each provide arenas for social exchange. In turn, these determine which school, shopping area, and local government will be the source of still other arenas. In all of them are the face-to-face social exchanges of individuals and of the groups they belong to in which people get and give those qualitative ingredients that so directly determine self-esteem, social reputation, and honor. In short, these are the arenas in which social order is enacted, for social order is not located in patterns mapped in physical space or set out in zoning classifications. It is born of the ways people deal with the inevitable differences among themselves. These are differences often presumed to inhibit their ability to work out amicable relationships, assumptions used in anticipating levels of social compatibility. The social geometry of sprawl, for example, puts the emphasis on circumscribing the arenas of exchange rather than on the social competences different kinds of arenas require.

Patterns of metropolitan development as manifestations of social thought can be best explained, therefore, by those *propositions* about social order, rather than by the social relationships people actually have and the social order they enact.

Direct evidence for enacted social order abounds in a fine work (1974) by William Kornblum, *Blue Collar Community*, a study of a steel mill neighborhood of South Chicago, where he lived for a few years and worked in the mills. Kornblum's discussion was not directly concerned with this topic, but in documenting how people having strong group identifications live and work together, it necessarily provides an array of evaluative criteria that Americans use. Culturally, the same kinds of social processes are occurring generally in American society, processes not limited to people of lower income or people recently arrived from other countries. All of us are borrowers from the American public library.

These are the subjects around which people working and living together in South Chicago form their evaluations of one another, resulting in their own "status" system. *Within* each nationality and each social group the same criteria are used as are used in sizing up and including new arrivals: age; arrival and settlement date; access to power of many kinds (union, neighborhood, church); ability to mediate, to bridge between groups; style of conflict-resolution; occupational performance—competence, work habits; how people raise their children, maintain their house, bear misfortune, how friendly they are coming and going, how a man's behavior inside the plant compares to that outside the plant.

Nothing here has to do with how much income people have, what kinds of things they own, or how they look. Ethnic and racial differences are well-noticed, but Kornblum finds that negative stereotypes are often changed by the work people share. Among the blacks, Poles, Serbians, Croatians, Italians, and Mexicans of this study, conflicts abound, as they do between and within any

176

so-called mainstream groups. Some conflicts may be wholly based on racial and ethnic differences: but not inevitably, the study makes clear. There are many close friendships, too.

Once generally oriented, people make important use of categories, definitions, and criteria, such as those Kornblum identifies, in the social exchanges through which they, among other things, evaluate themselves and others. Society is ordered by these relationships and the principles they are based on. How people form, maintain, repair, dissolve, and avoid social relationships constitutes a substantive sociology now lacking to parallel the formal sociology which, though plentiful in printouts, will remain underinterpreted and uninterpretable until the tunneling out of meaning begins from another side.

Local Control over Social Place

The process of status renegotiation that Kornblum finds in South Chicago, one occurring in response to growth and the newcomers it spawns, is a general one in American society. In the specific situation of metropolitan population growth, it provides the social and cultural wellsprings of local-level control.

Blacks in South Chicago can get just so far in their assumption of leadership: without residence in Irondale they are unable to lay full claim to the leadership skills they demonstrate inside the mill, skills that bring them the friendship and respect of whites. Irondale residents rioted against five black families who moved into a nearby public housing project that, even as an all-white project, had long been felt as a threat by the working-class residents. "Since 1954 the black population of the project has tripled, but blacks have not been successful in moving into the private homes in the old sections of Irondale" (73). Residential life there, as elsewhere, is also political life, in a situation where local power is tenuously held relative to other groups of the metropolitan area. The complexities of ethnicity, occupation, union leadership, and political activity are, according to Kornblum, mediated in important ways by residence in the mill neighborhood, where internal plant relationships and conflicts are often worked out through Irondale's institutions, formal and informal (church and tavern). Despite the variety of social sortings-out their occupational relationships result in, there is, however, no variation

177

in the residential pattern: the black men, and to a lesser extent the Mexicans, do not live, as the whites do, in the mill neighborhood.

That is, though, far from being a permanent fact: the blacks' and Mexicans' negotiation for a share of local power is the current phase of a long-term process repeated in the arrival of each ethnic group (often recruited for their special skills by the mill owners)—earlier, Poles, Italians, Croatians, Serbians, and now Mexicans and blacks. "Once they have proved to the white residents that their settlement will not be stopped, blacks and Mexicans can expect to compete with the white residents for respectability and power in communal institutions. In this way the time-worn processes of status negotiation can continue for the newcomers as it does for the various white ethnic groups who remain in the community" (214).

In metropolitan areas, as growth and change occur, once-settled boundaries (of place, of category) become unsettled, and people living on one or another side of these lines are forced to redefine themselves vis-à-vis others. Those events surrounding the adoption, enforcement, amendment, and variation of land-use regulations are, in these terms, significant sources of information about culture and social structure, waiting to be mined.

The defensive and delaying tactics citizens and public officials use to avoid lower-income households and higher densities are well known. But the strategies and adaptations people have used in moving over and making room are less well documented. The fact is, despite outcry and opposition, as often as not, the new development arrives down the street—else metropolitan growth would long since have used up *all* our agricultural land.

It is as an adaptive mechanism for old-timers that I examine here *the zoning game*, the appellation Richard Babcock, lawyer and land-use expert, gave to zoning after scrutinizing this public institution. What he found ten years ago persists:

> But the chaos in land-use planning is not the result of uncontrolled individual enterprise. It is a result of a combination of controls and lack of controls, of over-planning and anti-planning, enterprise and anti-enterprise, all in absolute disarray. I doubt that even the most intransigent disciple of anarchy ever wished for or intended the litter that prevails in the area of local land-use regulation. . . .
> . . . The ugly running sore of zoning is the total failure of this

178

system of law to develop a code of administrative ethics. Stripped of all planning jargon, zoning administration is exposed as a process under which multitudes of isolated social and political units engage in highly emotional altercations over the use of land, most of which are settled by crude tribal adaptations of medieval trial by fire, and a few of which are concluded by confused *ad hoc* injunctions of bewildered courts. . . .

. . . The indictment of zoning to which all critics subscribe is that its administration is arbitrary and capricious. Procedural due process is continually flaunted in our medieval hearings, our casual record keeping and our occult decision-making. . . . (Babcock 1966: 135, 154)

The greed, exploitiveness, and quick profiteering of developers and speculators on the rural and suburban scene doubtless account for most of the innings of this game. Developers and the people who sell to them *are* often enough the really bad guys, distorting local priorities and plans and corrupting a process that should give both of them only their fair share. Local officials may be greedy for the tax income and shortsighted in evaluating development's impact. Comprehensive planning and zoning control are essential bridles, and where citizens have not come out in force to insist on expressing a public interest in development details there is often enough suburban shoddiness and profligate uses of open space, for example. But at the same time developers are also the only people organized to build the housing a growing society has to have, and constraints in the public interest have to provide them incentives as well.

From the point of view of settled suburban residents, the developer has come to symbolize not only the harms he can do but the good he does as well: As Ream sees it, *any* change, any growth is resisted by settled suburbanites. Developers and, often enough, their requests for variances and zoning amendments, light up for old-timers the early warning system of social shifts to come.

The significant thing about the zoning game is that, as a game, it has, by definition, rules, even rules for subverting publicly legitimated rules. I view the outrages of disorganization, lack of regularized procedures, and exclusionary practices as an authentic and indigenous social process furiously signalling for recognition, a process symptomatic of other issues in modern society. If ever zoning or taxing powers are to be removed to a regional or state level, it will have been necessary to know first why they have been so insistently local. As a start, I propose that if local control over

179

zoning is instead viewed as local control over social place, disorganization will be seen to have, as an adaptive mechanism, rhyme, reason, and structure.

(By social place I do not mean "territory," and by "control" I do not intend an instinctive defense of turf. Among other things, the doctrine of innateness leaves out of account human language, persuasion, invention, and choice.)

I shift the customary focus on zoning from local control over resources per se to control over defining and redefining the scale by which resources are evaluated. Denis Brogan, a British observer, comments on "perpetual" social redefinition in American society:

> The American value system has formed "a society which, despite all efforts of school, advertising, clubs and the rest, makes the creation of effective social barriers difficult and their maintenance a perpetually repeated task. American social fences have to be continually repaired; in England they are like wild hedges, they grow if left alone." (Lipset 1967 [1963]: 128-29)

The zoning game is played out by repairing the social fences and taming the hedges newcomers break through. Time of arrival and settlement is a general principle organizing as much in Scarsdale as in Irondale. Evaluations of social place are not given once and for all, as those supposedly objective observer-measures of social status may deceive us into thinking, but are matters of changeable opinion. Zoning questions provide a public forum for arriving at them where opinions matter most—the locality of residence and all the arenas of social life it implies.[3]

[3] A cross-cultural note: The caste systems of South Asia, particularly outside of the cities, continue as a major social institution because there is so much local preoccupation with their maintenance. Caste systems are tied to territory, and they are myriad, differing even from village to village. The location of any one caste in the total system of social order, itself based on religious ideas, affects every other. Disputes over breaches are rife, and they are settled publicly by the territorial council, the *panchayat*. Villagers come before it to press their claim to be relieved of an unjustly low rank because, as they see it, an unjustly high status may have been allowed to others. Contrary to common Western perceptions, castes are not rigidly closed groups, and individuals and families can and do change their relative positions. The disputes coming before a *panchayat* reflect the innumerable fine points of the rules governing caste relations (the second- and third-hand use of objects, the parts of the village that may be traversed, or occupational relationships) (Marriott and Inden 1974).

180

Status renegotiation means finding out what new arrivals will do to the social position and to access to the many kinds of resources one has been accustomed to as a member of various block, social, and political groups. A larger population in an area previously settled sparsely, for example, may introduce social differentiation and social ranking, as both resources and social positions become scarcer and have to be allocated. I view the zoning mechanism, and especially its warts, as an institution through which this renegotiating process is carried out. The social mechanism for participating in this process is the neighborhood, block, or homeowners' association, as a membership group within the local municipal corporation. When it comes to changes, in hearings before zoning or appeals boards, these groups engage in a "cultural performance," a ritual of sorts, having a central role in the way Americans try to retain control over the scale by which local resources and their relationship to them are to be evaluated—resources of wealth, prestige, and opportunity.

In the four New Jersey counties forming the outer ring of the New York metropolitan areas, single-family zoning applies to 76 percent of the area (400,000 acres) and non-residential zoning covers 23 percent (124,000 acres) (New Jersey County and Municipal Government Study Commission 1974: 106). A mere one-half of 1 percent of the vacant and developable land, out of a total of about one million acres, is zoned for multi-family development—and yet between 1965 and 1972, multi-family building permits accounted for 40 percent of all residential building permits (107). In just one county, for example, 17,200 apartment units were authorized between 1965 and 1972, but only 307 acres were zoned for multi-family development (units with 5 or more apartments). Here, full-blown, is the process of status renegotiation in action, in communities where land use is earmarked "single family" but growth comes in at higher densities once all manner of local control has been exercised over it. The study whose data I am citing finds this to be a reprehensible "informal" land-use regulatory system, one used to subvert the "formal" system of "planning and zoning." A case where everyone but the experts is so far out of step bears looking into.

In New Jersey there are three mechanisms for changing land-use regulations: the use variance, the special exception variance, and the zoning amendment. The two types of variance pertain to individual parcels and they are decided in quasi-judicial proceedings by an appeals board; zoning amendments, by definition applying across the board, are decided legislatively by the local governing body. Either the prospective seller of the land or the developer initiates the petition for change with the local planning board. A public hearing date is set and property owners within a radius of 200 feet from the property are notified by mail that they have standing to appear and voice their opinions.

The New Jersey Supreme Court allows the use variance, one that most state laws explicitly forbid and that, if granted by a locality, courts often will refuse to uphold. Variances from zoning laws are more usually allowed for minor variations necessitated by the peculiarities of the piece of property (topography, soil conditions, location, and so on). The special exception variance (sometimes called a conditional use) is common practice. It allows for greater scrutiny of land uses problematic in some way for the community's legislated objectives, as, for example, the conversion of a single-family house into a nursery school, a use that may be allowed by right, but only after a hearing. One important feature of the variance mechanism is that in granting it special requirements may often be imposed—extra care in landscaping, a larger number of parking spaces, secondary access roads, and other such details intended to mute the local effects of development.

The study finds, however, that legislatively adopted zoning amendments are least used. They occur only after the fact: once a single-family district is well-populated with variances, only then are amendments passed that establish apartment zones. The effect is to reduce the amount of land within the locality for those uses (114).

The apartments going up are divided between 80 percent having one bedroom and 20 percent having two. Neither type of unit encourages households having many children. These apartments can be regarded—and indeed are by local leaders—as fiscal assets (perhaps even generating a "surplus" in revenues that "compensates" for single-family units with many school children who "exceed" their own property tax contribution). These are, as well, the zoning results that the New Jersey Supreme Court has declared unconstitutional, in that their size effectively keeps out middle- and low-income families having children, among whom some are also likely to be black or brown.

I have discussed other findings of this same study in Chapter Two, presenting its data on negative characterizations of apartment residents. Taken together, those characterizations of apartments and their residents and the case-by-case variance procedure are evidence of a social form used by those already settled to stand aside and make room—on terms they can control. Even though the bedroom configurations effectively guarantee against blacks and assure greater tax revenues, still this zealous control prevails.

The so-called informality of this process is all-important: the disturbance of growth is best cushioned (to use van Gennep's terms) if broken down into locally manageable fits and starts of development, each providing the ritual opportunity of venting grievances at neighborhood-level hearings. Zoning amendments, by definition community-wide, afford every local citizen a say, diluting the neighborhood role of gatekeeper. Sociologically, these old-timer groups exercise a superior social position toward newcomers, deciding the particular terms on which they will make their entry into their arenas. These rituals take time, time that drives developers to drink, bribery, or defeat (as their front-money interest costs add up and the conditions imposed eat into their hoped-for return).[4] But it is time that old-timers use to control the rate at which they adjust to all the differences it will make having those new people come in, redefining as they do the arena of one's address. Once allowed the position of gatekeeper, they unlatch it. Recall that Pope had to assure people in $60,000 houses that those in $40,000 houses would be "average human beings" like themselves.

Zoning is, then, one means by which people can retain control, certainly over the actual directions in which their community develops, and equally over the definition of their own category, in a complex, industrializing society. The process allows time for gradually defusing the magic circles of danger.

Babcock concludes: "In my judgment, social influences, far

[4] So regular are these "irregular" practices that developers may also know enough to come to the bargaining table with the compromise in hand that they know is feasible.

more than economic considerations, motivate the public decision-makers in zoning matters. Cost is not as important as status" (1966: 185). What is clear is that "public decision-makers" are responding to their constituents:

> The resident of suburbia is concerned not with *what* but with *whom*. His overriding motivation is less economic than it is social. His wife spends more at the hairdresser in a month than the proposed apartment house will add to her husband's tax bill in a year. What worries both spouses is that the apartment development is a symbol of everything they fled in the city. When they protest that a change in dwelling type will cause a decline in the value of their property, their economic conclusion is based upon a social judgment. (31)

A first rule of the zoning game is that only the players defined to have a decided interest in the matter at hand can be in it, and a second is that its present decisions should not presuppose its determinations in future.

The entire institution of zoning is based on an emphatic localism that is revealed in several ways. In public hearings or in law suits, the issue of standing is paramount, and there has been a "basic unwillingness of courts to accept that nonresidents of a community possess a requisite life, liberty, or property interest" in any other community's zoning laws (Fessler 1973: 186). As in New Jersey, for any given appeal or variance request often only those property owners within a certain number of feet of the lot in question have standing at public hearings. Each issue determines the radius of its influence: the assumption is that its radius is definable.

The "pleas for help" heard by Atlanta aldermen largely concern block and neighborhood changes: citizens show less concern for citywide changes or those in another neighborhood. Aldermen also respond personally, in contrast to the kind of help a "paid" city official can give on an issue so "close to the citizens":

> Many aldermen [in Atlanta] consider that zoning is the one function of the city government which remains close to the citizens. Therefore, they are more directly responsive to the pleas for help on zoning than they would be on other city functions where the citizens have access to paid city officials who can resolve most problems.
>
> Most of the aldermen say that they want to hear from local citizens about zoning matters rather than groups that may enter

184

many zoning actions. . . . Any citizen is entitled to give his views, but the aldermen are more likely to listen to those who can show clearly how their interests are affected by the change (Rupnow and Clarke 1972: 126, 127).

Historically, the judiciary has supported the supremacy of local-level control. Two U.S. Supreme Court decisions recently have upheld the right of referenda on local land-use issues heretofore delegated to local governing bodies, thereby popularizing even greater localized control.[5] Until hearing *Village of Belle Terre* v. *Boraas* in 1974, the Supreme Court had assiduously avoided letting any zoning matter come before it, a record that had prompted Babcock to observe: "I would like to believe that among the justices of our highest court, conservative or liberal, Democrat or Republican, Southerner of Yankee, corporate lawyer or ex-professor, there has been consensus on only one point: if we cherish our equilibrium, never agree to review a zoning case" (Babcock 1966: 110). Between 1949 and 1955, for example, appeals were dismissed or petitions for certiori denied in all twenty-one cases involving zoning and local planning matters (Haar 1959: 169).

A second rule of the zoning game is that its determinations should not last long. The records of zoning matters cannot be used as precedent or example because they are a "disorganized pile . . . found only in the third drawer of the village clerk's desk" (Babcock 1966: 155). "The indictment of zoning to which all critics subscribe is that its administration is arbitrary and capricious" (135). A Pittsburgh study found that out of seventy-six zoning hearings, the City Clerk could find the records for only thirty-two; the only data source for the others was the local newspaper (Davis and Reuter: 18). One Atlanta study reports that in fifty of 154 zoning cases (32 percent), there is even no record of the numbers of people attending the hearings, the usual index of political support.

In New York City, disputes over zoning changes are so structured that resolving them does not result in new sets of rules or power blocs or identifiable factions—nothing prevents subsequent

---

[5] In *James* v. *Valtierra*, the Court upheld a California requirement that the authorization for and location of every public housing project may be decided on by public referendum (402 U.S. 137 [1971]). The Court found in an Ohio case that the decisions of the local governing body can be remade in referenda (*City of Eastlake* v. *Forest City Enterprises*, decided 21 June 1976).

disputes. No new rules result to redefine what is disputable, so that the next request for a change will go through the same process, even if it is similar in kind or extent to one previously denied (Makielski 1966: 109, 153). An advocate of nonzoning cites the fact that just after citywide zoning was adopted in Chicago, of the many rezoning petitions and variances submitted, between 58 and 98 percent were granted, signifying to him that "control of property through zoning is more chaotic than it is orderly" (Siegan 1972: 15-16).

Why does zoning operate with rules that keep it so open and loose a process? The looseness and malfunctioning cause much consternation and many manifestoes for reform among land-use experts. Babcock, as a member of the bar, worries that "zoning is becoming a rule of men not of laws" (1966: 8). But no other than men are displacing jural with pragmatic rules (Nicholas 1968: 302). Why? Why such a fragile "equilibrium" that the judiciary has entered this field only recently, waiting until six years beyond the passage of Civil Rights legislation? The fragility has far from disappeared, as we know from the outcries accompanying redress in educational opportunity for blacks.

First, local control over zoning is a means of creating peer and reference groups under conditions of population growth and industrial specialization (Shils 1968: 126-29). Social arenas are literally redefined out from under, as rural and then suburban social organization yields to the scale associated with urban. Block and homeowner associations are the social form taking on the work of social redefinition. They are increasingly being legitimated in the public law governing citizen participation in land-use matters (Rosenbaum 1974; American Law Institute 1974: 99-103).[6] Their

---

[6] In its "Model Land Development Code," the American Law Institute proposed to recognize neighborhood organizations as having a statutory right to appear and be heard for the record at adjudicatory proceedings. "Participation by associations of individuals in land use decisions is a fact of life. Traditionally, this participation has been highly informal and disorganized. . . . The purpose of this Section is to encourage more or less permanent associations to undertake regular functions of commenting upon applications for development permits and thus to reduce the erratic participation in the existing process" (American Law Institute 1974: 101-2).

The "fact of life" will continue to be the erratic, informal, and disorganized participation of citizens who may be likely to become more interested in or more aggrieved over specific matters that they define as affecting them than over the larger issues they "ought" to be concerned with in the

186

power is undoubted. A study of developers in San Jose, California, found that they shied away from sprawl-reducing and higher-density projects because of "public opposition" by "well-organized homeowner associations."

> The third deterrent to mid-density development is the increasing public opposition to growth manifested in well-organized home-owner associations. Because these groups are concerned about the increased burdens more people place on the city's ability to provide services, and on the environment, they are especially adamant against mid-density projects. Moreover, mid-density projects frequently give citizens an opportunity for *public* opposition, because they often require major zoning changes or other planning commission action. Again, developers, preferring to avoid the delays and adverse publicity, either opt for a less controversial kind of project, the single-family detached house, or work in a different area. (Rolph 1973: 25)

A civic leader told me:

One thing that I think we *discovered* is that if they didn't have [neighborhood social life] they sure got together in a hurry when they heard that the [public] housing project was being considered for their area. You might say that only lately is there solidarity in a neighborhood like that. They have common interest in maintaining a neighborhood. There might have been some cleavages between different groups, but the threat of a housing authority will certainly drive them together. The same thing if a highway was going to pierce the neighborhood or something. The fantasy is that if you own a house you jump to the defense of your neighborhood, because first of all you want to keep a good place to live and secondly you want to protect the value. (Dial: 21)

---

development of their community. The land-use forum, I believe, should be as open as possible, allowing standing to all. A first draft of this ALI proposal would have recognized only organizations representing 50 percent of the adults within its boundaries, but subsequent discussion suggested it be lowered, ranging from 10 to 35 percent.

The proposal itself was framed in order to assure that a "qualified neighborhood organization can participate as a party and can commence a judicial proceeding free of a challenge that it is an intermeddler and not a proper party in interest" (1974: 102). The burden might better rest on those judicial criteria that rule in the first place that unorganized or otherwise "unqualified" citizens are but "intermeddling."

In Houston, about 200 of some 7,000 subdivisions have active "civic associations," that are often set up in the deed restrictions in order to collect and spend membership fees not only for maintenance and improvements but also for enforcement of the restrictions (Siegan 1972: 35). This particular form of civic association might be considered an indigenous ideal of the social corporation whose very purpose is to manage status renegotiation. As members, people work out concrete redefinitions of their social placement and control social risk personally, in that the convenants have the form of a private contract binding each to each. One citizens' group in St. Paul-Minneapolis recommends a similar form for conserving older neighborhoods (Citizens League Report 1973).

[In a new subdivision] you've got deed restrictions and covenants which will protect those kinds of uses. . . . Plus, you've got civic clubs which are very, very strong and very, very vocal in this area, because everybody knows there is this potential for change to take place over which they have no control or have limited control. And what limited control they do have, they stress through the civic club and renew their deed restrictions and stay on top of them and do not allow—if it's a single-family detached area, do not allow duplexes to be built in it. And fight City Hall and file injunctions against anybody who tries to do it. But it is strictly a matter of protecting your own. There is no City Hall that is going to protect you in terms of an urban environment. (Goss Group: 24, 25)

Secondly, this local control over residential self-definition takes much of its meaning from the control over self-definition available elsewhere in industrial society. Not only are people limited to being the "boss" of their own house, as the Goss Group put it, but they want to have a say in decisions about those most important resources, their own social reputation and self-respect. One objection to newcomers commonly voiced is not only that they will be too poor, but too rich as well. People want to define themselves by a scale of social value that assures that they will come out well.

To assess whether localism can be decreased means asking whether it is possible to change the emphasis on residence as so major a source of people's social self-esteem and social reputation. Their occupation is their other major source of social "sustenance and identity," and the less it provides them with a socially esteemed and rewarded position, the more their residential placement will matter.[7] As Pope and Gale have said, it is the "lower down" one goes in the socioeconomic hierarchy that there is resistance to whatever is believed to be threatening people's neighborhood and "good address." These may be people in dead-end jobs, marking their life cycle with consumption goods instead of promotions. Their address is the most significant accomplishment their work allows.

Last, in being frequently held, the judicial or quasi-judicial zoning forum makes more accessible the adjudication and mediation of felt wrongs. Other social mechanisms for settling disputes and hearing grievances are scarce elsewhere in American society:

> One of the frequently criticized aspects of life in America is the failure of the society's institutions to cope adequately with the people's grievances against each other. Ordinary courts cost money and time, are slow and mystifying, and tilted against the poor, the uninitiated and the occasional user . . . [in one study] the references to non-government institutionalized adjudication or mediation in the United States are very sparse except within organizations, within organized commercial activities and within some minority groups. (Felstiner 1974: 85)

For people who are not their own bosses elsewhere, what local control over the zoning process provides—to better-off suburbanites as well—is social efficacy in evening things up with other unpredictable and often unfair distribution of rewards: at least one's grievance will be heard and arbitrated.[8] Threats darken people's lives no matter their occupation and level of wealth. Higher densi-

---

[7] ". . . the search for acceptance and recognition, for esteem and prestige are in fact a quest for sustenance and identity, conducted in forms and patterns emphasized and standardized in the cultural milieu in which the status structure operates. The emphasis on cultural patterns is crucial, for one must play the status game by the existing rules or almost surely fail. The rules prescribe how one may legitimately defend his rating, search for more recognition, or react against his ranking; the social values and institutions determine how much of what kinds of recognition for what kinds of status will be accorded to how many people" (Tumin 1967: 102).

[8] In Appendix 4, excerpts appear from a case study of a zoning dispute in an exurban county about fifty miles from Manhattan, reporting the views of adjacent homeowners, civic association leaders, the planning board chairman, and the developer. Studies of "neighborhood organization" have concentrated on the poor and not the effective middle class of the suburbs; for example, see O'Brien 1976.

189

ties coming in down the street may arbitrarily redefine the family's social position, but in other arenas, too—job promotions, raises, chances at union membership, admission to college—its social rewards and denials can be felt as arbitrary, impersonal, and unfair. Bush understands some of the opposition to his plans for a 1,000-acre project that will include lower-income housing in just those terms:

> It is a highly mobile society, especially in the area we're dealing in, where General Electric Missile Lab was out there. They got shook up a couple of years ago. A missile lab cut 4,000 engineers out of there—4,000 guys who book themselves as professionals, as having security, were knocked out of jobs, that shook that whole community. They still haven't gotten over it. Introduced an uncertainty in their lives that never existed before. These are guys making $25-30,000 a year. It's not the kind of thing, it's not a blue-collar guy who is used to working by the hour. These are not people that are used to collecting unemployment. It's the world that we live in. It's changing at such a rapid rate that people are latching on to their . . . their local situation, something that they can get a handle on. They're fighting like hell trying to preserve some sanity. I'm not sure that I disagree with that and I try to understand that. (Bush: 7)

The fate of the less-well-off as future suburbanites is in the hands of middle-class taxpayers whose altruism, its limitations as well as its genuineness, has to be examined, not critically but as part of the same larger system. Whenever jobs, wages, and opportunity falter, the majority middle class begins to ask after its own general welfare. Its cyclic disappointments can turn into the poor's continued deprivations.

Indeed, as Bush says, the recent recession reveals just how tentative a place many can claim in the industrial system. Standing in line for unemployment checks, the college educated may come to understand better those situated permanently on one rung. But their ability to absorb more taxes and to pay higher prices is impaired, more than they might like it to be. Lowering their expectations means waking up at the best parts of the American dream: college tuitions they cannot afford, a house and garden no longer within their children's reach, and their old age spent in bitter dependency.

All together, the zoning game is a condensation of American life as a serious and unpredictable engagement where winning or losing may be less important than the overarching reassurance of fair play—the fair play often missing from life itself. Life's struggles are duplicated in a well-bounded setting, where an umpire or referee will listen and arbitrate (he will be right as often as he is wrong). Americans consistently endow the occupation of Supreme Court Justice with the highest prestige of any: in zoning disputes, Americans can come before their local "court," engaging fate in reasoned combat.[9] The central symbol is equity.

That is why the rules and the actors change repetitively, and why development arrives case by case. Living out each situation emotionally and exhaustingly in pursuit of equity, people ask that the exigencies of their lives be recognized. Each case is best argued on its own singular merits: the neighbors around the property are always different, the details of the use are different, the architectural and site planning features are unique. An Atlanta study of one year's zoning cases shows the chances of approval are fifty-fifty—an equal incentive for whichever side one's group is on. The rules, then, are best left imprecise, so that decisions can be made pragmatically; because modern life has so many exigencies, the rules should not be fixed and settled for all time.

A study of public opinion about land-use issues in Ohio found that those who fit the general label "Environmentalists" differed from those termed "Localists" in that the former emphasize the negative physical consequences of development and the latter emphasize the accountability of decision-makers. " 'Localists' characterize state control over land use as being in the hands of faceless, incompetent, and arrogant state bureaucrats . . . faceless bureaucrats responsible to no one" (Coke and Brown 1976: 107, 112).

> The Localists' identifications, rather than being abstract and conceptual, are specific and geographical: the local community— our friends and neighbors, those people who have to live with the land use decisions—ought to be the place where policy is made. The guiding principle is accountability rather than externalities, and the local community is favored since its decision-makers can

[9] "The 'middle-class' nature of zoning put an emphasis on certain political and behavior patterns: persuasion, bargaining, rationality, and organized, staffed activity . . ." (Makielski 1966: 158).

be more readily held accountable than can remote state officials.
(112)

In my terms, these "accountable" officials can be relied on to
keep zoning open, if not chaotic and disorganized, so that the
chances for winning one's particular, specific case remain good.
"Faceless bureaucrats," who use the same "arrogant" scale of
social value one place as another, themselves know no "friends'
and neighbors' " faces and reputations.

For Americans, the zoning game has become in these last fifty
years a cultural product of the tensions between the economic and
social opportunities industrialization offers and the social identities
upon which the gradually shrinking access to them depends.
These enticements reached a peak ten or so years ago, and their
withdrawal comes as a surprise. Suburban education, for example,
is no longer the undoubted best preparation for lifetime earning
power it once was believed to be. Yet, just when the promises
of college entrance and the good job are holding good for fewer
of their own, suburbanites are asked to share them.

I have so far not used the phrase "status symbols" for the
reason that, except perhaps for those trappings at the awesome
heights of wealth and political power, I do not think there is any
single set that carries the same social meaning everywhere. As I
have said, society is ordered through the esteem, respect, and
honor of social exchanges—their absence as well as their presence.
These are quite different from symbols of prestige as they are now
part of our cultural self-awareness (house and its furnishings,
car, travel, and other consumption abilities). Even those material
markers take on different meanings, depending on which system
of status they are used in. In being formed out of local agreement
on the values to be placed on the media of social exchange, there
are many American status systems, depending on factors such as
the time of arrival of various groups, the resources each controls,
local ecology and history, and so on.

The center-periphery (or elite-mass) model implies a single
center of resources and one point of control over their allocation.
Confusing social awe with social honor tends to blind us to the
fact of many centers and many peripheries created in their ambit
because valued resources and control over them are various and
dispersed. When access to the Board of Directors of the Chase
Manhattan Bank is valued and when access to the union's loan

192

fund is valued, each generates different "status systems" having different "symbols." People participate in several systems, including a national one, borrowing selectively to suit the arena—family, work, church, or school.

What an inside-out, or cultural, understanding of status systems would provide, then, is an alternative to the geologic model of social stratification. A major question in understanding this industrial society continues to be why it does not fly apart or face imminent revolution. Despite the American ideal of egalitarianism, inequalities, inequities, and invidious distinctions abound. A lack of earthquakes along those many faults of social stratigraphy must also be explained, and locally conceived and practiced systems of status evaluation and accommodation are one means of doing so.

A newspaper story about a town in North Dakota about to face a great increase in population appeared recently. The coal resources of the region were just beginning to be exploited, and a boom was in the making. One longtime resident said, "If I go downtown nowadays and find I've left my purse at home, I can just go right into my bank and they'll give me $40 for my groceries. In two or three years I don't know that that will be possible." Having more people in her town meant that her social reputation will no longer be a marker she can count on using. The local system for recognizing her in terms that she is accustomed to value will change. She cannot now think of any way to renegotiate her place in a larger scale of things, except perhaps to keep newcomers out.

THE RIGHTS OF PASSAGE: INCORPORATING NEWCOMERS

The social process now raising the most serious questions about the kind of social order we have is that of incorporating newcomers. Land-use regulations, backed as they are by legal and financial sanctions, directly affect the meanings newcomers are seen to have by those already settled. To become suburban residents, they have to pass zonal muster in order to establish whether they will raise or lower property values and whether it will strain municipal efficiency to provide them with schooling and other public services. The effect of growth on the "quality of life" for those already settled is debated, too, often as resistance to any change at all. As the safety-catch on growth, zoning regulations come to have powerful significance ˙for settled homeowners, legitimizing, if not

193

sanctifying, their "rights," "religiously defended," not only to a protected investment but, as Peat reports, to its guaranteed appreciation. In adding to the total supply, growth often dilutes prices.

Every society operates with rules and requirements governing the shifts of people out of one category into another. The rules are significantly influenced by the resources each category controls, so that the numbers of people who might qualify matter a great deal in figuring whether there will be enough to go around. Hence the rules are often rationing measures. Taken as a whole, zoning and taxing legislation as a system of rules regulating land use constitute the major publicly legislated mechanism for rationing access to financial, educational, and social resources. The rate of inclusion provides for the amounts of new growth and the rules of exclusion specify what form the new growth may take.

Simultaneously, the very continuation of society requires that it reproduce itself socially, and newcomers in many guises—as immigrants or as youngsters—are essential. But that continuity means social succession as well: those with power have to relinquish it eventually, just as those with resources have to share them eventually. How a society provides for these transitions is the heart of its social order.

In American society, a distinctive set of cultural conceptions about newcomers and old-timers arises out of our settlement history, the decision to restrict foreign immigration, and the history of zoning's emergence as a major rationing and categorizing device. This new-old distinction is based on time of arrival as a natural but not sufficiently explicit principle of social organization against which we have yet to devise effective counterweights when it is overdrawn and creates malignant distinctions among citizens.

The social movements favoring zoning and immigration restriction each culminated in legislation in the 1920s. Zoning was being promulgated by social reformers and real estate interests during the same years that the country was for the first time debating its policy of open immigration. The 1924 Immigration Act fixed quotas and set an annual limit on immigration; by the end of the same decade "only six states had cities with neither zoning ordinances nor a completed comprehensive plan." Then there were more than 37 million people living under zoning enactments in 768 cities, towns, and villages, constituting three-fifths of the urban population (Toll 1969: 204; Knauss 1929: 167). As far as I am able to tell, these were no more than simultaneous cross-currents, once in a while coming together in events and in a few of the leading personages in zoning and economics. They are interesting in parallel, however, because each was taken up with systems of social classification. "The immigrant is in the fiber of zoning" (Toll 1969: 29).

In the San Francisco "Laundry Cases" of the 1880s, local laws controlling the location of Chinese laundries were enforced as part of a virulent anti-Oriental movement. In *Soon Hing* v. *Crowley*, decided in 1885, the United States Supreme Court upheld the San Francisco regulations, despite the argument of the plaintiffs that "the controls were an expression of the hatred and antipathy which San Franciscans were directing against the Chinese, trying to force them to quit the city," amounting to the deprivation of property without due process (29). The New York City ordinance, the first one comprehensively covering the city, was the result of outlawing the garment industry's lofts on lower Fifth Avenue. Immigrants working in the needle trades took to the sidewalks during their lunch hour, mixing there with the carriage trade: ". . . the things which were the essences of the garment industry— the strange tongues, the outlandish appearance and the very smell of its immigrant laborers, its relentless drive to follow the retail trade wherever it went . . . violated the ambience in which luxury retailing thrives" (158). Toll comments on the lightweight grounds on which Fifth Avenue's "violations" were justified by the study report providing the basis of New York's ordinance, adopted July 25, 1916:

> Fifth Avenue really offered no facts which justified exercising the police power for reasons of health, safety, or the generally accepted meaning of the term order. Unlike the lower Manhattan skyscraper area, whatever street congestion existed did not tie the hands of the fire department. No one was bold enough to suggest otherwise. Objections to the congestion had always been posed in terms of shopping amenity and the related harm to the retail trade, essentially a private point of view. Despite its occasional resort to the light and air arguments for the avenue, the actual material on which the report was supposed to rest its recommendations turned out to be so sketchy that it was no more than a makeweight. The balance of the appeal to Fifth Avenue's case was simply a plea to protect the warm memory of a street which never existed, but which, if it had, was also not then the proper object of the police power. . . . It was more important to defend

195

the carriage trade by removing the garment industry than to protect life by being able to evacuate office workers from burning buildings in the financial district. (169-70)

Throughout those same years that zoning was being discussed and refined as the national land-use control mechanism (the first national conference on city planning, in which zoning was the major topic, was held in 1909), a major national commission, appointed by President Theodore Roosevelt, was working out recommendations on the immigration restriction question. The Dillingham Commission reported in forty-one volumes in 1907, and by 1926 its summary volume had been reprinted six times. Congress held annual hearings all during the Progressive Era on the question of immigration restriction (Higham 1955: 187).

During those years, and culminating in the 1924 Immigration Act, every possible attribute of every national origin group imaginable was named and characterized in public debates about the superiority and inferiority of various peoples. The premise of both social movements was that it was legitimate and important as part of the public business to make fine discriminations among the attributes of social groups and social space.

> The Committee on Scientific Problems of Human Migration [of the National Research Council] . . . seems to have been an outgrowth of correspondence initiated in 1922 by Robert De-Courcy Ward, one of the founders of the Immigration Restriction League. Organized just as the agitation to pass restrictive legislation was rising to its climax, the Committee was explicitly charged with the responsibility of determining the relative worth of different ethnic groups as a basis for such legislation. (Stocking 1968: 299)

In this, there was something, as one observer put it, "peculiarly American" at work. As I mentioned earlier, Delafons found Americans, in contrast to the British, to have predilections for the making of land-use distinctions. The United States' immigration policy relied more on tightly prescribed rules than did the policies of Canada and Australia.

> In regulating immigration Britain and the Commonwealth countries have relied less on legislative prescription and more on administrative flexibility. Within certain broad terms laid down by Parliament, government authorities in Canada and Australia have enjoyed wide discretion to alter totals and quotas from day to day. The United States, a less deferential society, has been

196

unwilling to allow officials shielded from the glare of publicity to make policy circumspectly. Congress, working in a turbulent milieu of competing pressures, had had to *spell out rules and exceptions in detail*. (Higham 1975: 30) (Italics supplied)

The zoning scholar Ernst Freund, who emigrated from Germany and became professor of law at the University of Chicago, wrote *The Police Power*, a study of the constitutional basis on which zoning came to rest. From this position of natural comparativist, he also observed differences in the way distinctions are drawn in the United States compared to the way they are in European cities:[10]

The whole zoning problem in this country is affected by two factors which I should like myself to learn a little more about than I know now. They are in a sense peculiarly American. The one is the extraordinary sensitiveness of property to its surroundings. I know something about foreign cities. As a boy, I lived in two German cities, and I have traveled somewhat in Europe. Conditions there are very different. People do not mind a little store around the corner a bit. When you go to Vienna, you find that the palace of one of the great aristocratic families has a big glass works display room on the lower floor. The family has glass works on its Bohemian estates, and thinks nothing of advertising the fact in its residence. We wouldn't have that in this country because it is not conformable to our ideas. One of the millionaires in Frankfurt built his house right across the way from an amusement establishment where there were concerts given twice a day. We wouldn't do that. (1926: 78)

The main point of the Dillingham Report—aside from its clear-cut bias toward greater restrictions on immigration—was that the "old" immigrants were superior to the "new." Maldwyn Jones, an historian of American immigration, argues against this claim, one many other historians had joined in, in a detailed comparison of the motivations for immigration in all periods, and, not least, of the conditions within the immigrants' countries of origin. The "old" and "new" distinction became so portentous, Jones finds, because

[10] Zoning was a literal import from Germany. People who were influential in the American planning and zoning movement went to Germany to see firsthand how it worked. The 1913 Report of the Heights of Building Commission for New York City includes "The German Zone Building Regulations," a definitive statement by Frank Backus Williams (1913: 94-119). At the Third National Conference on City Planning, in 1911, Frederick C. Howe reported on "The Municipal Real Estate Policies of German Cities" (1911: 14-41).

of the nativism of those times—the anti-foreign, anti-Catholic, and anti-Semitic movement running from about 1888 through the 1920s:

> As the "new" immigrants grew more numerous and conspicu-
> ous . . . the initial repugnance excited by their appearance and
> habits gave way to a dread of their subversive tendencies. Al-
> ready alive to the existence of a foreign menace nativists came to
> see a special danger in an influx of Slavs, Italians, and Jews who
> were associated in the prevailing ethnic stereotypes with disorder,
> violent crime, and avarice, respectively. . . . The notion that the
> "new" immigrants constituted a collective entity, different from
> and inferior to the old, arose not from popular antipathies but
> from the theorizing of a handful of race-conscious New England
> intellectuals. . . . As early as 1888 the social scientist Richmond
> Mayo-Smith was querying the economic value of immigration.
> . . . Three years later came an influential study by Francis A.
> Walker, President of the Massachusetts Institute of Technology
> [and Director of the U.S. Bureau of the Census], which attributed
> the declining birth rate of the native population to immigrant com-
> petition. . . . Early in 1894 the anxieties of the New England
> intelligentsia for the future of their "race" and class resulted in
> the formation of the Immigration Restriction League. . . . [In]
> about 1906 the Boston intellectuals . . . began to point to genetic
> principles as a scientific basis for their claim that immigration
> restriction was essential to preserve American racial purity.
> (Jones 1960: 257-59, 267)

Invidious distinctions were the order of those days, and other social scientists, Richard T. Ely, John R. Commons, and Edward A. Ross, joined Mayo-Smith and Walker as "active partners in the [Immigration Restriction] League during the 1900s and 1910s contributing in turn to the ideology of restriction and to the rec-ommendations of the Dillingham Commission that the 'illiteracy' test be used" (Solomon 1956: 131, 198). Commons published *Races and Immigrants in America* in 1907, and testified on behalf of the League's various proposals for federal legislation. Although his book was a study with an eye to the interests of organized labor, "he did not confine his arguments for restriction to economics," arguing that "even with the help of the American environment immigrants could hardly overcome the handicaps of race and her-edity" (Solomon 1956: 132; Jones 1960: 267).

Not all the New Yorkers active in the passage of the 1916 Zon-ing Law were interested only in the destiny of retailing. As ardent progressives and urban reformers, many were disturbed about the overcrowded and unhealthy tenement life to which so many immigrants were subject. Indeed, those very conditions made them ambivalent toward unlimited immigration:

> Nor was Progressivism entirely free of the taint of nativism, and its proponents, particularly in the social settlements, were often guilty of a condescension toward immigrants that could hardly fail to produce an unfavorable reaction. (Jones 1960: 230)

One of the first people to request a copy of the United States Supreme Court's Euclid decision in 1926 was a lawyer from Indianapolis, writing on behalf of his client, the "White People's Protective League" (Toll 1969: 242). This American Protective League, a nativist group provided with semi-official status as an auxiliary to the Justice Department to maintain American "security" from aliens in World War I, had members in 1,200 localities throughout the country in 1917 (Higham 1955: 211; Jensen 1968).[11]

The "social movement" of planning and zoning, as it was termed at Harvard in 1935, always had two purposes: to limit and channel new population growth and to encourage economic expansion (Bassett, Williams, Bettman, and Whitten 1935).[12] The use of

[11] Organized nativism, more virulent than before the Big Red Scare of 1919, led to the peak growth of the Ku Klux Klan to 2.5 million members by 1923 (Jones 1960: 275). With such widespread nativism a social fact, it is not surprising that those active in the planning and zoning movement would have some sort of attitude toward it. Frederick C. Howe, the most earnest of these, was a liberal and a Commissioner of Immigration who strongly favored the "Americanization" of immigrants, a position he held at the same time he promoted the future American city as one "destined to be the most generous, the most humane, the most democratic and possibly the most beautiful city in the world" (Wiebe 1967: 299; Higham 1955: 253; Toll 1969: 128). Newton D. Baker, Secretary of War under Woodrow Wilson and who later argued the case of Ambler in the U.S. Supreme Court, in *Euclid* v. *Ambler* in 1926, spoke up against the nativist tide in an address to the Annual Convention of Police Chiefs in 1917, "Problems of the Melting Pot":

> You and I are both too wise and we have had too much experience in this country to imagine that a broken accent means a broken mind, or that a non-American name, or the inability to speak readily our language means any lack of loyalty in the man or in his make-up (Baker 1918: 169).

[12] There is, of course, a long American history of restrictive covenants in real property that discriminate by race, religion, and national origin (Clark and Perlman 1948: 22-23). Predating present-day zoning laws, these

zoning as a legislative mechanism analogous to Congressional restriction of foreign immigration has not occurred until now, fifty years after both were instituted.

The prevailing axiom actively in use through the first half of this century was that there was a significant difference between the "old" and the "new" immigration. Even in 1952, Oscar Handlin testified to a Presidential Commission, after additional immigration restrictions had been imposed by the McCarran-Walter Act, solely to refute the presumedly factual basis of that distinction.

> The framers of the legislation of 1921-24, assumed that mankind was divided into biologically distinct races capable of mingling with one another only within very narrow limits. It was argued that the traditional American policy of free immigration had been appropriate in an era in which the bulk of immigration originated in the Nordic countries of Northern and Western Europe, because Englishmen and Germans were close kin of the original Anglo-Saxons and therefore easily Americanized. But the new immigration from Southern and Eastern Europe brought to our shores people who were racially different, and inferior, and therefore became Americanized only with difficulty.
>
> Such arguments were supported by reference to the difficulties new immigrants encountered in the course of their adjustment. People like the Italians, the Greeks, and the Poles, it was claimed, were more inclined than the old immigrants or than the native stock, to be illiterate, paupers, criminals, diseased, and the source of corruption in politics. Among the new immigrants, it was said, were a disproportionate number of anarchists and other disaffected individuals likely to be subversive of the American Government. It was on the basis of such arguments that the quota system favored the countries of Northern and Western Europe over those of Eastern and Southern Europe. (Handlin 1952: 327-28)

Today, the pervasive belief among most suburban communities, buttressed by cost-revenue analyses, is that new arrivals cost more in public services than do old-timers. These are the Dillingham Commission reports of today. An entire industry in econometric research has grown up around this local issue of "costing" newcomers, often with the result of rejecting any development that does not show a "profit" (Ellman 1976). Newcomers are made to appear to old-timers more expensive than they are.

How our cultural conceptions come about is, however, the ques-

---

restrictions were often the very basis on which zoning district lines were drawn in legislatively adopted official maps (Bassett 1936: 184).

tion here. Much remains to be explained about the universal fact of cultural criteria governing the incorporation and exclusion of people in the social categories of every social system. My view is that concentrating on the rules or principles governing this process will lead to better understandings of racial, ethnic, and wealth distinctions and discriminations—not, as much research today emphasizes, objective characteristics of the groups or "sub-cultures" themselves (their family structures, religious beliefs, customs, and income).

A proposition more fruitful for research and analysis is that the rules themselves—for incorporating and excluding—generate groups' characteristics. Groups do, of course, differ from one another as they define their common characteristics (beliefs, kinship systems, customs, and occupation). But in plural nations those characteristics as objective properties are of less importance to the formation of groups. Two things count above all: one group wants access to the resources another controls, and to get it, it complies with whatever the rules specify.

The history of American immigration and settlement alongside of the repetition of similar processes in the contemporary rationing of suburban access are evidence for this theoretical position.[13] At both ocean ports and suburban borders, new arrivals preoccupy their predecessors. The successive arrivals of nationality groups, each facing the necessity of settlement and livelihood and each claiming its own place and work under a set of rules controlled by those already there, are the features of our history I find significant, and not, as I have said, the attributes of nationality groups themselves. Peculiarly American cultural conceptions today still generate rules by which newcomers are allowed to locate, in many spheres of life.

Who the predecessors are and by what rules they ration access form the American cultural system for assimilating and generating

[13] Morton Fried raises the possibility that tribes are a "secondary phenomena," produced by "the appearance of relatively highly organized societies amidst others which are organized much more simply," citing evidence in colonial situations where groups having "considerable diversity in culture, language, and in physical type" were called tribes and "created by government action" (1967: 170-71). A recent critique of sociological approaches to American ethnicity also emphasizes its emergence from such structural features as occupation and residence, technology and transportation, and suggests that its salience depends on specific situations (Yancey, Ericksen, and Juliani 1976).

"ethnic groups," that is, groups of many kinds. The actual groups of American society are products of the strategies people use in dealing with, resisting, obeying, and changing the rules, for what the pot has ever melted down are ironclad rules governing access to a valued way of life. "Unmeltable ethnics" result from those "unbreakable rules" controlling access to jobs, skills, education, and housing. Whichever distinctive ethnic features come to matter do so because they matter to the rules by which a group is incorporated—or excluded.

Higham, an historian of immigration, emphasizes the "order of arrival" as a "crucial determinant of the subordinate status of ethnic groups."

> Since we know very little about the stratification of our society in any period, particularly in its ethnic aspects, I can offer only a few suggestions for inquiry. Probably one of the crucial determinants of ethnic status has simply been the order of arrival. In the founding of communities, in the settlement of new areas, and in the development of new industries, the first-comers secured a preferential position. Groups arriving later have usually had to enter on terms acceptable to their predecessors, who owned the land, offered the jobs, provided the credit, and controlled the sources of power and prestige. In these circumstances the new group had to accept or to struggle for a long time against a subordinate status. . . . (Higham 1975: 11)

More features than just their hierarchical position are a result of the rules is one point I am making—features emphasizing their heritage of language and beliefs. For example, in the West, the Irish "met far less resistance than they did in New England, where the social system had congealed long before their arrival." Attributes were not "universal stigma," but depended, instead, on the group's having a unique feature that became a social asset, as where Catholics established the first academies and colleges, attended as well by Protestants in Terre Haute and Cincinnati during the mid-nineteenth century.[14]

In San Francisco Jews acquired an especially favorable status from their large share in molding the basic institutions of the city.

[14] Higham introduces these data as evidence for a change of emphasis in his own view of nativism. He had previously (1955) defined it largely as a consequence of ideological fervor arising from national and international politics. In this reevaluation, he has moved to an analysis grounded in local and regional social organization where ethnic differences enter into competition for resources, social as well as material.

202

On the other hand, they have endured a particularly bad situation in Minneapolis where they had arrived late in the city's development. The same relationship applied to the Japanese in two adjacent California towns in the early twentieth century. In one the Japanese settled first and were accepted in the civic life of the American society that grew up around them; in the other they came later and met bitter persecution as their numbers grew. (Higham: 113)

The settlement history of the United States demonstrates, then, that acceptance of and antipathy toward any one nationality group was not uniform: region by region, a particular national origin translated variously as a mark of social status or stigma. In light of widespread beliefs that ethnic groups are by definition homogeneous, we must ask why that variable pattern came to be. The answer lies, I maintain, not in "ethnic" newcomers but in whoever was already there. Then as now, however, we know much more about "the uprooted" than we do about "the settled."

> Whatever particular phrase might serve the purpose of a particular author or speaker, [in the last part of the nineteenth century] all expressed the conviction that some hereditary element had given form to American culture. The conclusion was inescapable: to be Americanized, the immigrants must conform to the American way of life completely defined in advance of their landing. (Handlin 1951: 272)

For example, only upon their arrival in the United States did Italians think of themselves as members of a "nation state": their own group membership was at the more discrete level of the province (Jones 1960: 229). Their hosts' rules literally turned them into members of the larger nationality group, and if they wanted access to American resources, they used this distinguishing feature in the very way they were, in effect, being told to use it.

Artifacts of omnipresent scarcity and of the rationing device of exclusion, ethnic blocs and minorities are the political and economic creations of the rules controlling resource allocation. These are political groups equally as much as they are ethnic. In just the same way are the distinctive cultures of isolated groups maintained intact when they do not seek access to the resources controlled by others. Once they do, and once they begin to obey those rules and requirements, they become "assimilated" and "acculturated." The rules are familiar enough: residence requirements, literacy tests, educational achievement, seniority, initiation fees, language. Such rules apply to all sorts of situations: citizenship, job, and residence.

When the rules and requirements change, then, so do the groups that form as a result of them. When formal and inferrable rules for inclusion specify skin color, religion, national origin, we say that, according to the American constitution, they discriminate invidiously, creating "suspect classifications."

Commonly the analysis of minority-majority group relations emphasizes the "threatening" qualities of the minority and ignores the "fright" of the majority. One study of newly-arrived Puerto Ricans puts it that when these newcomers are in "strong, stable, immigrant communities" they will have the "confidence" to move into the American mainstream, but I would say that it is less any group's "confidence" that matters and more how charged their differences are for the in-group (Fitzpatrick 1971: 67). What are the social frights of the excluding group: loss of jobs? women? power? Robin Williams, an expert in these matters, finds it an "indispensable" insight for public policy to recognize that "discrimination often occurs—'not with the fist but with the elbow'— it is not so much directed against a victim as undertaken for someone's advantage or security" (1976: 661).

Newcomers are excluded or disparaged often on the same grounds as those used in discriminating against racial, religious, or nationality groups. That is, it may be the fact that the newcomer can be defined as a member of such a group, one which itself evokes prejudice, or: there is a separate cultural category of "newcomer" in American society, one encircled by its own set of axioms and propositions. Last hired, first fired; newcomers do not pay their way; newcomers start at the bottom; old money is superior to new; and so on. For even *within* the same national origin and racial group, time of arrival and settlement determines access to resources and leads to conflict (Kornblum 1974: 233-34).

The trouble is not that time of arrival is a potent principle of American social organization, but that it is not morally neutral: the "old" immigrants to the suburbs are defined as superior to and more valuable than the "new," entitled not to share the better education and public amenities available there.

Turning around the notion of ethnic differences themselves as the major determinant of social exclusion and treating instead the cultural category "newcomer," partakes of a recent ferment in anthropology reevaluating the approach to ethnic group differ-

204

ences. One major review of previous explanations of ethnic group boundaries comments that anthropologists working in nonliterate societies tend to "exaggerate the sharpness and impermeability of boundaries that have [actually] been transgressed and rearranged many times in the past, and the coherence and solidarity of recently formed ethnic groups" (LeVine and Campbell 1972: 102). Often enough, the pragmatic problem facing anthropologists in the field was to delineate, or to accept as defined, a unit to which a central, and usually colonial, government could minister. Using their own categories, boundaries were applied, not found from the inside out (Lehman 1967; see also LeVine and Campbell: 101-3).

I think it is not much different today in the United States. Social categories are being delineated for the many kinds of economic and social activities and entitlements of government and industry, using those socioeconomic data most ready to hand. Rather than perceiving group formation as the subject, the tendency is to keep analysis at the level of group characteristics. Not sub-cultures in plural societies therefore, but the social mosaic itself should be the subject, asking about the principles and forces holding it together. To learn how and why any one characteristic is stressed—ethnicity, race, or time of arrival—the rules should be examined to discover why they are as they are. To take an obvious example: In the United States, language is the single certain route to participation in economic life. Speaking a foreign language stands for ethnicity, a feature emphasized because of qualifying rules for jobs and, until recently, voting rights.

America's settlement history by so great a variety of groups also resonates in its notorious reputation for "joining." Thus do Americans continually create groups of equals from which others can be excluded. The belonging and excluding are one. These many memberships are possible because of those that are impossible, one way of reconciling the contradiction between our egalitarian ideology and the actual differences among people's capabilities and the distribution of power and wealth.

The cultural category of newcomer comes into play anticipatorily, in contrast to the social category that takes over after the fact of arrival. Earlier I suggested that the persistence of ethnic neighborhoods was insurance against the opprobrium of marginality, in that a group creates and fills its own category, socially and spatially. It is also insurance against being transformed from old-timer to newcomer status: the social security of the superior role of old-timer is as important as equity in property and a comfortable social network. People stay put for the social advantages of seniority and the greater control over the rules of inclusion it entails. Not only that, but these groups have already been newcomers once, and for those not venturing that may have been quite enough. But many do move yonder, and once they are the new family on the block, Americans, having had so much practice, are adept at hospitality.

The power of the principle of time of arrival is compounded in today's metropolitan areas: Newcomers to the suburbs who are lower income and who will live in other than a single-family-detached house contradict the cultural rule that there is a natural and correct order of life that suburban arrival preeminently symbolizes. Higher density in the suburbs confuses their public meaning. Reproducing the city in the suburbs is acceptable if it is an entire "new town," the "new" being a more highly valued cultural category in investment circles. Cluster development brings people of city ways who are rewarded *too soon* for their income and accomplishments by the suburban idyll. Out of order and out of place, they are dangerous to those already there.

The conservation of resources within the group having them is no new or inexplicable feature of social systems. Not yet asked is: To what resources are suburbanites rationing access? I suggested earlier that we need to know more about what they define as assets and liabilities in terms of their lifelong wealth strategies. Their houses certainly are assets and their current level of expenditure in taxes for public services are liabilities. Political power and social position are others. In addition, I speculate, a major resource is also very likely their children.

Resistance to integrated educational experiences perhaps expresses adults' fears of interracial and interclass liaisons among their children. The resistance to busing and to lower-income neighbors may signify less a concern with these actual relationships and more a worry about their own future good relationships with their children: parents want their children's loyalty and support into their old age, and if they and their children disagree about who their friends are and who they marry, familial amity can disappear. Positioning their children to make a match they approve of is as much a goal as it ever was. The sexual readiness of adolescents (which gets earlier all the time) provokes adults' passionate resistance to housing and educational integration by both race and class. In the South, for example, black and white children take separate paths only after elementary school when sex becomes more interesting. In integrated situations the self-segregation of blacks and whites expresses this same principle of sexual avoidance and, equally important, success in making sexual contact. Amity between generations is difficult enough over issues of premarital sex, drinking, drugs, and the family car. Parents avoid any added burden in order to conserve the emotional and economic assets of an intact family. Hence, I suggest, their rules and requirements for suburban access concentrate on assuring newcomers "like themselves," and, encouraged by realtors and social scientists, they use the insurance of differences of even $1,000 and $2,000 in house price as "rules" of thumb.

Another kind of resource is homeownership, for its other implications. There is evidence that once one crosses the threshold of admission to homeownership (a rationing rule), access to other resources becomes more possible. One study shows that the widespread exclusion of blacks from homeownership elaborates into a lower wealth position at all income levels (Kain and Quigley 1972). Once that threshold is attained, it is the cultural rule that social standing and access to better schools and to credit will follow. Mortgage lenders are the strict keepers of the rule for those in American society who are the latest newcomers to a legitimated social personhood, native American blacks, rationing, thereby, not merely their access to housing but to the accumulation of other resources as well.

A widespread, public preoccupation with social categorization thereby is continued, a consequence of American ideology, industrialization, and immigration. The egalitarian ideal de-emphasized ascriptive attributes, but the disparity between rates of industrial expansion and rates of population growth required social rationing. The distinction between the "old" and the "new" immigration at the turn of the century was the pivot of this qualifying process, a distinction reproduced today in rationing local resources, equally arising out of the context of our industrial structure and its capacity to provide enough for everyone.

CONCLUSION

This approach to metropolitan development issues as cultural and social processes reciprocal to growth should be taken as but the sketch of a model for studying the several regions of the United States. They are state and local variations on a federal theme. I have limited myself to cultural data and their manifestations in general, not speaking at all to the significance of particular historical records. For the actual characteristics of metropolitan areas throughout the country today differ considerably by size, ecology, economic base, and their dates of settlement, at the very least. Their occupational structures and the times of arrival of successive newcomers may provide one useful starting point for getting at their distinctive features in the sociology of tenure and suburbanization, the mechanisms for controlling social place, and present rules and processes in the formation of ethnic, political, and status groups. The unique statutory framework and the accompanying records of hearings and debate of each state are documents of the variety of public thoughts through time about criteria for defining social categories and the rules governing the relationships among them. What *Beyond the Melting Pot* did for New York needs to be done in every region (Glazer and Moynihan 1963).

The social forces shaping the metropolitan social landscape are alternatively analyzed as interest groups, each bent on maximizing its benefits and reducing its costs parochially. They can be labelled conservatives and liberals, localists and environmentalists, speculators and investors. Instead of compressing, this discussion has been taking them apart in order to replace them in the social and cultural contexts from which they get their strength and reinforcement. Without analysis grounded in the facts of both history and society, deterministic explanations, whether utilitarian or sociobiological, will continue to point only to the easy way out. In a country so vast, our own differences may provide "cross-cultural" models we can emulate. For example, the patterns of development and the social processes accompanying them in the Western United States may have much to teach the changing, older metropolitan areas of the middle-Altantic and Northeast as they try out new ways of adapting.

In context, homeownership, tenure, and the negotiation of social place turn out to raise broad questions about the organization and operations of those many interactions called society. Like other modern institutions whose meanings have come to be compartmentalized, land-use matters have never been the special province of any single perspective—law, economics, government—they are made to seem.

Not the properties of cities, but the properties of culture and social structure—the properties of humankind—are the subject. The fields on which they are displayed today are those metropolitan regions where most Americans live.

Chapter Six

Principles of Social Order

"Love calls for time, and we have hardly time for justice."
Albert Camus, *Les Justes*

Some of the principles from which American social order is generated have been the subject of this book. Principles of social order, the central concern of anthropology, can be many things to many people. In literate society, awareness of them can itself lead to their choice and their change by rearranging those features of social and economic systems reinforcing and sustaining them. I have tried to re-frame certain long-standing questions in the American system of land use in such a way that our responses might become more effective and lasting. These are not answers, but some new terms—a vocabulary of meanings—to use in thinking them through.

Uniquely, land-use ideas and practices translate American principles of social order into settlement patterns. They are actively and widely discussed in everyday life, as questions of physical proximity, social homogeneity, race relations, form of tenure, housing styles, income levels, privacy, and community. The cultural conceptions embedded in them have been addressed here as topics in their own right and as matters needing as much explanation as any other.

These principles bring a different perspective to classic concerns with class, status, and power, and as I have said, those observers' criteria for social categories take us only so far in comprehending the relationships among people actually filling the categories. The substance of social order is in the way people live with and work out their differences, always culturally defined.

The cultural conceptions providing social meanings to newcomers and old-timers, renters and owners, those arriving and those arrived, high and low density settlements, stability and change, and suburbs and cities powerfully guide actual practice in land-use matters. These conceptions also reveal more than we may have known before about some fundamental *sources* of stratification and differential social evaluation, more fundamental than

210

those conditions summed up in objective measures of wealth and power, for example.

For each of those distinctions guiding land-use practice also addresses the subject of differences between actual or implied social relationships: How these relationships as such are valued is the more fundamental source of the meanings that those objective measures take on. Not people in all their particulars of income, occupation, or education, but rather the *kinds of relationships* they are in with others—that, I have found repeatedly, is what is evaluated.[1] To recapitulate: There is first the different valuation put on relationships to landlords and to bankers. The highest status is accorded people having the most remote relationships with neighbors, and the lowest to those having the most proximate. People having blood relationships with those they share an abode with are more highly valued than those joining together out of friendship or explicit economic necessity. People already embedded in a network of social relationships—old-timers—are more highly esteemed than those newly arriving and starting afresh to create social connections. In property markets, new economic ventures and the kinds of relationships they set in motion are valued more highly than the maintenance of those previously established. Equal political rights signify equal access to valued relationships: voting rights are relations to the state, and employment opportunities signify the chance to participate in economic transactions (by definition relationships) for goods and services. The social relationships of men at work are more highly valued than those of women in their familial and neighborhood relationships. Legal relationships are more highly valued than those that are informal or customary.

These values placed on social relationships can and do change the import or connotations of apparently objective measures used in assessing social worth. The genteel poverty of old "first" families does not diminish the higher value put on the historical depth of their familial tree. Descent and lineage, basic elements in status, are, by definition, a veritable entourage of "relations,"

[1] I am not speaking of relationships with people having "high status" and the contagion of prestige implied, but about *kinds* of relationships being themselves ranked. For a stimulating discussion of status from a fresh perspective that has done much to inform this one by its differences, see Shils 1968.

when status is high; when the lineage is "shallow," status is lower. The pejorative connotation of the category *nouveau riche* is evidence of lineage outclassing wealth. On the other hand, the small earnings and manual labor of a local precinct captain are well compensated by the import of his being wired into a political network. In industrial society, the very numbers of relationships— the extent of one's connections—are an important criteria in social evaluation. The power content of the relationship matters, too, whether master or slave, patron or client, mother or father. The length of time a relationship endures matters, and the hurdles to overcome before achieving it affect its value, as do the sanctions involved in dissolving it. Each such component of a relationship has a value put on it, and the sum of them points to its level of social worth or status. These are not given once and for all, nor are they the same at all times and places in the same society.

Evaluations of kinds of relationships, being matters of opinion, change over time and under the influence of events. The signs of them can change. The apartment house does not inevitably for all times symbolize the disadvantaged relationship the tenant is in vis-à-vis the landlord. In earlier days, until the 1930s, the majority of people had a relationship with a landlord, before home-ownership and the debt relationship were elevated in social esteem. When skin color is socially evaluated, it is as a sign standing for kinds of social relationships, that more fundamental subject actually being addressed: Black is more beautiful in societies where the kinds of relationships blacks have been in are esteemed, but not where they have endured the relationship of slave to master.

The more equitable distribution of those components of wealth, income, and power is indispensable to the goal of a more just society. Equally important are the self-respect and social esteem only available through *being in* culturally valued relationships.

Life style is, then, the array of social relationships people are in. People do not possess either wealth or power in isolation from others. On the contrary: they are themselves consequences, even as they are causes, of relationships. Society structures a wide range of types of relationships in the different arenas of home, work, and leisure, and "life chances" constitute the opportunity to experience that array—to collect from a variety of situations a sum of social worth. That is the meaning of freedom of association, in residence, education, and occupation. That is the importance of assuring a more just society.

Other equally less familiar dimensions of land-use ideas and practices might be helpful in defining problems and getting to work on them. These dimensions are as amenable to research as any others, for having found them in the substance of social thought and action, we need not grope our way from theory to the data by which to test it.

Besides thinking of race, we need to think in terms of the rules applicable to and the meanings attaching to newcomers. Although it should not be so, blacks are our largest group of newcomers to citizenship, and the barriers and hurdles they find, much exacerbated by racism, are widespread. Women, renters, and younger people also find themselves outside the lines. First- and second-generation Americans, too, experience social hazing. And we all, in turn, do it to those coming next. The American cultural system has an abundant collection of axioms and propositions out of which a social geometry of insiders and outsiders, included and excluded, majority and minority, is formed. When we include familial and religious groups, just about everyone draws on some version of cultural criteria for membership. American conceptions of newcomers and old-timers are ubiquitous and are expressed everywhere in social and political life. How they are weighted and institutionalized is what needs vigilance. There are some methods by which people are taking turns at the privilege of having been first-come and first-served. For example, early retirement recognizes social succession, as do union demands for sharing out the work to give more people a start when there is not enough to go around.

Besides describing demographic and spatial differentiation, once looking also into the ways people negotiate their local differences, wholly new understandings of the substance and meanings of social life can blossom. From a substantive sociology of privacy, tenure, and social conflict—at all income levels—we can learn of principles and mechanisms used in neighborhood and community life and discover the social logic behind them.

Besides asking whether our legal and political institutions match in practice their ideal in outline, their symbolic uses need also to be taken into account in their reform and realignment. No less

213

important are their half-visible functions as social rituals using customary social practices for their performing stage. Legal and political institutions are equally sociological and cultural. That is, substantive relationships flesh out those formal outlines making use of various principles of social organization. We have yet to explore the culture and the sociology of tenure, of housing types, of homeownership, of neighboring, and of disputes as deeply as we have explored the economics and law of those subjects. Their details of custom, convention, relationship, and event will provide the ethnographic text with which we can carry on the science of social meanings, finding signs and what they stand for.

Besides the fact of numerical minorities, we can be alert to the social manufacture of marginality and the social meanings of danger and pollution that so automatically accompany it. Marginal categories in the system of land use are a demonology of the American civil "religion"—its dreamy ideology of progress, plenty, and equality contradicted by the waking reality. The ideology defines both achievement and failure in terms both more glorious and harsh than either need be cast.

One other trend in modern society is already a major source of marginality. The deepening of specialization results not only in differentiation and division, but in combinations as well, guided by criteria that are equally principles of social order. Dividing wholes into component parts and recombining the parts is a mode of thought giving rise to the major intellectual revolutions of this century, the Freudian, the atomic, and the cybernetic. What had appeared to be whole is split into its parts, thus posing the entirely new possibility of recombining each variously. In technology, modular building, multivariate regressions, hi-fi components, cafeteria menus, and "separates" in clothing are everyday commonplaces. Socially, even the "breakdown" of ideal family structure may be operating from these same principles, for instead of a seamless cluster of mother-father-children, the Freudian revolution created perceptions of it as sets of one-to-one roles, each component having unique dynamics and different consequences (mother-son, mother-daughter, father-son, father-daughter, wife-husband, and so on).

Groups living today as "families," though not "nuclear" families, consider themselves as "family." They are social atoms created by the greater freedom to divorce and to recombine. Singles

214

"swing"—swinging free of legal ties or living together by agreement rather than in wedlock, combining elements of friendship and marriage. Groups living communally put together some features of family and some of economic enterprise. Time, always interpreted culturally and socially and a basic arbiter of social categories, becomes broken into new kinds of segments when people put the social calendar together in different ways—"dropping out" of a single, temporal sequence or "dropping in" to school in later life. Tenure relationships: features of renting and owning combine into new forms of condominium and cooperative.

A componential society leaves much more in doubt, creating social categories that appear to be neither the one thing nor the other to which we have been accustomed. Unfamiliar combinations can become charged with those "trickster" meanings of marginality, with their serious implications for social order and social justice. We will need to be more careful in allowing what actually spells danger, for these different categories will also continue to be evaluated. Those rankings become a basis for distributing social rewards and entitlements and for acting upon social justice. As I have been trying to show, there is nothing inevitable about the social evaluations there are. Once that is better understood, the judicial question of discriminatory intent versus effect will become obsolete: our culture is intentional.

Last, besides the customary separations of land uses, the reasons for their presumed incompatibility need deeper understanding. The physical form of the suburbs as we know it today is, I believe, only a second-order effect of one central principle of American social order: the suburbs had transformed the greatest distance between home and work—often enough a logical separation as well—into the prime symbolic reward for achieving the American Dream. The necessities of the nineteenth-century factory system—separating work from the domestic group—have been transformed into twentieth-century virtues. Today in fullest flower, industrialism so drains energy resources that conservation, now as progress, may return us full circle to the shorter hop between home and work.

Those symbolic meanings of the reward have real consequences when they contrive to exclude from the suburbs the very people who must live close to their work—teachers, policemen, nurses, firemen, garbage collectors, construction workers, repair people,

215

students, houseworkers (Bergman 1974). They need to live close to their work because what they earn does not permit them to live far. Rewards there must be, but the form they take is entirely arbitrary.

Although the outward movement of cities has been going on throughout this century, the one new trend to occur within the life-time of most of us is an acceleration in the suburban location of significant industries of all kinds—manufacturing, corporate head-quarters, "downtown" shopping. The city is being reproduced else-where, and our present problems stem less from the logic of this fact than from its social meanings. Suburbanization, not just a visibly evolving geographical process, is equally a moral force. In American civil religion, the suburbs are a reward in the here-and-now. "God's in his heaven—All's right with the world" more so in the suburbs.

> . . . In the ancient city the organization of space was a symbolic re-creation of a supposed cosmic order. It had an ideological pur-pose. Created space in the modern city has an equivalent ideologi-cal purpose. In part it reflects the prevailing ideology of the ruling groups and institutions in society. In part it is fashioned by the dynamics of market forces. . . . Neither the activity of space cre-ation nor the final product of created space appear to be within our individual or collective control but fashioned by forces alien to us. We scarcely know how to grapple, either in reality or in the mind, with the implications of created space. (Harvey 1973: 310)

Today as in ancient times metropolitan space expresses the cosmic order, here of the American heaven and hell in the suburban pull toward salvation and the urban push of social pollution. By ac-knowledging that our culture, certainly no alien force, is as much in charge as culture ever is, the enemy as ourselves may begin to be faced.

Suburban residence has come to mean the final stage of a be-lieved-in natural social evolution, inevitable and right. The physical character of suburban communities is under pressure of change. More compact development and greater social heterogeneity are on the horizon. All together, these dislocate the moral significance of the suburbs, a cultural category created in antithesis to the city. For as the city loses its edges, so does the category suburb, at once physical and moral, disappear. Evolution is confused by history: what was is. And it is next door.

216

The rewards should take the form of authentic self-respect and social esteem in the social arenas of work and everyday life. Both respect and esteem depend on our catalogs of categories, those texts in which are translated American ideals for domestic tranquillity and equal justice under law. Once in better concordance, sharing may become more possible, and we may make time enough for love and justice both.

APPENDICES

These are examples of land-use regulations widely in use.

Appendix 1. Excerpts from "A Guide to the Philadelphia Zoning Ordinance," which summarizes the more important zoning requirements of the City of Philadelphia as amended to May 15, 1970, published by the Citizens' Council on City Planning.

Appendix 2. Excerpts from a typical residential deed restriction in Houston (Harris County, Texas).

Appendix 3. Excerpts from "A New Zoning Ordinance for Baltimore," 1968, by the Zoning Commission of Baltimore City. There are 5 pages here, out of a total of 29, which allocate various uses (about 500 in all) to each type of zoning district.

Excerpts from "A Guide to the Philadelphia Zoning Ordinance," which summarizes the more important zoning requirements of the City of Philadelphia as amended to May 15, 1970, published by the Citizens' Council on City Planning.

DISTRICT REQUIREMENTS

Philadelphia's Zoning Ordinance now establishes 50 different zoning district classifications: 28 Residential Districts, 10 Commercial Districts, 8 Industrial Districts and 4 Special Districts.

For each district, the ordinance lists permitted uses and prescribes regulations on the size and location on the lot of structures and open space. Before describing the specific requirements for each district, it is necessary to explore the purposes and effect of the regulations that are applied to the various districts.

PERMITTED USES

Zoning districts are ranked from "most restrictive" to "least restrictive". Uses permitted in highly restrictive districts are normally permitted in less restrictive districts. The ordinance usually specifies a list of uses permitted in a given district and, in addition, states that uses permitted in another district are also permitted. In inspecting the list of permitted uses, it is often necessary to refer to many other district requirements if one wishes to know all activities that may be conducted in a specific district.

YARDS

Yards are open, unoccupied areas between principal structures and property lines. In most residential districts, Front Yards, Side Yards and Rear Yards are required. Of course, side yard requirements do not apply along the common walls of row houses or semi-detached dwellings. Yards are also required in some commercial and industrial districts. Setbacks are established in most districts to preserve light and air along city streets and to improve visibility and safety for pedestrians, drivers and the occupants of structures.

MINIMUM LOT AREA AND WIDTH

In residential districts, the Ordinance specifies the minimum required area of every lot and either the minimum width of the lot, measured along the setback line, or in group housing districts, the minimum frontage of a lot on a public street. These regulations are intended to prevent construction of structures on lots which are too small for reasonable use.

OCCUPIED AND OPEN AREA OF LOT

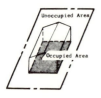

A control employed in most districts is a limitation on the percentage of lot that may be occupied by structures. The ordinance requires that some land be kept open to provide yards, setbacks, open parking spaces and other usable space for residents. These regulations are to prevent overcrowding of land with structures and to provide some space for the use and enjoyment of occupants.

MAXIMUM HEIGHT OF BUILDINGS

Many zoning ordinances specify the maximum height of buildings in every zoning district. The purpose of this limitation is to prevent erection of high buildings which rob neighboring buildings of light and air, and to discourage buildings which are so tall that they contribute to undue congestion on public streets. The Philadelphia ordinance specifies maximum heights of buildings for only some of its fifty districts: R-1 through R-10A, R-17 through R-19, C-1, C-2, Neighborhood and Area Shopping Center Districts, and Trailer Camp Districts. In other districts, building heights are controlled only indirectly through limitations on Gross Floor Area.

GROSS FLOOR AREA (FLOOR AREA RATIO)

A limitation on the Gross Floor Area of buildings related to lot size is used in the Philadelphia ordinance as a control over building height and bulk. This regulation is intended to encourage flexibility in building design and land use but still prevent over-crowding of land, excessive building bulk and unnecessarily high concentrations of population.

The Floor Area Ratio specifies the maximum amount of floor space in any building to the area of the lot upon which the structure is erected. A structure may have any number of floors within height specifications for the districts so long as the total area of all floors does not exceed the maximum permissible percentage.

Examples of the effect of the Floor Area Ratio are shown in the accompanying diagram. In a district in which the Gross Floor Area of all structures may be 150 per cent of the total lot area, the owner could erect a three-story building which covers one-half of the lot or a six-story building which covers 25% of the lot. A fifteen story building (not illustrated) could cover only 10% of the lot. In all of these cases, the total floor area would equal 150% of the lot area – the maximum permissible percentage.

In addition to the basic limitation on Gross Floor Area, in some districts a system of "bonuses" is employed. Under this system, additional floor area is permitted above the basic limitation if the builder will provide greater setbacks than are required or arcades, courts and other open spaces at ground level. Since the bonuses are based on complicated formulas, no attempt is made here to explain them in detail. However, the following charts identify those districts in which the bonuses apply.

DENSITY CONTROLS

Population density is the number of persons living in any area. Normally it is expressed in terms of persons or families per acre. Zoning ordinances often regulate density by specifying the minimum amount of land that must be provided for each family housed in a structure. Philadelphia's Ordinance does not, however, make such a requirement. Minimum lot area requirements apply to structures rather than families. Limitations on building height and bulk, requirements for off-street parking, land covering require-ments and minimum floor area requirements for dwelling units provide additional indirect controls over population density.

221

RESIDENTIAL DISTRICTS (R1 THROUGH R10)

Residential districts are intended primarily for dwellings and those non-residential uses which are normally associated with residential areas. The Philadelphia Zoning Ordinance provides 23 different classifications for residential districts and, in addition, five Residential-Commercial districts. The different categories provide for different kinds and sizes of residential structures, varying yard, height and lot coverage requirements, and, thus, different levels of population density. Use provisions and height, area and bulk requirements for these districts are summarized in the following tables.

District	Permitted Uses	Minimum Lot Area (Sq. ft.)	Minimum Lot Width (ft.)	Maximum % of Lot Occupied by Structures	Front Yard (ft.)	Side Yards (ft.)	Rear Yard (ft.)
SINGLE FAMILY DWELLINGS							
R-1 (14-202)	Single-family detached dwellings only.	10,000	75	35	35	15	30
R-2 (14-203)	Single-family detached houses and specified professional offices, places of worship, galleries, museums, libraries, railroad passenger stations and utility substations in enclosed buildings. Other specified non-residential buildings may be permitted if a Zoning Board of Adjustment Certificate is obtained.	5,000	50	30	25	15/10	25
R-3 (14-204)	Semi-detached (twin) dwellings and all uses permitted in R-2.	5,000	50	30	25	15/10	25
R-4 (14-205)	Uses in R-3.	3,150	35	40	15	Varies	20
R-5 (14-206)	Uses in R-4.	2,250	25	50	8	8	15
R-9A (14-210.2)	Uses in R-5 and attached single-family dwellings.	1,440	16	70 (80 on corner lots)	8	Varies	9
R-10A (14-221.1)	Uses in R-9A.	1,440	16	70 (80 on corner lots)	None	Varies	9

SINGLE-FAMILY AND DUPLEX DWELLINGS

District	Description						
R-5A (14-206.1)	Uses in R-4 plus detached and semi-detached duplex dwellings.	2,250	25	50	8	8	15 20 for duplex
R-6 (14-207)	Single-family row houses in groups of not more than ten are permitted, provided they are at least 24 feet wide. End houses may contain two families and shall be located on lots at least 36 feet in width. Detached dwellings and non-residential uses are not permitted.	1,920 (End of row 2,800)	24 (End of row 36)	50	15	8	20
R-7 (14-208)	All uses permitted in R-5 in addition to single-family or duplex row houses in groups of not more than ten houses.	1,620 (End of row 2,700)	18 (End of row 30)	50	15	8	20
R-8 (14-209)	Same uses as R-7 but the limitation of ten houses in a row is removed.	1,440	16	50	15	8	15

SINGLE-FAMILY, DUPLEX AND MULTIPLE-FAMILY DWELLINGS

District	Description						
R-9 (14-210)	Uses are those permitted in R-8 as well as multiple-family row houses.	1,440	16	70 (80 on corner lots)	8	Varies	9
R-10 (14-211)	Identical with R-9 except that no setback is required.	1,440	16	70 (80 on corner lots)	0	Varies	9

NOTE: Maximum Building Heights in R-1 through R-10A Districts:
for Dwellings – 35' or 3 Stories
for Non-Residential Buildings – up to 60' if building is set back from lot lines.

RESIDENTIAL DISTRICTS (R11 THROUGH R19)

GROUP HOUSING DISTRICTS

District	Permitted Use	Minimum Lot Area (sq. ft.)	Minimum Lot Frontage	Maximum % of Lot Occupied by Structures	Setback (ft.)	Maximum Gross Floor Area (% of Lot Area)
R-11 (14-202)	In these districts groups of single, duplex and multiple-family dwelling structures are permitted on a single lot. Garages as an accessory use and accessory signs are also permitted. These are districts in which several garden apartments or high-rise apartment buildings may be erected on large tracts. Since more than one structure may occupy the lot, conventional yard and height limitations are not imposed and formulas are used to provide for adequate spacing between buildings. The difference in these three districts are in the intensity of development permitted in each.	15,000	50	—	Formula	30
R-11A (14-212.1)		15,000	50	—	Formula	50
R-12 (14-213)		15,000	50	—	Formula	70
R-13 (14-214)		15,000	50	50	Formula	150

MULTIPLE HOUSING DISTRICTS

District	Permitted Uses	Minimum Lot Area (sq. ft.)	Minimum Lot Width (ft.)	Maximum % of Lot Occupied by Structures	Front Yard (ft.)	Side Yards (ft.)	Rear Yard (ft.)	Maximum Gross Floor Area (% of Lot Area)
R-14 (14-215)	In these districts one structure for single-family, duplex or multiple-family occupany is permitted on a lot. These apartment districts may be distinguished from Group Housing Districts (R-11, R-12, and R-13) because in Multiple Housing Districts, yard, area requirements are designed to regulate only one principal building on a lot.	10,000	50	50	20	Varies	20	150 (Bonuses)
R-15 (14-216)		5,000	50	70 (corner lots – 80)	0	Varies	Varies	350 (Bonuses)
R-16 (14-217)		—	—	Building 6 or more stories - 100 (5 or less stories - 80; 90 on corner lots)	Varies	Varies	Varies	500 (Bonuses)

District	Permitted Uses	Minimum Lot Area (sq. ft.)	Minimum Lot Width (ft.)	Maximum % of Lot Occupied by Structures	Front Yard (ft.)	Setback (ft.)	Yard Space required for each additional family to be housed in existing structure
CONVERSION DISTRICTS							
R-17 (14-218)	In these districts, regulations permit the conversion of residential structures to increase the number of dwelling units. A majority of floors shall have at least 700 square feet of floor area and yard space must be available for every family to be housed. Off-street parking must be provided and the total floor area in the structure must meet ordinance specifications. For existing structures the total number of families permitted is determined by formula based on the size of the floors in the structure. Minimum lot area and width requirements, and minimum standards for yards are based on types of residential structures and numbers of families occupying structures.	5,000	50	30	Formula	25	2,500 sq. ft.
R-18 (14-219)		2,250	25	50	Formula	8	800 sq. ft.
R-19 (14-220)		1,440	16	70	Formula	8	300 sq. ft.

225

RESIDENTIAL COMMERCIAL DISTRICTS (RC1 THROUGH RC5)

District	Permitted Uses	Minimum Lot Area (sq. ft.)	Minimum Lot Frontage	Maximum % of Lot Occupied by Structures	Setback (ft.)	Maximum Gross Floor Area (% of Lot Area)
RESIDENTIAL-COMMERCIAL DISTRICTS						
RC-1 (14-221)	Commercial uses are not permitted in most residential districts. However, because in some areas limited commercial operations are conducted within apartment buildings, the zoning ordinance provides five apartment districts in which such uses are permitted under strict limitations. The first floors in structures containing at least 25 dwelling units may be occupied by limited commercial uses having floor areas of not less than 500 nor more than 6,000 square feet. Professional offices are permitted on the first story of buildings of five or less stories and on the first and second stories of taller buildings.	15,000	50	50	Formula	150
RC 2 (14-222)		10,000	50	50	20	150 (Bonuses)
RC 3 (14-223)		none	none	100 Structures 5 stories or less: 80 (90 on corner lots)	none	350 (Bonuses)
RC-4 (14-224)		none	none	Same as RC-3	none	500 (Bonuses)
RC-5 (14-225)		none	none	Same as RC-3	none	1200; 500 for commercial and non-residential bonuses

and sold and in which personal and business services are conducted. They are also the sites for offices, commercial entertainments, and some wholesaling and related industrial uses. Ten different categories of Commercial districts are now provided, ranging from small convenience store areas, intended to serve adjacent residential districts, to general business districts and large shopping centers.

District	Permitted Uses	Maximum % of Lot Occupied Structures		Front Yard (ft.)	Side Yards (ft.)	Rear Yard (ft.)	Maximum Height of Structures	Maximum Gross Floor Area (% of Lot Area)
		Intermediate Lots	Corner Lots					
LIMITED BUSINESS								
C-1 (14-302)	A commercial district in which uses are limited to the sale of foods, drugs and confections, specified professional offices and residential uses permitted in the most restrictive abutting Residential district.	Area and height regulations are those of the most restrictive abutting district						
C-2 (14-303)	Retail sales, offices and personal and business services in enclosed buildings. Specified services and outdoor business and amusement enterprises may be permitted with a Zoning Board of Adjustment Certificate.	75	80	0	5	8	35' 3 stories	—
GENERAL BUSINESS								
C-3 (14-304)	Similar to above with some restrictions on uses removed.	Dwellings 75 / Structures other than Dwellings 90	80 / 95	0	0	0	—	Dwellings for 3 or more families 450% Other Structures 550%
C-4 (14-305)	Same uses as in C-3, subject to same conditions.	Structures 5 stories or less with one or more families 80 / Other structures 100	90 / 100	0	0	0	—	500% (Bonuses)
C-5 (14-306)	This district is for the Central Business District Core and is the same as C-4 except that a higher intensity of land development is permitted.	Structures 5 stories or less with one or more families 80 / Other structures 100	90 / 100	0	0	0	—	1,200% (Bonuses)

COMMERCIAL DISTRICTS (C1 THROUGH C7)

District	Permitted Uses	Minimum Lot Size (in sq. ft.)	Maximum % of Lot Occupied by Structures	Yards	Maximum Height of Structures	Maximum Gross Floor Area (% of Lot Area)
C-6 (14-306.1)	Uses permitted in this district include sales establishments, recreational, institutional, and entertainment facilities, and municipal buildings.	45,000	50	None required, but if provided must be 5'	35' or 3 stories	150
C-7 (14-306.2)	Sales facilities, municipal buildings, service and business establishments. No residential uses permitted.	5,000	60	None required, but if provided must be 5'	35' or 3 stories	75

228

District	Permitted Uses	Minimum Lot Width (ft.)	Minimum Lot Area (sq. ft.)	Maximum % of Lot Occupied by Structures	Front Yard (ft.)	Side Yards (ft.)	Rear Yard (ft.)	Maximum Gross Floor Area (% of Lot Area)
OTHER COMMERCIAL DISTRICTS								
Office Commercial (14-307)	A highly restricted district for offices, financial institutions, studies, research laboratories, and multiple dwellings.	100	10,000	50	20	12	35	150%
Neighborhood Shopping Center (14-308)	Small shopping centers for retail sales, offices and services in enclosed buildings of less than 4,000 sq. ft. floor area. A parking ratio of one square foot of parking for each square foot of floor area applies.	0	0	Maximum height of structures 3 stories or 35 feet				
Area Shopping Center (14-309)	Shopping centers permitting a wider range of activities than in NSC district and requiring twice as much parking per square foot of floor area.	200	80,000	Maximum height of structures 3 stories or 35 feet (may be increased to 65 feet under conditions specified in Ordinance)				

Industrial Districts

The Zoning Ordinance provides eight industrial districts for manufacturing, processing, assembly, fabrication, bulk storage and refining, freight terminals and similar industrial operations. These districts fall into four different classes: Limited Industrial, General Industrial, Least Restricted and Port Industrial. Distinctions among these classes lie primarily in the kinds of uses permitted. Within each class of districts different ranges of intensity of development are permitted. Dwellings, hotels, cultural activities, and hospitals are not permitted in these districts.

District	Permitted Uses	Front Yard (ft.)	Side Yards (ft.)	Rear Yard (ft.)	Maximum % of Lot Occupied by Structures	Building Bulk (times floor area)	Maximum Gross Floor Area (% of Lot Area)
LIMITED INDUSTRIAL							
L-1 (14-503)	Four districts are provided in which uses are limited to light manufacturing uses which cause a minimum of noise, smoke, odors, glare, vibration and similar disturbances. Industrial operations, excluding off-street parking and loading, must be conducted within enclosed buildings. Finished products manufactured in these districts shall not exceed 2000 lbs. in weight unless a Zoning Board of Adjustment Certificate is obtained.	50	50	50	35	20	70
L-2 (14-504)		40	12	12	60	20	180
L-3 (14-505)		20	12	12	75	20	225
L-4 (14-506)		0	0	0	100	—	500 (Bonuses)

GENERAL INDUSTRIAL

G-1 (14-507) — A broader range of industrial activities is permitted to be conducted than in Limited Industrial Districts and the qualifications imposed on uses in the Limited Districts are removed. In the G-1 District, uses must still be conducted within enclosed buildings but this does not apply in the G-2 District. In the G-2 District, a wide range of industrial activities, including many which normally have considerable emissions of smoke and odors, are permitted.

G-2 (14-508)

LEAST RESTRICTED INDUSTRIAL

LR (14-509) — In this district, any legal industrial use may be conducted. Included are many uses which may create the undesirable effects often associated with heavy industry.

PORT INDUSTRIAL

PORT (14-510) — This district is intended for docks, wharves, piers, storage sheds and similar facilities associated with the transfer, storage and incident processing of waterborne cargo.

G-1 (14-507)	20	12	12	65	20	195
G-2 (14-508)	0	0	0	100	20	500
LR (14-509)	0	0	8	100	20	500
PORT (14-510)	0	0	0	100	—	—

Excerpts from a typical residential deed restriction in Houston (Harris County, Texas).

CANDLELIGHT HILLS, SECTION ONE
RESTRICTIONS, COVENANTS, CONDITIONS AND
MAINTENANCE CHARGE

THE STATE OF TEXAS   )(
COUNTY OF HARRIS   )(

KNOW ALL MEN BY THESE PRESENTS:

. . . CANDLELIGHT HILLS, SECTION ONE, for the benefit of the present and future owners of said lots, [does] hereby adopt and establish the following reservations, restrictions, covenants and easements to apply uniformly to the use, occupancy and conveyance of all residential building sites in CANDLELIGHT HILLS, SECTION ONE, and each contract or deed which may be hereafter executed with regard to any of the lots in said CANDLELIGHT HILLS, SECTION ONE, shall be conclusively held to have been executed, delivered and accepted subject to the following reservations, restrictions, covenants, easements, liens and charges, regardless of whether or not said reservations, restrictions, covenants, easements, liens and charges are set out in full in said contract or deed.

1. RESERVATIONS

In authenticating the Subdivision map for record, and in dedicating the streets, drives, lanes, roads, parks, walks and easements to the use of the present and future owners of said lots and to the public, there shall be and are hereby reserved in Grantor, his heirs, successors and assigns, the following rights, title and easements, which reservations shall be considered a part of the land and construed as being adopted in each and every contract, deed, or other conveyance executed or to be executed by or on behalf of Grantor in the conveyance of said property or any part thereof, to-wit:

1:1 - The streets, drives, lanes, roads, parks, walks and ease-

232

ments as shown on said map or plat are hereby dedicated to the use of the public.

1:2 - Grantor reserves the necessary utility easements and rights-of-way as shown on the aforesaid recorded plat, which easements are reserved for the use and benefit of Candlelight Service Company and any public utility operating in Harris County, Texas, as well as for the benefit of Grantor and the property owners in the Subdivision to allow for the construction, maintenance and operation of a system or systems of electric light and power, telephone lines, gas, water, sewers or any other utility or service which Grantor may find necessary for the proper service of lots. . . .

1:3 - Grantor reserves the right to impose further restrictions and dedicate additional easements and roadway rights-of-way on any unsold sites in said Subdivision. . . .

1:4 - Neither Grantor nor any utility company using the above mentioned easements shall be liable for any damage done by either of them or their assigns, agents, employees or servants, to shrubbery, trees, flowers or other property of the owner situated on the land covered by said easements.

1:5 - It shall be and is expressly understood and agreed that the title conveyed by Grantor to any lot or parcel of land by contract, deed or other conveyance shall not in any event be held or construed to include the title to the water, gas, sewer, storm sewer, electric light, electric power, or telephone lines, poles, or conduits or any other utility or appurtenances thereto constructed by Grantor or public utility companies through, along, or upon the herein dedicated public easements, premises, or any part thereof to serve said property and the right to maintain, repair, sell or lease such lines, utilities and appurtenances to the City of Houston, or to any public service corporation, or to any other party, is hereby expressly reserved in Grantor, his heirs, successors and assigns.

1:6 - Grantor expressly reserves unto himself, his heirs, successors and assigns,

> (i) the right to receive all payments from others for the purpose of connecting into the utility system for the purpose of serving property outside of CANDLELIGHT HILLS, SECTION ONE, and

(ii) the right to grant the right of passage over any access easements running from CANDLELIGHT HILLS, SECTION ONE to serve other properties in the vicinity.

2. ARCHITECTURAL CONTROL COMMITTEE

2:1 - There is hereby created an Architectural Control Committee comprised of Three (3) members. . . . In the event any one of said members should die, resign or become ineligible to act, the remaining Two (2) members of the Committee may appoint a successor. Any one of said members may be removed by Grantor or his successors, with or without cause, and a successor appointed by Grantor or his successors.

2:2 - No building or other improvements shall be erected, placed or altered on any lot until complete copies of the construction plans and specifications, and a plot plan showing the location of any such building or improvements have been approved in writing by the Architectural Control Committee as to use, quality of workmanship and materials, conformity and harmony of external design with existing structures and as to location of the building or improvements with the respect to topography and finished ground elevation. Grantor or his successors may designate a representative with authority to act for the Committee. In the event said Committee, or its designated representative, fails to give written approval or disapproval within Thirty (30) days after said plans and specifications have been submitted to it, or in any event, if no suit to enjoin the erection of such building or improvements or the making of alterations have been commenced prior to Sixty (60) days after the completion thereof, such approval will not be required and this provision as to approval will be deemed to have been satisfied. Neither the members of said Committee, nor its designated representative, shall be entitled to any compensation for services performed pursuant to this provision. The duties and powers of said Committee, or of any designated representative, shall cease on January 1, 1978, or upon the resignation of all Three (3) members, which ever occurs earlier. Thereafter, the approval of plans and specifications shall not be required unless prior thereto and effective thereon a written instrument is executed by the then record owners of a majority of the lots subject hereto appointing a new committee composed of Three (3) members to exercise the same powers delegated to be exercised by the committee first named, and the instrument creating said new committee is recorded in the office of the County Clerk of Harris County, Texas.

2:3 - Grantor or his successors may, at his sole option, approve the re-subdividing of more than Two (2) residential lots as shown on the recorded plat of CANDLELIGHT HILLS, SECTION ONE, provided that no residence shall be constructed on any building site having a frontage of less than five (5') feet from that shown on the recorded plat of said Subdivision. In this connection, it is intended that building sites shall not be subdivided into smaller plots than as shown on the recorded plat, with the exception of the five (5') foot reduction hereinbefore provided. However, this will not prohibit the construction of a residence on a larger building site, and in this connection the subdivider or any builder may build a single residence on a building site composed of One and One-half (1-1/2) lots, or Two (2) lots.

3. RESTRICTIVE COVENANTS ON RESIDENTIAL LOTS

3:1 - All lots shall be used only for residential purposes and the term "residential purposes" as used herein shall exclude hospitals, clinics, hotels, duplex houses, apartment houses, motels, boarding houses or any commercial or professional uses whether from houses, residences or otherwise, and all such uses of said property are hereby expressly prohibited, provided, however that Grantor reserves the right to maintain a sales office in said Subdivision until all lots are sold to individual home owners.

3:2 - No building shall be erected, altered, placed or permitted to remain other than (a) One (1) detached single family dwelling not to exceed Three (3) stories in height, a private garage or carport for the storing of not less than Two (2) cars and not more than Four (4) cars, and servants' quarters for use of domestic servants employed on the premises; and (b) a tool shed or work shop, attached or unattached to the residence building.

3:3 - No buildings shall be located nearer to the front lot line or nearer to any side street property line than the building setback line shown on the recorded plat of said Subdivision, except as provided in Paragraph 2:3 hereof. In any event, no building shall be located on any residential building site nearer than Ten (10') feet to any side street property line, or nearer than Five (5') feet from the rear lot line, or nearer than Five (5) feet from any side property line; provided, however that any unattached garage may be constructed within Two (2) feet of the side property line of the residence lot.

3:4 - All detached garages must be located at the rear of the main residence building and no attached garage shall be located nearer to the street than the front line of the main residence building unless its location is approved in writing by the Architectural Control Committee prior to its construction.

3:5 - All buildings shall be constructed to front on the street upon which the lot faces and all corner lots shall be considered to face on the street on which the lot has the smallest frontage.

3:6 - No noxious or offensive trade or activity shall be carried on upon any residential lot nor shall anything be done thereon which may be or become an annoyance or nuisance to the neighborhood.

3:7 - No trailer, basement, tent, shack, garage or other outbuilding erected on any residential building site shall at any time be used as a residence, temporarily or permanently, nor shall any structure of a temporary character be used as a residence. Nor may any vehicle, trailer, camper, boat, boat trailer or machinery of any type be kept or stored within said Subdivision except within a garage or in such a place as may be completely out of view from any public street or adjacent lot.

3:8 - No main residential structure shall be placed on any lot unless its living area has a minimum of Twenty-Two Hundred (2,200) square feet of floor area, exclusive of porches and garages, and in the event the dwelling is in excess of One (1) story in height, the ground floor must contain no less than Fourteen Hundred (1,400) square feet of living area, exclusive of porches and garages.

3:9 - The exterior walls of any single story residence constructed or placed in said Subdivision exclusive of outbuildings, shall be constructed of at least Seventy-Five (75%) per cent brick, brick veneer, stone, stone veneer, or brick on hollow tile. In the event a residence is in excess of One (1) story in height, Seventy-Five (75%) per cent of the exterior walls of the ground floor shall be constructed of brick, brick veneer, stone, stone veneer, or brick on hollow tile. All residences shall have a roof pitch of not less than

3″ vertical to 12″ horizontal pitch. All roofs are to be wood shingle, or of such other material as may be approved by the Architectural Control Committee.

3:10 - No animals, livestock or poultry of any kind other than dogs, cats or other household pets, shall be kept on any residential lot, and not more than Two (2) of each household pets shall be kept on the premises.

3:11 - No water well, septic tank or cess pool shall be permitted on any residential lot, but each lot owner shall be required to enter into a utility service contract with Candlelight Service Company, and to use the water, sewer and meter services provided by Candlelight Service Company, its successors and assigns, until such time as such facilities shall be sold to a State, County, Municipal or other governmental agency. Each lot owner shall be required to subscribe to all three of the abovementioned services. Connections to such facilities shall be at the lot owner's expense. . . .

3:12 - No spiritous, vinous or malt liquors, or medicated bitters, capable of inducing intoxication, shall ever be sold, or offered for sale, on any residential lot, and said premises shall not be used for any vicious, illegal or immoral purposes, or for any purpose in violation of any state or federal law, or of any police, health, sanitary building or fire code, regulation or instruction relating to or affecting the use, occupancy or possession of any of said residential lots.

3:13 - No sign of any kind shall be displayed to the public view on any residential lot except one sign of not more than Five (5) square feet advertising the merits of the property for sale or rent or signs used by a builder to advertise the property during the construction and sales period.

3:14 - No drilling, oil development operations, oil refining, gas recycling, quarrying or mining operations of any kind shall be permitted on any residential lot, nor shall oil wells, gas wells, tanks, tunnels, mineral excavations or shafts, be permitted upon any residential lot; and no derrick or other structure designed for use in drilling or boring for oil or gas shall be erected, maintained or permitted on any lot.

3:15 - No lot shall be used or maintained as a dumping ground for rubbish. Trash, garbage or other waste shall not be kept on any lot except in sanitary containers. All equipment for the storage

237

or disposal of such material shall be kept in a clean and sanitary condition.

3:16 - No fence, wall or hedge or any pergola, carport or other detached structure shall be erected, placed, grown or maintained on any lot nearer to the street than the front line of the main residence building, or in the case of a corner lot, nearer to the street than the side line of the main residence, nor shall any fence exceed Six (6') feet in height. No clothes line shall be constructed or maintained on any lot within sight of the street or any adjacent lot. No fence shall be constructed on any lot out of any material except brick, wood or wrought iron without permission of the Architectural Control Committee.

3:17 - Grass and weeds are to be cut on all vacant lots so as to prevent an unsightly appearance and this is the obligation of the owner of the lot at his expense.

3:18 - No repair work, dismantling or assembling of motor vehicles or any other machinery or equipment shall be done in any street, or front or side yard on any lot.

3:19 - No garage apartment for rental purposes shall be permitted. Living quarters on the property other than in the main building may be used for bonafide servants only.

3:20 - No single family dwelling shall be occupied for residence purposes unless the exterior of such dwelling is entirely finished and the interior has been finished to the extent required by the Architectural Control Committee, whose approval in writing is required before any residence which is not entirely completed shall be occupied.

3:21 - Any violation of any of the covenants, agreements, reservations, easements and restrictions set out above shall not have the effect of impairing or affecting the rights of any mortgagee, trustee, or guarantor under any mortgage or Deed of Trust, or the assignee of any mortgagee, trustee or guarantor under any such mortgage or Deed of Trust outstanding against the property covered by any such mortgage or Deed of Trust at the time the easements, agreements, restrictions, reservations or covenants may be violated.

3:22 - Grantor, his successors and assigns, with the written approval of the Architectural Control Committee, may make reasonable alterations in any building setback line on any lot.

3:23 - Grantor, his successors and assigns, or any other person, firm or corporation owning a residential lot shall have the right to prosecute any action at law or in equity that it or they may deem advisable to enjoin any violation or attempted violation of any of the covenants and restrictions contained herein, and to prosecute the same against the person or persons violating or attempting to violate the same. In addition, violation of any restrictions, or covenants herein shall give Grantor, his successors and assigns the right to enter upon the property where such violation exists and summarily abate or remove the same at the expense of the lot owner, and such entry and abatement or removal shall not be deemed a trespass. Failure to enforce these restrictive covenants as to one or more persons shall not be construed as a waiver thereof, nor shall such an action be used as an estoppel against Grantors or any owner of the property in enforcing the restrictions against other persons subject thereto.

3:24 - Should any one or more of the covenants or restrictions set forth herein be held to be invalid or unenforcible by final judgment of any court at law or in equity, the same shall in no wise affect the remainder of the covenants and restrictions contained herein not directly affected by such final judgment.

3:25 - The covenants and restrictions set forth herein shall be binding upon Grantor, his heirs, successors and assigns, and any other person, firm or corporation owning or occupying a residential lot in CANDLELIGHT HILLS, SECTION ONE, until January 1, 2002, after which time said covenants, conditions and restrictions shall be automatically extended for successive periods of Ten (10) years each unless by a written instrument duly executed by the owners of at least Eighty (80%) percent of the residential lots in all sections of this Subdivision covered by these restrictions, duly acknowledged in recordable form by each of said owners and duly recorded in the office of the County Clerk in Harris County, Texas, it is agreed to modify, amend or terminate any of said covenants, conditions and restrictions in whole or in part; *provided, however,* that notwithstanding any modification, amendment or termination of said covenants, conditions and restrictions in whole or in part, Grantor, his heirs, successors and assigns, and any other person, firm or corporation owning or occupying a lot in this Subdivision shall be bound by the terms, covenants and conditions of (a) Contract No. CC-CSC-10 entered into between Candlelight Service Company and the San Jacinto River Authority, recorded under

239

County Clerk's File No. *D 725354* in the Official Public Records of Real Property in the office of the County Clerk of Harris County, Texas, and (b) Agreement No. CC-SA-CSC-10 entered into between San Jacinto River Authority, T. D. Gardner and Candlelight Service Company, recorded under County Clerk's File No. *D 725354* in the Official Public Records of Real Property in the office of the County Clerk of Harris County, Texas, and all amendments and supplementary agreements thereto which may be executed and recorded from time to time, all as more fully described under Section 5 hereof, entitled "UTILITY CHARGES."

4. ANNUAL MAINTENANCE CHARGE

4:1 - Each residential building site or lot shall be subject to an annual maintenance charge at an initial rate of Sixty and No/100 ($60.00) Dollars per year for the purpose of creating a fund to be known as "CANDLELIGHT HILLS MAINTENANCE FUND," hereinafter referred to as "MAINTENANCE FUND," and to be paid by the owner of each building site.

4:2 - The maintenance charge is to be paid to the "CANDLELIGHT HILLS MAINTENANCE FUND, INC.," a Texas non-profit corporation, hereinafter referred to as "the Association," annually in advance on January 1st of each year, and shall commence from the date of the sale of the lot by Grantor.

4:3 - The maintenance charge may be adjusted by the Association, its successors and assigns, from year to year as the needs of the Subdivision may, in its or their judgment require. The amount of the maintenance charge may be increased by the Board of Trustees of the Association to Eighty ($80.00) Dollars per year by majority vote of the Trustees. Adjustments in the maintenance charge in excess of $80.00 per year may be recommended by the Trustees to the members of the Association, and shall become effective at such time as the owners of at least Fifty-One (51)% per cent of the lots in the Subdivision have voted in favor of such adjustments.

4:4 - To secure the payment of the maintenance charge, a vendor's lien upon and against each residential lot is created by this instrument in favor of the Association, its successors and assigns, and the title to said lot sold or conveyed by Grantor shall be subject to the vendor's lien securing said charge. . . .

4:5 - Delinquent payments of any maintenance charge, shall

bear interest from the date the same became due until paid, at the rate of Ten (10%) per cent per annum.

4:6 - The total fund accumulated from this annual maintenance charge, insofar as the same may be sufficient, may be applied towards the payment of maintenance expenses incurred for any or all of the following purposes:

Lighting, improving and maintaining streets, parks, parkways, bridle paths and esplanades; subsidizing bus service; collecting and disposing of garbage, ashes, rubbish and the like; caring for vacant lots; payment of legal and all other expenses incurred in connection with the collection, enforcement and administration of the "MAINTENANCE FUND" and the enforcement of all covenants and restrictions for the Subdivision; employing private policemen and watchmen; doing any other thing necessary or desirable in the opinion of the Trustees of the Association to keep the property in the Subdivision neat and in good order, or which they consider of general benefit to the owners or occupants of the Subdivision. It is understood that the judgment of the Trustees of the Association in the expenditure of said funds shall be final and conclusive so long as such judgment is exercised in good faith.

4:7 - The maintenance charge shall remain effective until January 1, 1987, and shall automatically be extended thereafter for successive periods of Five (5) years provided, however, that owners of at least Eighty (80%) per cent of all residential lots in the Subdivision subject to such maintenance charge may revoke the maintenance charge on January 1, 1987, or at the end of any successive five-year period thereafter, by executing and acknowledging an appropriate agreement or agreements, in writing, for such purpose and filing the same for record in the office of the County Clerk of Harris County, Texas, at any time prior to January 1, 1987, or at any time prior to the expiration of any successive five-year period thereafter. . . .

5. UTILITY CHARGES

5:1 - Sewer Services will be provided to this Subdivision by the Candlelight Service Company pursuant to Contract No. CC-CSC-10 (the "Contract") between Candlelight Service Company and the San Jacinto River Authority, (which contract is filed under Document No. *D 725354*, Harris County Real Property

241

Records and made a part hereof for all purposes) and Agreement No. CC-SA-CSC-10 between San Jacinto River Authority, T. D. Gardner and Candlelight Service Company (a copy of which Agreement is filed under Document No. *D 725354*, Harris County Real Property Records and made a part hereof for all purposes), together with all amendments and supplementary agreements thereto which may be executed and recorded from time to time. Pursuant to the Contract, Candlelight Service Company must establish and maintain and from time to time adjust the rates, fees and charges for the services provided by its sanitary sewer collection system such that the gross revenues therefrom will be sufficient at all times to provide payment for the expenses of operating and maintaining such sanitary sewer collection system and for Candlelight Service Company's obligations to the San Jacinto River Authority under the Contract. . . .

6. JOINDER OF LIENHOLDERS

The undersigned lienholders join in the execution of this instrument for the purpose of evidencing their consent and agreement to the establishment of the foregoing restrictions on the land described herein. . . .

Appendix 3

Excerpts from "A New Zoning Ordinance for Baltimore," 1968, by the Zoning Commission of Baltimore City.

INDEX OF USES

USE	R-1	R-2	R-3	R-4	R-5	R-6	R-7	R-8	R-9	R-10	O-R	B-1	B-2	B-3	B-4	B-5	M-1	M-2	M-3
Abattoirs																			P
Abrasives--manufacturing																		AI	P
Accessory or non-accessory radio and television antennas and towers when free standing or when they extend higher than 25 ft. above the building on which they are mounted												C	C	C	C	C	C	P	P
Accessory or non-accessory radio and television antennas and towers when less than 25 ft. above the building on which they are mounted												P	P	P	P	P	P	P	P
Accessory radio and television antennas when free standing or when they extend higher than 12 ft. above the building on which they are mounted	C	C	C	C	C	C	C	C	C	C	C								
Accessory radio and television antennas when less than 12 ft. above the building on which they are mounted	A	A	A	A	A	A	A	A	A	A	A								
Accessory uses	P	P	P	P	P	P	P	P	P	P	P	P	P	P	P	P	P	P	P
Acids--manufacturing																		AI	P
Adhesive products--manufacturing																	P	P	P
Agricultural uses	P	P	P	P															
Aircraft--manufacturing																		P	P
Alcoholic distillation																		AI	P
Alkalies--manufacturing																		AI	P
Ambulance service													P		P				
Ammonia--manufacturing																		AI	P
Amusement establishments--including archery ranges, shooting galleries, kiddie parks, golf driving ranges, pitch and putt, miniature golf courses, and other similar facilities													P		P				

P = Permitted Use   AI = Additional Industrial Use
C = Conditional Use   A = Accessory Use

243

INDEX OF USES

USE	R-1	R-2	R-3	R-4	R-5	R-6	R-7	R-8	R-9	R-10	O-R	B-1	B-2	B-3	B-4	B-5	M-1	M-2	M-3
																	DISTRICTS		
Amusement parks and permanent carnivals														C		C			
Animal by-products (not for human consumption)-- processing																			P
Animal hospitals													P		P			C	C
Antenna towers and microwave relay towers and installations for communications transmission or receiving	C	C	C	C	C	C	C	C	C	C	C	C	C	C	C	C	C	P	P
Antique shops													P	P	P	P			
Apartment hotels								P	P	P			P	P	P	P			
Apparel and other finished products--manufacturing																	P	P	P
Arsenals																			C
Art and school supply stores												P	P	P	P	P			
Art needlework shops												P	P	P	P	P			
Artisans' and craft work													P		P	P	P	P	P
Asbestos products-- manufacturing																		AI	P
Asphaltic mix plants																			P
Athletic fields	P	P	P	P	P	P	P	P	P	P	P	P	P	P	P	P	P	P	P
Atomic reactors																	C	C	C
Auction rooms													P	P	P	P			
Auditoriums																	C	C	C
Auditoriums and concert halls, with capacity greater in each case than 1,000 seats													C	C	C	C			
Auditoriums and concert halls, with capacity limited to 1,000 seats in each case													P	P	P	P			
Automobile accessory stores-- including repair and installation services													P		P				

P = Permitted Use AI = Additional Industrial Use
C = Conditional Use A = Accessory Use

244

INDEX OF USES

USE	DISTRICTS																		
	R-1	R-2	R-3	R-4	R-5	R-6	R-7	R-8	R-9	R-10	O-R	B-1	B-2	B-3	B-4	B-5	M-1	M-2	M-3
Automobile accessory stores--with no repair or installation services													P		P				
Automobile dismantling or scrapping																			C
Automobile glass and mirror shops													P		P				
Automobile laundries													C		C		P	P	
Automobile painting shops													P		P				
Automobile seat cover and convertible top establishments													P		P				
Automobile service stations												C	C	C	C			C	C
Automobiles--manufacturing and fabrication																		P	P
Automotive parts--manufacturing																	P	P	P
Automotive testing grounds																			C
Awnings, storm windows, and doors--sales and service													P		P				
Bakeries--including the sale of bakery products to restaurants, hotels, clubs, and other similar establishments													P		P				
Bakery goods--manufacturing																	P	P	P
Banks and building and loan associations											P	P	P	P	P	P	P	P	P
Barber shops												P	P	P	P	P			
Batteries--manufacturing and rebuilding																		P	P
Battery and tire sales and service													P		P			P	P
Beauty shops												P	P	P	P	P			

P = Permitted Use
C = Conditional Use
AI = Additional Industrial Use
A = Accessory Use

245

INDEX OF USES

USE	DISTRICTS																		
	R-1	R-2	R-3	R-4	R-5	R-6	R-7	R-8	R-9	R-10	O-R	B-1	B-2	B-3	B-4	B-5	M-1	M-2	M-3
Beverages--manufacturing																	P	P	P
Bicycle sales, rental, and repair stores													P	P	P	P			
Bituminous products-- processing																			P
Bleacheries																		AI	P
Blood donor centers													P	P	P	P			
Blueprinting and photostating establishments													P	P	P	P		P	P
Boat sales, rental, and repair establishments														P		P			
Boats less than 65 ft. in length--manufacturing and repairing																	P	P	P
Boiler works																		AI	P
Bone--distillation																		AI	P
Bone and ivory products-- processing																		AI	P
Book and magazine stores and similar establishments (Class A)												P	P	P	P	P			
Book and magazine stores and similar establishments (Class B)															C	C			
Bookbinding														P		P	P	P	P
Bottles--manufacturing																		P	P
Bottling works																	P	P	P
Boxes--manufacturing																	P	P	P
Bowling establishments													P	P	P	P			
Brewing, beer and ale																		P	P
Bricks--manufacturing																		AI	P
Brooms--manufacturing																	P	P	P

P = Permitted Use
C = Conditional Use

AI = Additional Industrial Use
A = Accessory Use

INDEX OF USES

U S E	R-1	R-2	R-3	R-4	R-5	R-6	R-7	R-8	R-9	R-10	O-R	B-1	B-2	B-3	B-4	B-5	M-1	M-2	M-3
Brushes--manufacturing																		P	P
Building and lumber material sales establishments with shops and yards														P		P		P	P
Bus and transit passenger stations and terminals													C	C	P	P	C	P	P
Bus and transit turn-arounds and passenger shelters	C	C	C	C	C	C	C	C	C	C	C	C	P	P	P	P	P	P	P
Business and office machine sales, rental, and service													P	P	P	P			
Camera and photographic supply stores													P	P	P	P			
Cameras and other photographic equipment--manufacturing																	P	P	P
Candy--manufacturing																	P	P	P
Candy and ice cream stores												P	P	P	P	P			
Canvas products--manufacturing																	P	P	P
Carbon black--manufacturing																		AI	P
Carpet and rug cleaning establishments													P		P		P	P	P
Carpet and rug stores													P	P	P	P			
Carpets--manufacturing																	P	P	P
Carry out food shops													P	P	P	P		P	P
Cartage and express facilities													P		P				
Catering establishments, food													P	P	P	P		P	P
Cellulose--manufacturing																		AI	P
Cement--manufacturing																		AI	P
Cemeteries--including accessory crematoriums and mausoleums	C	C	C	C	C	C	C	C											
Cereals--manufacturing																	P	P	P
Charcoal--manufacturing																		AI	P

P = Permitted Use AI = Additional Industrial Use
C = Conditional Use A = Accessory Use

Excerpt from *Zoning Controversies In The Suburbs: Three Case Studies,* published in 1968 by the Douglas Commission (The National Commission on Urban Problems). The cases were reported by Raymond and May Associates, planning consultants.

Below are excerpts from a case study of a zoning dispute in an exurban county about fifty miles from midtown Manhattan. Residents of single-family houses on one-acre lots faced the prospect of clustered development on an adjacent 300-acre site, which, developed under the existing one-acre zoning, would have permitted 265 lots in a conventional grid plan. The developer wanted to preserve the terrain of farmland, open fields, woods, and lovely views by building 165 houses on half-acre lots and donating the remaining land (not all of it buildable, of course, due to water levels and topography) to the town for park, recreation, and school use. The town denied him the permit, the case went to court, and the developer lost. The excerpts are quotations from residents, the planning board chairman, and the developer.

Adjacent Homeowner, Housewife: . . . The proposed houses were not in keeping with this particular area. The developer has said he would have three models, ranging from about $15,000 to $25,000. We became a bit fearful when he said at a public meeting that if the more expensive houses didn't sell, he'd build what the market indicated, with no regard for the surrounding area. He was honest in stating that if the $15,000 house wouldn't sell, he'd make some changes if necessary and sell it for $13,000. Adjacent homes at the time were selling for $23,000-$25,000 or more. It is wrong to develop land between two such areas with houses selling for as little as $13,000. Such a disparity would have brought down property values. . . .

President, Adjacent Civic Association; Attorney; Planning Board Member: . . . The proposed prices—in the $17,000 range—upset all of our area, where houses are in the $25,000-$30,000 range. We objected to cheaper houses in a prestige area. We could have done something about the other problems, but it

248

never got to that point. The developer made a mistake when asked at a public hearing what he would do if the $17,000 houses weren't selling; he said he would have to cheapen the house and sell it for $14,000.

Chairman, Town Planning Board: . . . This was the first cluster proposal in the county. It was made prior to a Town election, when Town Board members were more sensitive to public opinion. People didn't fully understand the concept then, but things are changing, and the Town may now be ready for such a development. . . .

The two major issues in the 1965 case were price differential and schools. Area residents feared depreciation of their property if $14,000-$16,000 houses were built near their $24,000-$30,000 houses. Two of the original five members of the Planning Board felt that the proposed houses would be below the area's standard and would degrade the neighborhood. The developer later talked of building houses selling for $21,000. . . . The adjacent civic organization opposed the plan; most civic associations elsewhere in the town took no position, though some opposed it as a precedent for lower-priced houses. . . . Problems related to lower-priced houses were never specified by opponents. Negroes and Puerto Ricans were never mentioned, but some people may have had them in the back of their minds.

Developer: . . . The hearing was attended by surrounding home-owners who were belligerent. They objected to the price of the house (I said I intended to sell in the range of $16,000 to $23,000), to having houses near the gas line (we had adhered to state regulations), and to effect on the schools, which they said were already overcrowded, and which would be forced into double sessions. One speaker said that "for $16,000 we're only going to get scum." The chairman of the Planning Board said, "Well, then I must be scum—that's what my house cost." There was no doubt a fear that lower-priced houses might bring colored people into the area. You must earn about $7,500 a year to buy a $16,000 house, and that's not out of line with this area.

The Planning Board was surprised at the reaction. We met with the Town Board to present the plan, but all logic failed; they

249

were determined. In response to the concern about price, I said I would create a buffer zone by having houses adjoining existing houses at the same tax valuation. It would be necessary to have $16,000 houses where the superhighway was planned. But people who live in $30,000 houses will feel kindly only to $40,000 houses next door. . . . (Raymond and May 1968: 64, 65, 66, 68, 69)

TABLES

TABLE 1

PERSONAL TAX LIABILITIES OF RENTER AND HOMEOWNER WITH
EQUIVALENT EARNINGS, ASSETS, AND EXPENSES[a]

In dollars

Item	Renter	Home-owner
Income		
Earnings	15,000	15,000
From assets of $37,500		
Interest (at 4 percent)	1,500	900
Imputed net rent on $15,000 equity in house	—	(600)
Money income	16,500	15,900
Housing cost[b]		
Money expenditure	3,750	3,150
Imputed net rent	—	(600)
Residual money income	12,750	12,750
Taxable income		
Money income	16,500	15,900
Less standard deductions and personal exemptions	5,000	5,000
Less mortgage interest and property taxes	—	2,100
Total	11,500	8,800
Tax liability	2,150	1,556

SOURCE: Adapted from Richard Goode, "Imputed Rent of Owner Occupied Dwellings Under the Income Tax," *Journal of Finance*, Vol. 15 (December 1960), pp. 505-06.

[a] Based on 1972 tax rates for a four-person household with no members age 65 or over. Renter claims standard deduction of $2,000 and personal exemptions of $3,000; homeowner itemizes and claims as deductions $2,100 in mortgage interest and property taxes, $2,000 in other deductions, and personal exemptions of $3,000.

[b] Real housing costs are 25 percent of earnings for both renter and owner. Costs of homeownership include $600 net profit or net imputed rent, $1,350 in mortgage interest (6 percent on a $22,500 mortgage), $750 in property taxes, and $1,050 for maintenance and depreciation.

SOURCE: Henry J. Aaron, *Shelter And Subsidies: Who Benefits From Federal Housing Policies?* (Washington: The Brookings Institution, 1972), p. 54.

TABLE 2

OWNERSHIP CHARACTERISTICS OF HOUSING UNITS: 1973 AND 1970
(Numbers in Thousands)

	Total		Total Inside SMSA's		In Central Cities		Not In Central Cities		Outside SMSA's	
	1973	1970	1973	1970	1973	1970	1973	1970	1973	1970
U.S.										
Occupied	69,337	63,445	47,725	43,859	22,493	21,395	25,231	22,464	21,612	19,586
Owner Occupied	44,653	39,886	28,942	26,090	11,087	10,300	17,854	15,790	15,711	13,796
Percent of All Occupied	64.4	62.9	60.6	59.5	49.3	48.1	70.8	70.3	72.7	70.4
Renter Occupied	26,684	23,560	18,783	17,769	11,406	11,095	7,377	6,674	5,901	5,790
Owner-Occupied by Region (Percent)										
Northeast										
Occupied	16,152	15,483	12,943	12,507	6,001	5,963	6,942	6,543	3,209	2,977
Percent of All Occupied	59.2	57.6	55.7	54.3	37.5	36.0	71.4	70.9	73.1	71.6
North Central										
Occupied	18,742	17,536	12,368	11,616	5,715	5,644	6,653	5,972	6,374	5,919
Percent of All Occupied	69.1	68.0	66.0	64.9	54.2	53.0	76.1	76.1	75.1	74.1
South										
Occupied	21,806	19,257	12,349	10,856	6,265	5,747	6,084	5,110	9,456	8,401
Percent of All Occupied	66.5	64.7	62.0	61.5	53.8	54.4	70.4	69.5	72.4	68.7
West										
Occupied	12,638	11,169	10,064	8,880	4,513	4,041	5,552	4,838	2,574	2,290
Percent of All Occupied	60.6	59.0	58.8	57.3	52.5	50.2	63.9	63.2	67.5	65.6

SOURCE: U.S. Department of Commerce, Bureau of the Census, *Annual Housing Survey: 1973, Part A: General Housing Characteristics*, 1975. Table A-1, p. 1; Table B-1, p. 28; Table C-1, p. 43; and Table D-1, p. 58, Table

TABLE 3

Estimates of the Net Income Tax Subsidy Granted Homeownership in the U.S. as a Percent of Housing Gross Rents

| Household Marginal Income Tax Bracket | Capital Costs of Equity and Mortgage Debt Assumed to Equal: | | | | | |
| | A. 4 Percent Rent Value Ratio Equals: | | B. 6 Percent Rent Value Ratio Equals: | | C. 8 Percent Rent Value Ratio Equals: | |
	(a) 6.5 Percent	(b) 10 Percent	(a) 6.5 Percent	(b) 10 Percent	(a) 6.5 Percent	(b) 10 Percent
14	−0.5	−0.4	3.8	2.5	8.1	5.3
20	5.0	3.3	11.2	7.3	17.3	11.3
30	14.2	9.3	23.5	15.3	32.7	21.3
50	32.7	21.3	48.1	31.3	63.5	41.3
70	51.2	33.3	72.7	47.3	94.2	61.3

NOTE: The effective property tax rate was assumed to amount to 3.5 percent of structure value. Excess annual depreciation allowances were assumed to amount to 3.5 percent of structure value. The income tax rate assumed to apply to landlord income was 25 percent. Assumed values of other parameters are listed in the Table. The following formula was used to calculate the net tax subsidy of homeownership as a percent of housing gross rents:

$$S = \frac{t^o \cdot (i + p) - t^L \cdot (N - 1) \cdot d}{RV}$$

where: S = the subsidy of homeownership;
t^o = the marginal income tax rate applied to household income;
i = the capital costs of equity and mortgage debt;
t^L = the marginal income tax rate applied to landlord incomes;
$(N - 1) \cdot d$ = excess depreciation allowances permitted landlords as a percent of housing value; and
RV = the appropriate rent to value ratio taking into account the subsidy granted landlords.

SOURCE: Franklin James, *Income Taxes and Homeownership* (Washington: The Urban Institute, Land Use Center Working Paper 5031-03, January 1975), p. 2-46.

TABLE 4

OCCUPIED HOUSING UNITS BY STRUCTURAL TYPE
PERCENT RENTER OCCUPIED

	1940	1950	1960	1970
1 Unit Detached	42.5	27.0	21.7	18.4
1 Unit Attached	52.2	40.8	54.9	41.6
2 Units	74.7	63.5	65.0	66.6
3 or More Units	90.7	91.0	91.5	92.5
Trailer	59.3	20.6	11.7	15.5

SOURCE: Franklin James, *Income Taxes and Homeownership* (Washington: The Urban Institute, Land Use Center Working Paper 5031-03, January 1975), p. 2-55. Compiled from U.S. Census of Housing 1940-1970.

TABLE 5

MORTGAGED AND NONMORTGAGED SINGLE-FAMILY HOMES
BY AGE OF PRINCIPAL OWNER

	Total Properties		Mortgaged Properties (In Thousands)		Nonmortgaged Properties	
	Number	Percent	Number	Percent	Number	Percent
United States 1-Housing Unit Properties	31,145	100	19,099[a]	61	12,045	39
Age of Principal Owner						
Less than 25 years	416	01	374	02	42	– 01
25-34	4,418	14	4,116	22	302	03
35-44	6,509	21	5,662	30	847	07
45-54	7,257	23	5,136	27	2,121	18
55-64	5,748	18	2,575	13	3,173	26
65 years and over	6,294	20	930	05	5,364	45
Not Reported	503	02	307	02	196	02
		100		100		100

SOURCE: Table 1a Mortgage Status, 1-Unit Homeowner Properties: 1971, U.S. Bureau of the Census, Census of Housing, *Residential Finance*, Vol. V, pp. 67, 68.

[a] The total number of mortgaged properties (19,099) is as given by this Census publication, even though the column adds to 19,100.

TABLE 6

SINGLE-FAMILY HOMES: AGE OF PRINCIPAL OWNER BY MORTGAGE STATUS
(Number of Properties in Thousands)

	Total		Less than 25		25-34		35-44		45-54		55-64		65 & Over		Not Reported	
	Number	%	Number	%	Number	%	Number	%	Number	%	Number	%	Number	%	Number	%
Mortgaged	19,099[a]	61	374	90	4,116	93	5,662	87	5,136	71	2,575	45	930	15	307	61
Non-mortgaged	12,045	39	42	10	302	7	847	13	2,121	29	3,173	55	5,364	85	196	39
TOTAL	31,145	100	416	100	4,418	100	6,509	100	7,257	100	5,748	100	6,294	100	503	100

SOURCE: Table 1a Mortgage Status, 1-Unit Homeowner Properties: 1971, U.S. Bureau of the Census, Census of Housing, *Residential Finance*, Volume V, pp. 67, 68.

[a] See Note a in Table 5.

TABLE 7

RENTAL AND VACANT HOUSING-UNIT PROPERTIES, 1971:
TYPE OF OWNER AND RENTAL VACANCY LOSSES
AS PERCENT OF POTENTIAL RECEIPTS

TYPE OF OWNER	Housing Unit Properties					
	Number of Properties					
United States	1-4	%	5-49	%	50 or more	%
Total	6,969		482,065		30,579	
Type of Owner						
Individual	6,210	89.	356,544	74.	6,744	22.
Partnership	218	3.	58,132	12.	11,087	36.
Real Estate Corporation	179	3.	42,848	9.	8,909	29.
Real Estate Investment Trust	13	—	4,959	1.	522	2.
Financial Institutions	27	—	2,106	—	342	1.
Housing Cooperative Organization	—	—	2,640	1.	1,224	4.
Other	283	4.	11,548	2.	1,539	5.
Not Reported	38	—	3,288	1.	182	1.

RENTAL VACANCY LOSSES AS PERCENT OF POTENTIAL RECEIPTS	Housing Unit Properties					
	Number of Properties					
United States	1-4	%	5-49	%	50 or more	%
Acquired Before 1970—Total	5,256		419,915		26,909	
Less than 1.0 percent	2,476	41.	117,605	28.	8,318	31.
1.0 to 2.9 percent	31	1.	39,788	9.	4,430	16
3.0 to 4.9 percent	86	2.	32,185	8.	2,757	10
5.0 to 6.9 percent	43	1.	26,267	6.	1,756	7
7.0 to 8.9 percent	139	3.	18,352	4.	936	3
9.0 to 10.9 percent	62	1.	21,432	5.	1,109	4
11.0 to 12.9 percent	40	1.	9,164	2.	487	2
13.0 to 14.9 percent	43	1.	10,230	2.	454	2
15 percent or more	752	14.	59,451	14.	1,739	6
Not Reported or Not Computed	1,583	30.	85,442	20.	4,896	18

SOURCE: Table 1a, U.S. Bureau of the Census, Census of Housing: 1970, Vol. V *Residential Finance*, U.S. Government Printing Office, Washington, D.C. 1973, pp 373-374, 561-562, 639-640. N.B. The columns do not always add up to the total fig ures as given by the source; hence the percentage total is sometimes less than 100.

TABLE 8

HOMEOWNERSHIP
SECULAR CHANGE IN ALL NON-FARM HOUSING UNITS—UNITED STATES
1890-1970

Year	Number of Occupied Units (single, row and multifamily) (in thousands)	Percent in One-Family Detached Homes[a]	Percent in All One-Family Structures[a] (includes row and townhouses)	Percent of All Housing Units Owner occupied (includes multifamily units)
1890	7,923	41.9	55.7	36.9
1900	10,274	41.9	54.9	36.5
1910	14,132	44.1	56.2	38.4
1920	17,600	47.7	58.8	40.9
1930	23,300	51.6	61.6	46.0
1940	27,946	55.2 (54.8)[b]	64.6 (64.4)[b]	40.9
1950	37,105	57.1	64.7	53.4
1960	49,460	66.4	73.2	61.0
1970	60,351	65.0	68.2	62.0

[a] The 1940 Census performed the first Census of Housing. Descriptions of the structural characteristics of the housing stock prior to 1940 are based on tabulations presented from the 1940 Census of housing unit age and 1940 structural characteristics. As a result of housing conversion, 1940 structural characteristics may be misleading indicators of initial structural characteristics: Housing structures still standing in 1940 may not be a representative sample of earlier housing structures. Structure characteristics 1940 and earlier refer to all units, occupied and vacant; after 1940 only occupied housing units are considered. Distinction between one-family detached structures and duplex structures were not consistent over the entire period. Estimates of number of one-family attached structures were made to conform to current definitions as much as possible.

[b] Occupied units in one-family structures as percent of total occupied units. See above note.

SOURCE: 1940 U.S. Census of Housing, *Characteristics by Type of Structure*, Table A-1; 1950 U.S. Census of Housing, *General Characteristics, Volume I, Part 7*, U.S. Summary, Table 5; 1960 U.S. Census of Housing, Volume I, *States and Small Areas, Part 1: United States*; 1970 U.S. Census of Housing, Volume I, *States and Small Areas, Part 1: United States*. In, Franklin James, "Income Tax Subsidies of Homeownership and Urban Density," draft, mimeo, The Urban Institute, May 20, 1975, p. 19.

Aaron, Henry J.
  1973 Federal Housing Subsidies: History, Problems, And Alternatives. Washington, D.C.: Brookings Institution.
  1972 Shelter And Subsidies: Who Benefits From Federal Housing Policies. Washington, D.C.: Brookings Institution.
Altman, Irwin, and Martin Chemers
  1975 Cultural Aspects Of Environment-Behavior Relationships. Salt Lake City: University of Utah, Department of Psychology. Mimeo.
The American Law Institute
  1974 A Model Land Development Code. Philadelphia: The American Law Institute. Draft, April 15, 1974.
Babcock, Richard F.
  1966 The Zoning Game: Municipal Practices And Policies. Madison: The University of Wisconsin Press.
Babcock, Richard F., and Fred P. Bosselman
  1973 Exclusionary Zoning: Land Use Regulation And Housing In The 1970s. New York: Praeger Publishers, in cooperation with the American Society of Planning Officials, Chicago, Illinois.
Babcock-Abrahams, Barbara
  1975 "A Tolerated Margin Of Mess": The Trickster And His Tales Reconsidered. Journal Of The Folklore Institute 9: 147-86.
Baker, Newton D.
  1918 Frontiers Of Freedom. New York: George H. Doran.
Barlow, Robin, Harvey E. Brazer, and James N. Morgan
  1966 Economic Behavior Of The Affluent. Washington, D.C.: Brookings Institution.
Barth, Frederik
  1972 Analytic Dimensions In The Comparison Of Social Organization. American Anthropologist 74: 207-20.
  1969 Ethnic Groups And Boundaries: The Social Organization Of Culture Difference. Boston: Little, Brown.
  1966 Models Of Social Organization. Occasional Paper No. 23. London: Royal Anthropological Institute.
Barthes, Roland
  1970 [1964] Elements Of Semiology. Boston: Beacon Press.
Bassett, Edward M.
  1936 Zoning: The Laws, Administration, And Court Decisions During The First Twenty Years. New York: Russell Sage.
Bassett, Edward M., Frank B. Williams, Alfred Bettman, and Robert Whitten
  1935 Model Laws For Planning Cities, Counties, And States Including Zoning, Subdivision Regulation, And Protection Of Official Map. Cambridge, Mass.: Harvard University Press.

261

Beaglehole, Ernest
  1931   Property: A Study In Social Psychology. London: School of Economics and Political Science. Study No. 1.
Berger, Bennett M.
  1960   Working-Class Suburb: A Study Of Auto Workers In Suburbia. Berkeley: University of California Press.
Bergman, Edward M.
  1974   Eliminating Exclusionary Zoning: Reconciling Workplace And Residence In Suburban Areas. Cambridge, Mass.: Ballinger Publishing Co.
Berkhofer, Robert F.
  1973   Clio And The Culture Concept: Some Impressions Of A Changing Relationship in American Historiography. *In* The Idea Of Culture In The Social Sciences. Louis Schneider and Charles Bonjean, Eds. Cambridge: Cambridge University Press.
Berry, Brian J. L., and Robert S. Bednarz
  1975   A Hedonic Model Of Prices And Assessments For Single-Family Homes: Does The Assessor Follow The Market Or The Market Follow The Assessor? Land Economics 21: 22-40.
Beuscher, J. H., and Jerry W. Morrison
  1955   Judicial Zoning Through Recent Nuisance Cases. Wisconsin Law Review Vol. 1955: 440-57.
Birch, David et al.
  1973   America's Housing Needs: 1970 To 1980. Cambridge, Mass.: Joint Center for Urban Studies of the Massachusetts Institute of Technology and Harvard University.
Black, Mary B.
  1973   Belief Systems. *In* Handbook Of Social And Cultural Anthropology. John J. Honigmann, Ed. Chicago: Rand McNally.
Blanton, Richard E.
  1976   Anthropological Studies Of Cities. *In* Annual Review Of Anthropology 5: 249-64. Bernard J. Siegel, Alan R. Beals, and Stephen A. Tyler, Eds. Palo Alto: Annual Reviews.
Boskin, Joseph
  1972   Sambo: The National Jester In The Popular Culture. *In* Race And Social Differences, Paul Baxter and Basil Sansom, Eds. London: Penguin Books.
Boulding, Kenneth
  1973   Toward The Development Of A Cultural Economics. *In* The Idea Of Culture In The Social Sciences. Louis Schneider and Charles Bonjean, Eds. Cambridge: Cambridge University Press.
Bracey, Howard E.
  1964   Neighbours: Subdivision Life In England And The United States. Baton Rouge: Louisiana State University Press.
Broom, Leonard, F. Lancaster Jones, and Jerzy Zubrzycki
  1968   Social Stratification In Australia. *In* Social Stratification, J. A. Jackson, Ed. Cambridge: Cambridge University Press.

Bryant, R. W. G.
1972   Land: Private Property, Public Control. Montreal: Harvest House.

Burger, Warren E.
1974   Barnacles On Our Legal Practices. Address to American Law Institute. May 21, 1974.

Burns, Emile
1935   A Handbook Of Marxism. New York: International Publishers.

Campbell, Angus, Philip E. Converse, and Willard L. Rodgers
1976   The Quality Of American Life: Perceptions, Evaluations, And Satisfactions. New York: Russell Sage Foundation.

Caplovitz, David
1974   Consumers In Trouble: A Study Of Debtors In Default. New York: The Free Press.

Charsley, S. R.
1974   The Formation Of Ethnic Groups. *In* Urban Ethnicity. Abner Cohen, Ed. London: Tavistock.

Citizens League Report
1973   Building Confidence In Older Neighborhoods. Minneapolis: Citizens League.

Clark, Tom C., and Philip B. Perlman
1948   Prejudice And Property: An Historic Brief Against Racial Covenants. Washington, D.C.: Public Affairs Press.

Clark, W. A. V., and Gerard Rushton
1970   Models Of Intra-Urban Consumer Behavior And Their Behavior Implications For Central Place Theory. Economic Geography 46: 486-97.

Clawson, Marion
1971   Suburban Land Conversion In The United States: An Economic And Governmental Process. Baltimore: The Johns Hopkins University Press for Resources for the Future.

Clawson, Marion, and Harvey S. Perloff
1973   Alternatives For Future Urban Land Policy. *In* Modernizing Urban Land Policy. Marion Clawson, Ed. Baltimore: The Johns Hopkins University Press for Resources for the Future.

Coke, James G., and Steven R. Brown
1976   Public Attitudes About Land Use Policy And Their Impact On State Policy-Makers. Publius—The Journal Of Federalism 6: 97-134.

Coke, James G., and Charles S. Liebman
1961   Political Values And Population Density Control. Land Economics 37: 347-61.

Colby, Benjamin N.
1975   Culture Grammars. Science 187: 913-19.

Coleman, Richard P.
1973   Seven Levels Of Housing: An Exploration In Public Imagery. Working Paper No. 20. Cambridge, Mass.: Joint Center for Ur-

ban Studies of the Massachusetts Institute of Technology and Harvard University.

Cox, Kevin R., and John A. Agnew
1974   The Location Of Public Housing: Towards A Comparative Analysis. Department of Geography, The Ohio State University. Mimeo.

Crecine, John P., Otto A. Davis, and John E. Jackson
1967   Urban Property Markets: Some Empirical Results And The Implications For Municipal Zoning. Journal Of Law And Economics 10: 79-99.

Dahrendorf, Ralf
1968   Essays In The Theory Of Society. Stanford: Stanford University Press.
1959   Class And Class Conflict In Industrial Society. Stanford: Stanford University Press.

Danielson, Michael N.
1976   The Politics Of Exclusion. New York: Columbia University Press.

Davis, Otto A., and Frederick H. Reuter
N.d.   A Simulation Of Municipal Zoning Decisions. Regulatory Process Workshop Paper No. 1. Pittsburgh: Graduate School of Industrial Administration, School of Urban and Public Affairs, Carnegie-Mellon University.

Dean, John P.
1945   Home Ownership: Is It Sound? New York: Harper & Row.

De Huszar, William I.
1972   Mortgage Loan Administration. New York: McGraw-Hill Book Co.

Delafons, John
1962   Land-Use Controls In The United States. Cambridge, Mass.: Harvard University Press.

Dexter, Lewis Anthony
1970   Elite And Specialized Interviewing. Evanston: Northwestern University Press.

Douglas, Mary
1970 [1966]   Purity And Danger: An Analysis Of Concepts Of Pollution And Taboo. London: Penguin Books.
1970   Natural Symbols: Explorations In Cosmology. New York: Pantheon Books.
1973   Rules And Meanings: The Anthropology Of Everyday Knowledge. Editor. Harmondsworth: Penguin Books.

Downie, Leonard, Jr.
1974   Mortgage On America: The Real Cost Of Real Estate Speculation. New York: Praeger.

Downs, Anthony
1973   Opening Up The Suburbs: An Urban Strategy For America. New Haven: Yale University Press.

264

Dumont, Louis
1970   Homo Hierarchicus: The Caste System And Its Implications. Chicago: University of Chicago Press.

Duncan, Otis Dudley
1969   Inequality And Opportunity. Population Index. July–September: 361-66.

Durkheim, Emile, and Marcel Mauss
1963 [1903]   Primitive Classification. Chicago: The University of Chicago Press.

Eco, Umberto
1976   A Theory Of Semiotics. Bloomington: Indiana University Press.

Elder, Glen H., Jr.
1975   Age Differentiation And The Life Course. *In* Annual Review Of Sociology 1: 165-190. Alex Inkeles, James Coleman, and Neil Smelser, Eds. Palo Alto: Annual Reviews.

Ellickson, Robert C.
1973   Alternatives To Zoning: Covenants, Nuisance Rules, And Fines As Land Use Controls. University Of Chicago Law Review 40: 681-781.

Ellman, Tara
1976   Fiscal Impact Studies In A Metropolitan Context. *In* Economic Issues In Metropolitan Growth, Paul R. Portney, Ed. Baltimore: The Johns Hopkins University Press for Resources for the Future.

Farley, Reynolds
1976   Is Coleman Right? Social Policy 6:14-23.

Federal Housing Administration, United States Department of Housing and Urban Development
1968   Suggested Legal Documents For Planned-Unit Developments, FHA Form 1400, VA Form 26-800. Washington, D.C.: U.S. Government Printing Office.

Felstiner, William
1974   Influences Of Social Organization On Dispute Processing. Law and Society Review 9: 63-94.

Fernea, Robert A., and James M. Malarkey
1975   Anthropology Of The Middle East And North Africa: A Critical Assessment. *In* Annual Review Of Anthropology 4: 183-204. Bernard J. Siegel, Alan R. Beals, and Stephen A. Tyler, Eds. Palo Alto: Annual Reviews.

Fessler, Daniel Wm.
1973   Casting The Courts In A Land Use Reform Effort: A Starring Role Or A Supporting Part? *In* Modernizing Urban Land Policy. Marion Clawson, Ed. Baltimore: The Johns Hopkins University Press for Resources for the Future.

Firey, Walter
1947   Land Use In Central Boston. Cambridge, Mass.: Harvard University Press.

Firth, Raymond
  1973 Symbols: Public And Private. Ithaca: Cornell University Press.
  1967 Themes In Economic Anthropology: A General Comment. *In* Themes In Economic Anthropology. Raymond Firth, Ed. London: Tavistock.
Fitzpatrick, Joseph P.
  1971 Puerto Rican Americans: The Meaning Of Migration To The Mainland. Englewood Cliffs: Prentice-Hall.
Franklin, Herbert M., David Falk, and Arthur J. Levin
  1974 In-Zoning: A Guide For Policy-Makers On Inclusionary Land Use Programs. Washington, D.C.: The Potomac Institute.
Freund, Ernst
  1929 Some Inadequately Discussed Problems Of The Law Of City Planning And Zoning. *In* Planning Problems of Town, City, and Region. Philadelphia: William F. Fell.
  1926 Discussion. *In* Planning Problems Of Town, City, And Region: Papers and Discussions. 18th National Conference on City Planning. St. Petersburg and Palm Beach, Fla.
Fried, Marc
  1973 The World Of The Urban Working Class. Cambridge, Mass.: Harvard University Press.
Fried, Morton H.
  1967 The Evolution Of Political Society. New York: Random House.
Frost, Robert
  1969 The Poetry Of Robert Frost. Edward Connery Lathem, Ed. New York: Holt, Rinehart, and Winston.
Gaffney, Mason
  1973 Tax Reform To Release Land. *In* Modernizing Urban Land Policy. Marion Clawson, Ed. Baltimore: The Johns Hopkins University Press for Resources for the Future.
Gans, Herbert J.
  1967 The Levittowners: Ways Of Life And Politics In A New Suburban Community. New York: Vintage Books.
Geertz, Clifford
  1973 The Interpretation Of Cultures: Selected Essays. New York: Basic Books.
Geertz, Hildred, and Clifford Geertz
  1975 Kinship In Bali. Chicago: The University of Chicago Press.
Glazer, Nathan, and Daniel P. Moynihan
  1975 Introduction. *In* Ethnicity: Theory And Experience. Nathan Glazer and Daniel P. Moynihan, Eds. Cambridge, Mass.: Harvard University Press.
  1963 Beyond The Melting Pot: The Negroes, Puerto Ricans, Jews, Italians, And Irish Of New York City. Cambridge, Mass.: The MIT Press.

266

Goffman, Erving
  1963 Stigma: Notes On The Management Of Spoiled Identity.
  Englewood Cliffs: Prentice-Hall.
Goldschmidt, Walter
  1955 Social Class And The Dynamics Of Status In America.
  American Anthropologist 57: 1209-17.
Goodenough, Ward H.
  1974 *Review*, The Interpretation Of Cultures By Clifford Geertz.
  Science 186: 435-36 (1 November).
  1970 Description And Comparison In Cultural Anthropology. Chi-
  cago: Aldine Publishing Co.
Gottlieb, Manuel
  1976 Long Swings In Urban Development. New York: National
  Bureau of Economic Research.
Gould, Roger L.
  1972 The Phases Of Adult Life: A Study In Developmental Psy-
  chology. American Journal Of Psychiatry 129: 33-43.
Grezzo, Anthony D.
  1972 Mortgage Credit Risk Analysis And Servicing Of Delinquent
  Mortgages. United States Department of Housing and Urban
  Development, Office of International Affairs. Washington, D.C.:
  U.S. Government Printing Office.
Gries, John M., and James Ford, Eds.
  1932 Home Finance And Taxation, The President's Conference
  On Home Building And Home Ownership. Washington, D.C.
Guttenberg, Albert Z.
  1967 The Social Evaluation Of Non-Residential Land Use: Sub-
  standardness Criteria. Bureau of Community Planning, University
  of Illinois, Urbana.
  1965 New Directions In Land Use Classification. Chicago: Ameri-
  can Society of Planning Officials.
Haar, Charles M.
  1975 Suburban Problems: Report Of The President's Task Force.
  Ed. Cambridge, Mass.: Ballinger Publishing Co.
  1959 Land-Use Planning: A Casebook On The Use, Misuse And
  Re-Use Of Urban Land. Boston: Little, Brown.
Haar, Charles M., and Demetrius S. Iatridis
  1974 Housing The Poor In Suburbia: Public Policy At The Grass
  Roots. Cambridge, Mass.: Ballinger Publishing Co.
Haefele, Edwin T.
  1973 Representative Government And Environmental Manage-
  ment. Baltimore: The Johns Hopkins University Press for Re-
  sources for the Future.
Halper, John B.
  1967 The Influence Of Mortgage Lenders On Building Design.
  Law And Contemporary Problems 32: 266-73.

267

Hamilton, Richard F.
  1971 Black Demands, White Reactions, And Liberal Alarms. *In* Blue Collar Workers: A Symposium On Middle America. Sar A. Levitan, Ed. New York: McGraw-Hill Book Co.
Handlin, Oscar
  1952 Statement And Memorandum Concerning The Background Of The National Origin Quota System, Hearings before the President's Commission on Immigration and Naturalization, September-October 1952: 327-33, 1839-64.
  1951 The Uprooted: The Epic Story Of The Great Migrations That Made The American People. New York: Grosset & Dunlop.
Hannerz, Ulf
  1974 Ethnicity And Opportunity In Urban America. *In* Urban Ethnicity. Abner Cohen, Ed. London: Tavistock.
Hartshorne, Thomas L.
  1968 The Distorted Image: Changing Conceptions Of The American Character Since Turner. Cleveland: Case Western Reserve University Press.
Harvey, David
  1973 Social Justice And The City. Baltimore: The Johns Hopkins University Press.
Hawley, Amos H., and Vincent P. Rock
  1975 Metropolitan America In Contemporary Perspective. Eds. New York: Sage Publications.
Herbert, David T.
  1973 Urban Geography: A Social Perspective. New York: Praeger.
Herzog, John P., and James S. Earley
  1970 Home Mortgage Delinquency And Foreclosure. New York: National Bureau of Economic Research.
Higham, John
  1975 Send These To Me: Jews And Other Immigrants In Urban America. New York: Atheneum.
  1955 Strangers In The Land: Patterns Of American Nativism, 1860-1925. New Brunswick: Rutgers University Press.
Hills, Carla A.
  Remarks Before The American Bar Association, August 13, 1975.
Hodge, Robert W., and Donald J. Treiman
  1968 Class Identification In The United States. American Journal Of Sociology 73: 535-47.
Hofstadter, Richard
  1963 [1944] Social Darwinism In American Thought. Revised Edition. Boston: The Beacon Press.
Home Mortgage Disclosure Act of 1975
  1975 Hearings, Part 1, Committee on Banking, Housing and Urban Affairs, United States Senate. May 5-8.
Hoover, Herbert
  1924 Foreword. A Standard State Zoning Enabling Act. Washington, D.C.: United States Department Of Commerce.

268

Howe, Frederick C.
  1911   The Municipal Real Estate Policies Of German Cities. Pro-
    ceedings of the Third National Conference on City Planning.
    Boston: The University Press.
Huber, Joan, and William H. Form
  1973   Income And Ideology: An Analysis Of The American Po-
    litical Formula. New York: The Free Press.
Hughes, Everett C.
  1928   A Study Of A Secular Institution: The Chicago Real Estate
    Board. Ph.D. Thesis, Department of Sociology and Anthropology,
    The University of Chicago.
Ineichen, Bernard
  1972   Home Ownership And Manual Worker's Life-Styles. Socio-
    logical Review 20: 391-412 (New Series).
Jacobs, Jane
  1961   The Death And Life Of Great American Cities. New York:
    Random House.
James, Franklin
  1975a   Income Taxes And Homeownership. Land Use Center Work-
    ing Paper 5031-03. Washington, D.C.: The Urban Institute.
  1975b   Income Tax Subsidies Of Homeownership And Urban Den-
    sity. Draft. Washington, D.C.: The Urban Institute.
James, Franklin J., Jr., with Oliver Duane Windsor
  1976   Fiscal Zoning, Fiscal Reform, And Exclusionary Land Use
    Controls. Journal Of The American Institute Of Planners 42:
    130-41.
Janowitz, Morris
  1967   The Community Press In An Urban Setting. Second Edition.
    New York: The Free Press.
Jensen, Joan M.
  1968   The Price Of Vigilance. Chicago: Rand McNally.
Jones, Maldwyn Allen
  1960   American Immigration. Chicago: The University of Chicago
    Press.
Kain, John F., and John M. Quigley
  1972   Housing Market Discrimination, Homeownership, And Sav-
    ings Behavior. American Economic Review 62: 263-77.
Kaiser Committee (The President's Committee on Urban Housing)
  1969   A Decent Home. Washington, D.C.: U.S. Government Print-
    ing Office.
Kee, James Edwin, and Terrence A. Moan
  1976   The Property Tax And Tenant Equality. Comment. Harvard
    Law Review 89: 531-51.
Keesing, Roger M.
  1974   Theories Of Culture. *In* Annual Review Of Anthropology 3:
    73-98. Bernard J. Siegel, Alan R. Beals, and Stephen A. Tyler,
    Eds. Palo Alto: Annual Reviews.

Keller, Suzanne
  1968   The Urban Neighborhood: A Sociological Perspective. New York: Random House.
Kimball, Solon T.
  1960   Introduction. Arnold van Gennep, The Rites Of Passage. Chicago: The University of Chicago Press.
  1946   A Case Study In Township Zoning. The Quarterly Bulletin, No. 28. Michigan State College Experimental Station. East Lansing.
Knauss, Norman L.
  1929   768 Municipalities In United States Now Protected By Zoning Ordinances. *In* The American City 20: 167-71.
Koch, Edward
  1973   Testimony. Hearings on H.R. 702 "Tax Deductions For Renters," before The U.S. House of Representatives, Ways and Means Committee (April).
Kornblum, William
  1974   Blue Collar Community. Chicago: The University of Chicago Press.
Laumann, Edward O.
  1973   Bonds Of Pluralism: The Form And Substance Of Urban Social Networks. New York: J. Wiley.
  1966   Prestige And Association In An Urban Community: An Analysis Of An Urban Stratification System. Indianapolis: Bobbs-Merrill.
Laumann, Edward O., and Richard Senter
  1976   Subjective Social Distance, Occupational Stratification, And Forms Of Status And Class Consciousness: A Cross National Replication And Extension. American Journal Of Sociology 81: 1304-38.
Leach, Edmund
  1976   Culture And Communication: The Logic By Which Symbols Are Connected. Cambridge: Cambridge University Press.
  1964   Anthropological Aspects Of Language: Animal Categories And Verbal Abuse. *In* New Directions In The Study Of Language. Eric H. Lennenberg, Ed. Cambridge, Mass.: The MIT Press.
  1954   Political Systems Of Highland Burma. Boston: Beacon Press.
Lehman, F. K.
  1967   Ethnic Categories In Burma And The Theory Of Social Systems. *In* Southeast Asian Tribes, Minorities, And Nations. Peter Kunstadter, Ed. Princeton: Princeton University Press.
Lévi-Strauss, Claude
  1967   The Scope Of Anthropology. London: Jonathan Cape.
LeVine, Robert A., and Donald T. Campbell
  1972   Ethnocentrism: Theories Of Conflict, Ethnic Attitudes, And Group Behavior. New York: J. Wiley.

270

Lipset, Seymour Martin
  1967 [1963] The First New Nation. New York: Anchor Books.
  1963 [1960] Political Man: The Social Bases Of Politics. New York: Anchor Books.
Lowenthal, David
  1972 Environmental Assessment: A Comparative Analysis Of Four Cities. New York: American Geographical Society.
Lynch, Kevin
  1960 The Image Of The City. Cambridge, Mass.: The MIT Press.
Lynd, Robert S., and Helen Merrell Lynd
  1937 Middletown In Transition: A Study In Cultural Conflicts. New York: Harcourt, Brace & World.
Makielski, S. J. Jr.
  1966 The Politics Of Zoning: The New York Experience. New York: Columbia University Press.
Mandelker, Daniel R.
  1971 The Zoning Dilemma. Indianapolis: Bobbs-Merrill.
Marcuse, Peter
  1973 Tenure And The Housing System: The Relationship And The Potential For Change. Working Paper, No. 209-1-5. Washington, D.C.: The Urban Institute.
  1972a The Financial Attributes Of Homeownership For Low And Moderate Income Families. Working Paper No. 209-1-2. Washington, D.C.: The Urban Institute.
  1972b The Legal Attributes Of Homeownership For Low And Moderate Income Families. Working Paper No. 209-1-1. Washington, D.C.: The Urban Institute.
  1971 Homeownership For The Poor: Economic Implications For The Owner/Occupant. Working Paper 112-26. Washington, D.C.: The Urban Institute.
Marquis, Albert G.
  1975 Constitutional Law—Zoning For Single-"Family" Dwellings Is Not Denial Of Equal Protection To Unrelated Persons. Washington Law Review 50: 421-39.
Marriott, McKim
  1976 Hindu Transactions: Diversity Without Dualism. *In* Transaction And Meaning: Directions In The Anthropology Of Exchange And Symbolic Behavior. Bruce Kapferer, Editor. Philadelphia: Institute for the Study Of Human Issues.
Marriott, McKim, and Ronald B. Inden
  1974 Caste Systems. *In* Encyclopaedia Britannica, Macropaedia 3: 982-91.
Maser, Steven, William H. Riker, and Richard N. Rosett
  1975 The Effects Of Zoning And Externalities On The Prices Of Land In Monroe County, New York. Mimeo. July.
Mauss, Marcel
  1967 [1925] The Gift. New York: Norton.

271

McPherson, James Alan
  1972   The Story Of The Contract Buyers League. The Atlantic Monthly. April.
Merton, Robert K.
  1951   The Social Psychology Of Housing. *In* Wayne Dennis et al., Editors. Current Trends In Social Psychology. Pittsburgh: University of Pittsburgh Press.
Miller, S. M.
  1971   The Future Of Social Mobility Studies. American Journal Of Sociology 77: 62-65.
Mixon, John
  1967   Jane Jacobs And The Law—Zoning For Diversity Examined. Northwestern University Law Review 62: 314-56.
Morrison, Peter A., and Judith P. Wheeler
  1975   Local Growth Control Versus The Freedom To Migrate. Santa Monica: The Rand Corporation.
Murray, Robert K.
  1955   Red Scare: A Study In National Hysteria 1919-1920. Minneapolis: University of Minnesota Press.
Muth, Richard
  1969   Cities And Housing. Chicago: The University of Chicago Press.
National Academy of Sciences and National Academy of Engineering
  1972   Freedom Of Choice In Housing: Opportunities And Constraints. Report of the Social Science Panel, Division of Behavioral Sciences. Washington, D.C.
National Association of Homebuilders
  1973   Economic News Notes. 19, No. 4.
National Association of Realtors
  1976   Headlines. 43, No. 34. (August 23).
National Committee Against Discrimination In Housing and The Urban Land Institute
  1974   Fair Housing And Exclusionary Land Use. ULI Research Report No. 23. Washington, D.C.
National Institute of Mental Health
  1971   Summary. NIMH Working Conference On Behavioral Effects Of Extended Property Ownership. Mimeo.
Needham, Rodney
  1972   Belief, Language, And Experience. Chicago: The University of Chicago Press.
  1968   *Review of* Seth, God Of Confusion: A Study Of His Role In Egyptian Mythology And Religion by H. Te Velde. American Anthropologist 70: 987-88.
Neutze, Max
  1968   The Suburban Apartment Boom: Case Study Of A Land Use Problem. Washington, D.C.: Resources for the Future, Inc.

New Jersey County and Municipal Government Study Commission
  1974   Housing And Suburbs: Fiscal And Social Impact Of Multi-family Development. New Brunswick: Rutgers University Press.
The New York Times
  25 August 1975.
Nicholas, Ralph W.
  1968   Rules, Resources, And Political Activity. *In* Local-Level Politics: Social And Cultural Perspectives. Marc J. Swartz, Ed. Chicago: Aldine Publishing Co.
Noyes, C. Reinold
  1936   The Institution Of Property: A Study Of The Development, Substance And Arrangement Of The System Of Property In Modern Anglo-American Law. New York: Longmans, Green.
O'Brien, David J.
  1975   Neighborhood Organization And Interest-Group Processes. Princeton: Princeton University Press.
Orfield, Gary
  1974   Federal Policy, Local Power, And Metropolitan Segregation. Political Science Quarterly 89: 777-802.
Orlans, Harold
  1953   Utopia Ltd.: The Story Of The English New Town Of Stevenage. New Haven: Yale University Press.
Ortner, Sherry B.
  1973   Sherpa Purity. American Anthropologist 75: 49-63.
Oser, Alan S.
  1976   Role Of Community Associations Widens. The New York Times, August 25, p. 55.
Packard, Vance
  1959   The Status Seekers. New York: David McKay.
Parsons, Talcott
  1973   Culture And Social System Revisited. *In* The Idea Of Culture In The Social Sciences. Louis Schneider and Charles Bonjean, Eds. Cambridge: Cambridge University Press.
Pauline, David
  1971   Constitutionality Of The Pennsylvania Spite Fence Statute. Dickinson Law Review 75: 281-302.
Perin, Constance
  1975   Social Governance And Environmental Design. *In* Responding To Social Change. Basil Honikman, Ed. New York: Halstead Press.
  1974   Social Order In Environmental Design. *In* Designing For Human Behavior. Jon Lang et al., Eds. Stroudsburg, Pa.: Dowden, Hutchinson, and Ross.
  1972   Concepts And Methods For Studying Environments In Use. *In* Environmental Design: Research And Practice. William J. Mitchell, Ed. Proceedings of the EDRA/3 Conference, Los Angeles, January 1972.

1970 With Man In Mind: An Interdisciplinary Prospectus For Environmental Design. Cambridge, Mass.: The MIT Press.

1967 A Noiseless Secession From The Comprehensive Plan. Journal Of The American Institute Of Planners 33: 336-47.

The Potomac Institute, Inc.

1974 Zoning For The Living Welfare Of People: The New Jersey Supreme Court Mt. Laurel Decision. Washington, D.C.

1973 Controlling Urban Growth—But For Whom? Washington, D.C.

Rainwater, Lee

1974 What Money Buys: Inequality And The Social Meanings Of Income. New York: Basic Books.

Rapoport, Amos

1969 House Form And Culture. Englewood Cliffs: Prentice-Hall.

Rawls, John

1971 A Theory Of Justice. Cambridge, Mass.: Harvard University Press.

Raymond and May Associates

1968 Zoning Controversies In The Suburbs: Three Case Studies. Research Report No. 11. Washington, D.C.: The National Commission on Urban Problems.

Reilly, William K.

1973 The Use Of Land: A Citizens' Policy Guide To Urban Growth. New York: Thomas Y. Crowell.

Richmond, Anthony H.

1969 Sociology Of Migration In Industrial And Post-Industrial Societies. *In* Migration. J. A. Jackson, Ed. Cambridge: Cambridge University Press.

Riesman, David

1954 Individualism Reconsidered. New York: Doubleday.

Riesman, David, with Nathan Glazer and Reuel Denney

1961 [1950] The Lonely Crowd. Abridged Edition. New Haven: Yale University Press.

Ring, Alfred A., and Nelson L. North

1967 Real Estate Principles And Practices. Sixth Edition. Englewood Cliffs: Prentice-Hall.

Rolph, E. S.

1973 Decisionmaking By Residential Developers In Santa Clara County. Santa Monica, Calif.: The Rand Corporation.

Rose, Jerome G.

1973 Landlords And Tenants: A Complete Guide To The Residential Rental Relationship. New Brunswick: Transaction Books.

Rosenbaum, Nelson M.

1974 Citizen Involvement In Land-Use Governance: Issues And Methods. Draft, Working Paper 0785-04-01. Washington, D.C.: The Urban Institute.

274

Rosow, Jerome M.
1971 The Problems Of Lower-Middle-Income Workers. *In* Blue-Collar Workers: A Symposium On Middle America. Sar A. Levitan, Ed. New York: McGraw-Hill Book Co.

Roth, Julius A.
1963 Timetables: Structuring The Passage Of Time In Hospital Treatment And Other Careers. New York: Bobbs-Merrill.

Rupnow, Roger F., and Frank J. Clarke
1972 Zoning Problems In Atlanta: Two Studies Of Policy, Practice And Community Acceptance And Their Problem-Solving Applications. Atlanta: Atlanta Urban Observatory.

Sahlins, Marshall
1976 Culture And Practical Reason. Chicago: The University of Chicago Press.
1972 Stone Age Economics. Chicago: Aldine-Atherton.
1965 On The Sociology Of Primitive Exchange. *In* The Relevance Of Models For Social Anthropology. M. Banton, Ed. London: Tavistock.

Salaman, Graeme
1974 Community And Occupation: An Exploration Of Work/Leisure Relationships. Cambridge: Cambridge University Press.

Sauer, Carl
1963 Land And Life: A Selection From The Writings Of Carl Ortwin Sauer. Berkeley and Los Angeles: University of California Press.

Schafer, Robert
1974 The Suburbanization Of Multifamily Housing. Lexington, Mass.: Lexington Books.

Schiffman, Irving
1975 The Limits Of The Local Planning Commission: A Study Of Three California Communities. Institute of Governmental Affairs, University of California, Davis.

Schneider, David M.
1976 Notes Toward A Theory Of Culture. *In* Meaning In Anthropology. Keith H. Basso and Henry A. Selby, Eds. Albuquerque: University of New Mexico Press.
1972 What Is Kinship All About? *In* Kinship Studies In The Morgan Centennial Year. Priscilla Reining, Ed. Washington, D.C.: The Anthropological Society of Washington.
1969 Kinship, Nationality And Religion In American Culture: Toward A Definition of Kinship. *In* Forms Of Symbolic Action. Proceedings of the 1969 Annual Spring Meeting of the American Ethnological Society. Seattle: University of Washington Press.
1968 American Kinship: A Cultural Account. Englewood Cliffs: Prentice-Hall.

Schneider, David M., and Raymond T. Smith
1973 Class Differences And Sex Roles In American Kinship And Family Structure. Englewood Cliffs: Prentice-Hall.

275

Schrödinger, Erwin
  1967 [1958]   What Is Life? & Mind And Matter. Cambridge: Cambridge University Press.
Schussheim, Morton J.
  1975   An Analysis Of House Resolution 34—The Proposed "Emergency Homeowners' Relief Act." *In* Hearings Before The Committee On Banking, Housing And Urban Affairs, United States Senate, Ninety-Fourth Congress, February 13 and March 17, 18, 19, and 20, 1975. 586-92.
Schwartz, Gary, and Don Merten
  1971   Participant Observation And The Discovery Of Meaning. Philosophy and Social Science 1: 279-98.
Scott, Mel
  1969   American City Planning Since 1890. Berkeley and Los Angeles: University of California Press.
Sexton, Patricia Cayo, and Brendan Sexton
  1971   Blue Collars And Hard Hats: The Working Class And The Future Of American Politics. New York: Vintage Books.
Shelton, John P.
  1968   The Cost Of Renting Versus Owning A Home. Land Economics 44: 59-72.
Shils, Edward
  1968   Deference. *In* Social Stratification. J. A. Jackson, Ed. Cambridge: Cambridge University Press.
Siegan, Bernard H.
  1972   Land Use Without Zoning. Lexington, Mass.: D. C. Heath.
Singer, Milton B.
  1972   When A Great Tradition Modernizes. New York: Praeger.
  1968   The Concept Of Culture. *In* Encyclopedia Of The Social Sciences. New York: The Macmillan Company and The Free Press.
Smith, David Horton
  1975   Voluntary Action And Voluntary Groups. *In* Annual Review Of Sociology 1: 247-70. Alex Inkeles, James Coleman, and Neil Smelser, Eds. Palo Alto: Annual Reviews.
Smith, Halbert C., Carl J. Tschappat, and Ronald L. Racster
  1973   Real Estate And Urban Development. Homewood, Ill.: Richard D. Irwin.
Smith, Henry Nash
  1970   Virgin Land: The American West As Myth And Symbol. Revised Edition. New York: Vintage Books.
Solomon, Barbara Miller
  1956   Ancestors And Immigrants: A Changing New England Tradition. Cambridge, Mass.: Harvard University Press.
Sopher, David E.
  1973   Place And Location: Notes On The Spatial Patterning Of Culture. *In* The Idea Of Culture In The Social Sciences. Louis Schneider and Charles Bonjean, Eds. Cambridge: Cambridge University Press.

Stocking, George W. Jr.
   1968   Race, Culture, And Evolution. New York: The Free Press.
Straszheim, Mahlon R.
   1975   An Econometric Analysis Of The Urban Housing Market.
   National Bureau of Economic Research. New York: Columbia
   University Press.
Stull, William J.
   1975   Community Environment, Zoning, And The Market Value
   Of Single-Family Homes. Journal Of Law And Economics 17:
   535-57.
Sutherland, Anne
   1975   Gypsies: The Hidden Americans. New York: The Free Press.
Suttles, Gerald
   1972   The Social Construction Of Communities. Chicago: The
   University of Chicago Press.
   1968   The Social Order Of The Slum. Chicago: The University of
   Chicago Press.
Sutton, Francis X., Seymour E. Harris, Carl Kaysen, and James Tobin
   1956   The American Business Creed. Cambridge, Mass.: Harvard
   University Press.
Szalai, Alexander
   1972   The Use Of Time: Daily Activities Of Urban And Suburban
   Populations In Twelve Countries. The Hague: Mouton.
Tambiah, S. J.
   1969   Animals Are Good To Think And Good To Prohibit. Eth-
   nology 8: 424-59.
Tiebout, Charles M.
   1956   A Pure Theory Of Local Expenditures: Journal Of Political
   Economy 64: 416-24.
Timms, Duncan
   1971   The Urban Mosaic: Towards A Theory Of Residential Dif-
   ferentiation. Cambridge: Cambridge University Press.
Toll, Seymour
   1969   Zoned American. New York: Grossman Publishers.
Tumin, Melvin M.
   1967   Social Stratification: The Forms And Functions Of Inequality. Englewood Cliffs: Prentice-Hall.
   1953   Some Principles Of Stratification: A Critical Analysis. *In*
   Class, Status, And Power. Reinhard Bendix and Seymour Martin
   Lipset, Eds. Second Edition. New York: The Free Press.
Turner, Victor W.
   1974   Dramas, Fields, And Metaphors: Symbolic Action In Human Society. Ithaca: Cornell University Press.
   1969   The Ritual Process: Structure And Anti-Structure. London:
   Routledge & Kegan Paul.
   1968   Myth And Symbol. *In* International Encyclopedia Of The
   Social Sciences. New York: Crowell Collier and Macmillan, Inc.
   1957   Schism And Continuity In An African Society: A Study Of
   Ndembu Village Life. Manchester: Manchester University Press.

277

United States Kerner Commission
1968 Report. (National Advisory Commission On Civil Disorders)
New York: Bantam Books.
United States Senate Committee on Banking and Currency
1973 The Central City Problem And Urban Renewal Policy.
Washington, D.C.: U.S. Government Printing Office.
United States Supreme Court
1974 Transcript Of Oral Argument, Village Of Belle Terre v.
Boraas. February 19 And 20, No. 73–191.
Urban Land Institute
See National Committee Against Discrimination In Housing.
van Gennep, Arnold
1960 [1908] The Rites Of Passage. Chicago: The University of
Chicago Press.
Veblen, Thorstein
1953 [1899] The Theory Of The Leisure Class: An Economic
Study Of Institutions. New York: Mentor.
Village of Belle Terre v. Boraas.
1975 416 U.S. 1.
Wagner, Roy
1975 The Invention Of Culture. Englewood Cliffs: Prentice-Hall.
Warner, Sam Bass, Jr.
1972 The Urban Wilderness: A History Of The American City.
New York: Harper & Row.
Warner, W. Lloyd
1959 The Living And The Dead: A Study Of The Symbolic Life
Of Americans. New Haven: Yale University Press.
1953 American Life: Dream And Reality. Chicago: The Univer-
sity of Chicago Press.
Warner, W. Lloyd, Marchia Meeker, and Kenneth Eells
1960 [1949] Social Class In America: The Evaluation Of Status.
New York: Harper & Row.
The Washington Post
31 July 1975.
Weaver, Robert C.
1973 Housing And Associated Problems Of Minorities. *In* Mod-
ernizing Urban Land Policy. Marion Clawson, Ed. Baltimore:
The Johns Hopkins University Press for Resources for the Future.
Weber, Max
1947 The Theory Of Economic And Social Organization. New
York: Oxford University Press.
Werner, Oswald, and Joann Fenton
1973 Method And Theory In Ethnoscience Or Ethnoepistemology.
In A Handbook Of Method In Cultural Anthropology. Raoul
Naroll and Ronald Cohen, Eds. New York: Columbia Univer-
sity Press.
Werthman, Carl, Jerry S. Mandel, and Ted Dienstfrey
1965 Planning And The Purchase Decision: Why People Buy In
Planned Communities. Berkeley, Calif.: Institute for Urban and

278

Regional Development, Center for Planning and Development Research, University of California.

Westin, Alan F.
1970   Privacy And Freedom. New York: Atheneum.

Whiteside, Thomas
1975   Credit Bureaus. The New Yorker. April 21.

Wiebe, Robert H.
1967   The Search For Order 1877-1920. New York: Hill and Wang.

Willhelm, Sidney
1962   Urban Zoning And Land Use Theory. New York: The Free Press.

Williams, Frank Backus
1914   Comment. *In* Proceedings Of The Sixth National Conference On City Planning. Toronto, May 25-27. Boston: The University Press.
1913   The German Zone Building Regulations. Appendix III. *In* Report Of The Heights Of Buildings Commission To The Committee On The Height, Size, And Arrangement Of Buildings Of The Board Of Estimate And Apportionment Of The City Of New York.

Williams, Robin M. Jr.
1976   *Review of* Towards The Elimination Of Racism. Phyllis A. Katz, Ed. Science 192: 660-62 (14 May).
1975   Race And Ethnic Relations. *In* Annual Review Of Sociology 1: 125-64. Alex Inkeles, James Coleman, and Neil Smelser, Eds. Palo Alto: Annual Reviews.

Winder, R. Bayley
1967   The Lebanese In West Africa. *In* Immigrants And Associations. L. A. Fallers, Ed. The Hague: Mouton.

Winger, Alan R.
1973   Some Internal Determinants Of Upkeep Spending By Urban Home-Owners. Land Economics 49: 474-79.

Wirth, Louis
1936   Preface. *In* Karl Mannheim, Ideology And Utopia: An Introduction To The Sociology Of Knowledge. New York: Harcourt, Brace & World.

Wood, Robert C.
1972   The Necessary Majority: Middle Americans And The Urban Crisis. New York: Columbia University Press.
1958   Suburbia: Its People And Their Politics. Boston: Houghton-Mifflin.

Yancey, William L., Eugene P. Ericksen, and Richard N. Juliani
1976   Emergent Ethnicity: A Review And Reformulation. American Sociological Review 41: 391-403.

279

281

Library of Congress Cataloging in Publication Data

Perin, Constance.
Everything in its place.

Bibliography: p.
Includes index.
1. Land use, Urban—United States. 2. Home-
ownership—Social aspects. 3. Housing—United
States. 4. Zoning—United States. 5. Social
structure. 6. Social values. I. Title.
HD7287.8.P47   333.7'7'0973   77-72133
ISBN 0-691-09372-5